SxI - Springer for Innovation / SxI - Springer per l'Innovazione

Volume 16

SxI – Springer per l'Innovazione : L'Innovazione riveste nella società attuale un ruolo di fondamentale importanza, sia a livello di ricerca sia di implementazione in ambito scientifico, tecnologico, organizzativo, finanziario, legale, economico e commerciale. Springer, con il lancio di questa serie, intende proporre una serie di contributi, italiani e stranieri, nati da realtà che sviluppano, in vari settori e da diversi punti di vista, aspetti ed esperienze innovative. I volumi risultano essere uno strumento di approccio e approfondimento per tutti coloro che lavorano per la ricerca e l'innovazione, siano essi in ambito accademico, istituzionale o industriale.

SxI - Springer for Innovation : Innovation plays a fundamental role in our Society, at a research and also at an implementation level in the scientific, technological, financial, legal, economical and commercial areas. Springer, launching this series, aims at offering a wide range of contributions born in many – Italian and International - fields which develop, from different points of view, innovative aspects and experiences. The works included in this series are a useful tool meant to approach and deepen these aspects for all those who are involved in research and innovation, at an academic, institutional and industrial level.

Giuseppe Conti • Rosa Grimaldi

Knowledge Share: the (R)evolution of Technology Transfer

Foreword by Tom Hockaday

Springer

Giuseppe Conti
IUSS Pavia
Pavia, Italy

Rosa Grimaldi
University of Bologna
Bologna, Italy

Foreword by
Tom Hockaday
Wykham Farm
Banbury, UK

ISSN 2239-2688 ISSN 2239-2696 (electronic)
SxI - Springer for Innovation / SxI - Springer per l'Innovazione
ISBN 978-3-031-51383-1 ISBN 978-3-031-51384-8 (eBook)
https://doi.org/10.1007/978-3-031-51384-8

Knowledge Share

This Springer imprint is published by the registered company Springer Nature Switzerland AG
The registered company address is: Gewerbestrasse 11, 6330 Cham, Switzerland

To our sons: Lorenzo, Giulia, Anna,
Francesco and Isabella

Foreword

Universities do three things. The first two are comfortably labelled as teaching and research, usually in that order, with some liking to expand teaching into teaching and education. Labelling the third activity has been the subject of much discussion over the decades. For some it is an attempt to capture everything a university does that is not teaching and research; for others, it is all rolled into teaching and research in any case. In this book, the authors aim to bring the debate to a close with the term Knowledge Share, as the last stage of an evolutionary process.

Knowledge Share is presented as a new way of thinking about how universities (and Public Research Organizations, PROs) operate in both their external environment and within their organization, and also at the individual level. Knowledge Share can apply to the activities of teaching and research, but it is most applicable in the third activity. Knowledge Share encompasses the unintentional flow of knowledge and emphasizes the socialization of knowledge; it is a concept, a domain, and requires new approaches and new organizational forms within universities.

In my career I have seen the labelling of this activity change from industrial liaison to technology transfer, knowledge transfer, knowledge exchange, knowledge co-creation, knowledge mobilization, wider engagement, valorization, maturation—all considered parts of the third activity, third stream or Third Mission of universities; a minestrone of labels. Decades ago, I worked in a Technology Transfer Office, my colleagues may soon be working in Knowledge Share Offices.

The COVID-19 pandemic dominated our lives for three years, 2020, 2021, 2022. COVID changed everything for those three years and has changed many things forever. It helps provide an understanding of Knowledge Share: during COVID, universities shared their knowledge with the world.

The response from universities to the pandemic was instant, varied and hugely impressive, saving countless lives. Amongst the many examples, we saw university laboratories and equipment turned over to focus on the pandemic, with 3d-printing labs rapidly producing protective equipment; collaborations with industry generating new breathing apparatus; university academics at the forefront of public information campaigns, experts helping us understand every aspect of the science and social impact of the virus; universities as trusted sources of infection rates, mortality rates, making sense of the diverse data across the world; and creating one of the most effective vaccines against the virus. Universities shared their knowledge with the world, in every conceivable way.

It is no accident that this new thinking on the third activity has emerged from Italy. Italian university academics, leaders and administrators have given great attention to the philosophy, purpose, procedures and operations underpinning what the authors now describe as Knowledge Share. The Italian national network, NETVAL brings together the community to share knowledge, within Italy and internationally. The Italian Patent Office (UIBM, Ufficio Italiano Brevetti e Marchi) provides generous support, and the Cassa Depositi e Prestiti has invested significantly into early-stage investment funds for university-derived opportunities.

The more we understand about how universities share knowledge the better; the more universities do share their knowledge the better; hence the importance of this book.

Oxford, UK
May 2023

Tom Hockaday

Preface

We decided to write this book to provide answers to very common and basic questions that we happen to hear every day. Our daily work brings us in touch with large, diverse audiences of colleagues from universities (faculty members and professionals), students, policymakers, institutional decision-makers, financial institutions, local contexts, private companies, national governors, etc. This book talks to people interested in creating the conditions in which effective knowledge share (KS) can happen. We aim to offer insights into how universities and public research organizations (PROs) should approach KS. In order to do that, we all need to understand the rationale behind KS, the main theoretical and practical issues involved and their evolution over the years. Only if we grasp these aspects will we be able to design and implement effective actions that support KS. This is the vision the two authors have agreed upon and that is offered throughout the book, based on our 20 years of experience and our different perspectives.

The book is built on the experience of the authors in university contexts, and many of the examples focus on university settings. However, almost all of the theories, models and practices we talk about also apply to PROs and, more specifically, to public entities that invest in research, produce knowledge and practice knowledge sharing.

An important driver for us to write this book was that we noticed there was not a comprehensive approach to analysing KS in the existing literature. There are several reports/studies that focus on single aspects of KS, or on specific characteristics of the environmental system (laws, funding, country systems, ecosystems), the organizations involved (strategies, actions and tools) or the people (individual characteristics, traits, personalities and motivations). However, we couldn't find a broad, comprehensive picture that takes all these factors and their interrelationships into account, bringing them into a unitary framework. Also, there is no widespread awareness of how KS can positively influence economic, cultural, social and human progress.

Yet, it is important to describe KS from a wider perspective in order to identify future developmental trajectories, with both policy and managerial implications, paying attention to the role that different actors in various contexts can have.

Also, in writing this book we were moved by the urgency of bringing together theories and models with evidence and concrete examples of actions, activities and processes to implement support for KS. Theory and practice are the two pillars of this book, which brings together the theoretical perspective—which is necessary to develop awareness, contextualize and have a better understanding of KS—and the practitioners' perspective, which is relevant for making things happen.

Offering insights to audiences outside universities and PROs was another driver for writing the book. Both public and private entities in the contexts surrounding universities and PROs can gain terrific benefits from interacting with universities and PROs and from being part of knowledge sharing.

Private companies, regardless of their size, the industry they are in and the type of business they carry out understand that, in a fast-changing environment and an uncertain world, the only way to stay ahead is to leverage innovation to deliver a clear and unique value proposition to the right market segments. Also, in order to navigate uncertainty, companies need to be fluid, embrace change and orchestrate resources, while being aware that they do not (and cannot) have all the competencies and resources that are necessary to succeed in the face of change; nevertheless, in an increasingly open, knowledge-based society, they can access the knowledge and competencies that they require outside the company. Producing, accessing, co-creating knowledge, and socializing and distributing it are key behaviours for companies to stay competitive and keep innovating. Small and medium-sized enterprises need dramatically better relationships with universities and public research entities and more effective KS mechanisms, which will go beyond the more traditional use of patents and licences. In this sense, the transfer of knowledge and the enhancement of research results are urgent and important activities for countries to be competitive. In addition to the commercial impact, there is also impact in terms of the production of public goods with educational, cultural and social value. The metaphor of universities as ivory towers is old but always effective, and these towers must be demolished not only through the active involvement of research institutions in Third Mission/academic engagement, but also through more proactive involvement of those who can benefit from it (profit and non-profit organizations and citizens).

This book intends to reach out to different communities, raise awareness around KS and hopefully trigger a conversation that will result in a better understanding of KS dynamics now and in the future.

Pavia, Italy
Bologna, Italy

Giuseppe Conti
Rosa Grimaldi

About the Book

This book targets different audiences who are interested in better understanding knowledge share (KS). The book aims to generate in-depth knowledge and better awareness of the phenomenon, as well as new ideas and concrete actions to favour KS.

We aim to provide inspiration and support for developing strategies and actions to promote KS and to encourage the adoption of behaviours that will maximize its effectiveness. We see KS as a broad 'umbrella' concept that we analyse from the perspective of universities and PROs. KS applies to research, education and third mission activities (TM). Yet, we believe that it is within TM activities that KS finds its best application.

In this book we focus on KS in a specific domain of TM activities relating to the commercial valorization of research results.

The book creates value for different targets:

Policymakers will gain a broader view and understanding of the phenomenon, which will allow them to elaborate ideas and solutions based on knowledge of national and international best practices.

Practitioners/professionals (e.g. Knowledge Transfer Office personnel) will find organizational, procedural and instrumental solutions to introduce in their work context.

Researchers will find a review of the literature and insights for new studies.

Instructors who teach courses and seminars on these topics (e.g. university professors and professionals) will find a textbook and a reference for specific sessions within the KS domain.

Students will find, within a single textbook, elements of theory and practice, accompanied by examples of good practice that may be useful for their growth and learning.

Entrepreneurs, managers and people in industry will gain a better understanding of how to build stronger bridges with the public research system. While it is desirable to have greater involvement in the Third Mission through the public research system and to make an effort to move closer to the business system by identifying the most effective ways to collaborate (especially for small and medium-sized enterprises), more proactive behaviour by companies is also essential. The knowledge offered by this book on the mechanisms that govern

KS can promote awareness and more active behaviours for more effective industry–university interactions.

Individual citizens will become more proactive in meeting the challenges of knowledge transfer and exchange, with a particular focus on the ways in which public goods have educational and social value.

This book responds to the expectations of the different audiences listed above through its original structure and fully comprehensive design, which includes the analysis of environmental, organizational and individual factors. This structure reflects the multifaceted nature of KS and of the factors that are likely to influence its success. These include the characteristics of the organizations that produce and transfer knowledge (strategic objectives and organizational aspects) and the characteristics of the individuals involved—from the researchers who generate knowledge worthy of transfer and exchange, to those who manage and organize it for exchange, to those who study it and try to understand its dynamics and impact. Finally, KS is influenced by the external context/environment (legal, funding, demographic and cyclical dynamics, and the country system in general). This holistic approach aims to stimulate a constructive debate that can lead to new policies and concrete actions.

The book is divided into six chapters.

Chapter 1 introduces the concept of KS. We provide our definition and explain why KS is now the widest and most all-encompassing concept to represent how knowledge is produced and how it flows. This chapter introduces a holistic model of KS, reminding us of the complexity of different factors that come into play at an environmental, organizational and individual level and that affect KS success. These three levels of analysis are explored in the following chapters.

Chapter 2 is dedicated to external environment dynamics. The environment is the broader context in which organizations and individuals live and operate. Its characteristics are key in the KS context. We will describe how the environment in which universities and public research organizations (PROs) operate can affect their KS processes.

Chapter 3 focuses on organizational factors. Specifically, we distinguish between strategy and organization, actions and initiatives, processes and tools. This chapter is dedicated to strategy, exploring how policies and strategies can have a successful impact through KS.

Chapter 4 continues to explore organizational factors, with a focus on Knowledge Transfer Offices. We will describe all the factors related to Knowledge Transfer Offices, from their relationship with the governance of the university/PRO to make-or-buy strategies for delivering services. We will go through a detailed analysis of macro- and micro-organizational models and describe processes, cycles of activity and tools.

Chapter 5 addresses the role of individuals. Individual-level characteristics are relevant for KS dynamics within universities and PROs. While individuals are at the heart of KS as engines of knowledge production, diffusion and socialization, they have been given scant attention in the literature on KS, which has devoted more room to organizational mechanisms and policy/environmental factors.

Chapter 6 closes the book with a reflection on entrepreneurial universities. The concept of the entrepreneurial university is central to knowledge sharing. The extent to which universities pay to reach out to different audiences and generate impact through KS has increased over the years. In this chapter we describe their efforts to accomplish this 'new' and 'more entrepreneurial' mission, with the aim of making them more central and visible in society and of generating impact.

The authors are experts in knowledge transfer from different points of view. Both have accumulated 20 years of experience in the university context.

Rosa Grimaldi, a university professor, has been researching knowledge transfer, new venture creation from research and university-industry collaborations with a focus on both managerial and policy aspects and implications.

Giuseppe Conti, now general director of a university and in the past head of a KTO, has a long-term experience in third mission and technology transfer.

More recently, the two authors have complemented their knowledge with additional experience. As past Deputy Rector for entrepreneurship and business relations at the University of Bologna (from 2015 to 2021), Rosa Grimaldi has put her studies into practice through the development of university strategies for transferring knowledge (with particular reference to the creation of new companies), paying specific attention to policy at regional, national and international levels.

As President of NETVAL, the Italian association for the enhancement of the results of research and technology transfer, Giuseppe Conti has had the opportunity to leverage the experience he developed as Director of Knowledge Transfer Offices, first at the Polytechnic of Milan and then at the University of Bologna, and to develop a thorough knowledge of organizational mechanisms and policies at the national level, with regard to different universities and research institutions in the country.

The two authors have recently contributed to the design and launch of a national master's programme. The Master in Intellectual Property Valorization for Knowledge Exchange and Impact—coordinated at national level by Rosa Grimaldi—targets Knowledge Transfer Office professionals and aims at training experts in the domain of KS.

Contents

About the Authors

Giuseppe Conti is General Director of IUSS, Institute of advanced university studies in Pavia. He is President of NETVAL (Italian Network for research exploitation), an association of Italian universities and public research institutes collaborating on the valorization of research results.

He has worked from 2010 to 2020 as head of third mission and industrial relationships, within the central administration at the University of Bologna. He has worked from 2003 to 2010 as head of Technology Transfer Office (TTO) at the polytechnic of Milan.

In the domain of Universities' third mission and technology transfer, he has served as expert evaluator in the national Assessment of third mission and engagement of Italian Universities run buy ANVUR (National Agency for Assessment of Universities).

He has been Deputy Italian representative 'SME and Access to Risk Finance' EU programme—Horizon 2020.

He has been board member of the University of Bologna Foundation (FAM) and of Almacube, the incubator of the University of Bologna.

He has been member of CTS (Comitato Tecnico Scientifico) ART-ER—Regional Agency in support of Research, Innovation and Technology.

Rosa Grimaldi is full Professor of entrepreneurship and innovation management at the University of Bologna, Department of Management. She teaches the courses of 'Technology Entrepreneurship' and 'Innovation Management' at the School of Engineering of the University of Bologna.

From 2021 she is Deputy Major in the city of Bologna for Innovation, Economic Development and International Attractiveness.

She is the Director of the Executive Master in Technology and Innovation Management (EMTIM) at BBS (Bologna Business School). Since 2022 she is the scientific director of a national Master programme (University of Bologna in collaboration with NETVAL and MIMIT) on Intellectual property Valorization for Knowledge Exchange and Impact.

From 2015 to 2021 she has been Vice Rector for Entrepreneurship and relations with companies at the University of Bologna.

In the domain of Universities' third mission and technology transfer, in 2020 she has served as expert evaluator in the national Assessment of third mission and engagement of Italian Universities run buy ANVUR (National Agency for Assessment of Universities).

Most of her scientific production is about New Business Creation, Entrepreneurship and Technology Transfer. On these topics she has publications on national journals and international journals (including Research Policy, Technology and Innovation Management, Journal of Business Venturing, Small Business Economics, Scientometrics, Entrepreneurship Theory and Practice, Journal of Technology Transfer, Technological Forecasting and Social Change, Journal of Business Research).

According to a study published in the Journal of Technology Transfer (Bengoa et al., 2021), she is listed (and she is the only woman) among the 25 most prominent and influential authors of scientific articles on the subject of technology transfer in top international journals.

List of Abbreviations

AI	Artificial Intelligence
EE	Entrepreneurial Education
IoT	Internet of Things
IP	Intellectual Property
KE	Knowledge Exchange
KIC	Knowledge and Innovation Community
KPI	Key Performance Indicators
KS	Knowledge Share
KSO	Knowledge Share Office
KT	Knowledge Transfer
KTO	Knowledge Transfer Office
PoC	Proof of Concept
PRO	Public Research Organization
R&I	Research and Innovation
STEM	Science, Technology, Engineering and Mathematics
TM	Third Mission
TRL	Technology Readiness Level
TT	Technology Transfer
TTO	Technology Transfer Offices
UES	University Entrepreneurial Strategy

List of Tables

Understanding Knowledge Share 1

This chapter aims to introduce the concept of knowledge share (KS). We provide our definition and explain why the term 'knowledge share' is the widest and most comprehensive *conceptual domain* to represent how knowledge is generated and how it flows.

We present a holistic model of university and public research organization (PRO) KS, which takes into account the role of environmental dimensions, individual characteristics and organizational-level factors. This model represents the architecture of the book, and all the subsequent chapters will be devoted to exploring different dimensions of this model.

1.1 What Is Knowledge Share? A Definition

In knowledge management literature, there are different ways to refer to the movement of knowledge from one individual to another, or between two or more different entities (Hayter et al., 2020; Azagra-Caro et al., 2020): KS, knowledge transfer (KT), technology transfer (TT), knowledge exchange (KE), etc. Scholars have provided definitions for each of these over the years, many of which overlap but have different nuances of meaning.

Figure 1.1 represents the increase over time of scholarly papers that use the terms 'knowledge sharing', 'knowledge transfer' and 'knowledge exchange', from 1224 in 2011 to 2246 in 2020 (an overall growth rate of 83.5%, albeit with a small decrease in 2012).[1] This increase indicates the attention that the topic has received over the last 20 years.

[1] The computation is based on SciVal data for 2011–2020 using as keywords 'knowledge 'AND 'sharing' OR 'transfer' OR 'exchange' and filtering for business, management and accounting subject area (data collected 21 January 2022, last updated 12 January 2022).

G. Conti, R. Grimaldi, *Knowledge Share: the (R)evolution of Technology Transfer*, SxI - Springer for Innovation / SxI - Springer per l'Innovazione 16,
https://doi.org/10.1007/978-3-031-51384-8_1

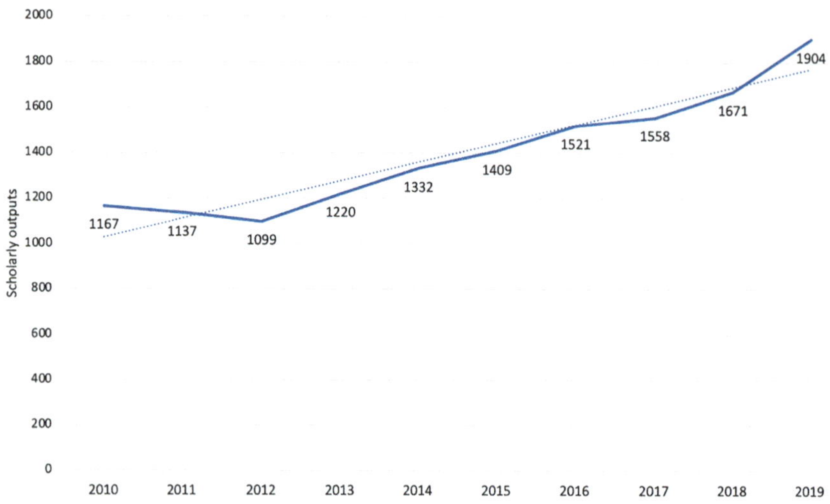

Fig. 1.1 Scholarly output trend 2011–2020

In this book, we have decided to use the term 'knowledge share'. We see KS as a new domain that encompasses previous concepts like TT, KT and KE and that is more in line with new modes of generating and disseminating knowledge.

We use the term KS to mean: *proactive and collaborative behaviours encompassing the distribution, connection and co-production of knowledge, through a circular, multi-sourced and multidirectional process that unfolds in both an intentional and an unintentional way.*

Let us explore this definition further, starting with the word 'knowledge'. From a definitory point of view, knowledge has both tacit and explicit types of contents. The concept of tacit knowledge is attributed to Michael Polanyi (1958). In his work *The Tacit Dimension*, he asserted that 'we can know more than we can tell'. He stated that not only is there knowledge that cannot be adequately articulated by verbal means, but also that all knowledge is rooted in tacit knowledge. Tacit knowledge can be defined as the skills, ideas and experiences people have, but that are not codified and may not necessarily be easily expressed (Polanyi, 1966; Nonaka & Takeuchi, 1995).

Tacit knowledge is intuitive and unarticulated; it cannot be communicated, understood or used without the 'knowing subject'. The transfer of tacit knowledge requires close interaction and the construction of shared understanding and trust. Tacit knowledge is personal and contextual. Its development is subjective as it depends on the characteristics of individuals/organizations and, as such, it has an intrinsic meaning that originates and stays within the context in which it is produced, making it difficult to aggregate and transfer in the absence of its 'originator' (i.e. the knowing subject). The realization of the full potential of this kind of knowledge requires the close involvement and cooperation of the knowing subject.

On the other hand, explicit knowledge can be codified (i.e. written down, put into words) and easily transferred without the knowing subject. Explicit knowledge can be clustered at a single location, stored in objective forms (e.g. books, manuals, artefacts), exchanged and appropriated without the participation of its originator.

Going back to our definition, we see knowledge sharing as an action through which different behaviours coexist and take place almost simultaneously: distribution, connection and co-production.

Specifically, sharing knowledge means distributing both explicit and tacit knowledge, socializing it and making it available and accessible.

Sharing knowledge means connecting and bringing together different content, information, pieces of knowledge and people and/or organizations.

Sharing knowledge means co-producing, leveraging others' knowledge contents and bringing them together to build new ones.

KS enables (Fig. 1.2) us to bring together data/information/knowledge from different sources (connecting) to favour joint generation (co-producing) of new knowledge that is socialized and diffused (distributing).

In the KS domain, knowledge is not created in a specific moment (time) or context (space); it is created through a process in which an initial spark of knowledge is socialized within a broader context, where it is enriched by different perspectives, as various contributors come into play to voluntarily or involuntarily co-produce.

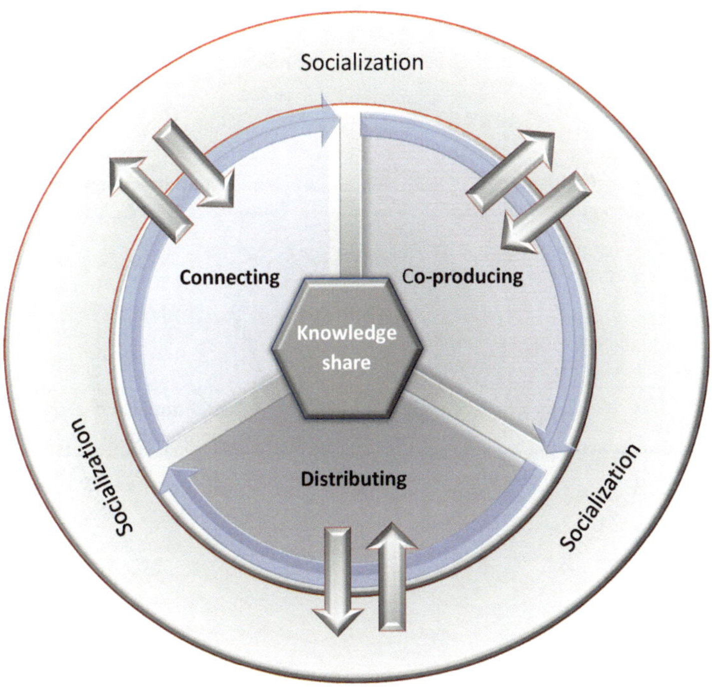

Fig. 1.2 Actions and sources of knowledge share

Finally, in the definition of KS that we have provided, we stressed specific attributes of the process, which we describe below in contrast with other, more traditional views of the process (Fig. 1.3).

1.1.1 Multi-sourced vs. Single-sourced

The process through which knowledge is shared can be multi/inter/transdisciplinary and as such may see the participation of many actors. Knowledge is the final outcome of a process that reflects the contributions of many in different spatial and temporal moments.

1.1.2 Circular vs. Linear

The linear process emphasizes start and end points. In the KS domain, knowledge flows according to a circular process. Along this process different actors come into play, and it is not possible to predict through a traditional causation process (cause–effect) what the final outcome will be, as knowledge is co-created through continuous iterative actions and cross-contamination. Causation is still at play, but it is no longer the prevailing logic.

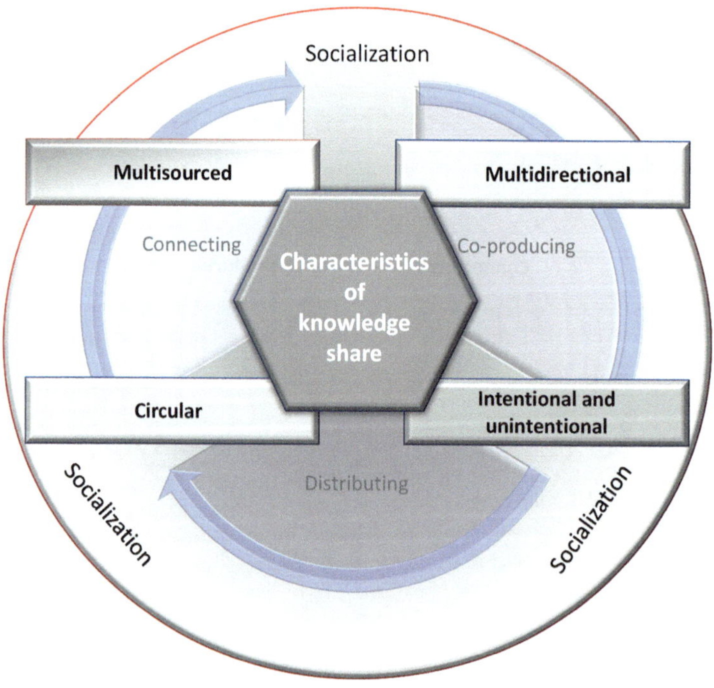

Fig. 1.3 Attributes of the knowledge share process

1.1.3 Multi-directional vs. Monodirectional

In the past, the focus has been on knowledge flowing from point A to point B (monodirectional). In our KS domain, there is a tendency also to consider return flows of knowledge. Flows can be bidirectional when two actors are involved and multidirectional when multiple actors are involved.

1.1.4 Unintentional and Intentional vs. Only Intentional

In the KS domain, knowledge unfolds according to intentional as well as unintentional processes. The unintentional perspective builds on the possibility that unexpected events may take place during the process and that unplanned externalities of knowledge may occur. While actors interact to share knowledge on top of planned outcomes, it is likely that novel and unplanned knowledge will be co-created. Some of this might be in line with the initial goal of collaboration/interaction; some might be totally innovative and unexpected.

As we described in the preface in this book, we look at KS from the perspective of universities and PROs, with a specific focus on their Third Mission (TM) activities.

1.2 From Technology Transfer to Knowledge Share: New Perspectives

Our new, broad definition of KS builds on (and encompasses) previous concepts such as technology transfer, knowledge transfer and knowledge exchange and flow (Hayter et al., 2020). In the 1970s the literature started to pay attention to knowledge, which began to be seen as a key asset for growth and development, and the term 'knowledge economy' was coined. Soon after, the idea that this asset could be an object of exchange led to consideration of intra- and interorganizational collaborations as relevant for organizations' growth, from a strategic as well as an organizational point of view (Drucker, 1993).

In the 1980s this idea of collaboration also started to circulate with regard to organizations characterized by different institutional logics, like universities and companies. In those years the term 'technology transfer' emerged (Friedman & Silberman, 2003). TT highlighted a source of technology whereby technological knowledge was produced and codified to be transferred via formal agreements to external third parties.

The literature on university–industry TT exploded, and increasing attention was paid to universities' outward-looking attitudes and engagement in TM activities (Siegel et al., 2001; Phan & Siegel, 2006). Organizational units, known as Technology Transfer Offices, started to proliferate within universities and PROs worldwide to take care of TT.

In general, technical knowledge was produced within universities, embodied in patents and transferred (via licence agreements) to outside industries. The emphasis was on a linear and monodirectional flow of a specific type of knowledge (mainly codified science, technology, engineering and mathematics—STEM—knowledge) from the place where it was produced to a place where it could be used, contextualized and valorized.

The term 'technology transfer' has been at the centre of debate because:

- It emphasizes STEM and not other types of knowledge (e.g. social sciences and humanities). Specifically, TT seems to pay attention to the technological, explicit component of knowledge, rather than to tacit components.
- It focuses mainly on intellectual property (IP)-based knowledge and exclusive licences, addressing a university–industry-specific dyad.

Bradley et al. (2013) found that the TT literature conceptualizes technology transfer linearly and places too much emphasis on patenting and licensing. Easy-to-observe outputs such as disclosures, patents, licences, licensing revenue and spin-off companies have been used as a proxy for the innovation-based contributions of research universities (Gulbrandsen & Rasmussen, 2012). According to Hayter et al. (2020), a patent-centric, linear view of TT overlooks the diversity of Technology Transfer Office practices in other university policies, programmes and options that might lead to better innovation outcomes (Link et al., 2007; Rasmussen, 2006). The use of linear approaches can slow down and inhibit the dissemination of new knowledge flowing from publicly funded research, making current conceptualizations suboptimal or even socially irresponsible (Grimaldi et al., 2011; Rasmussen, 2006). Carlile (2004) holds that knowledge cannot merely be transferred but needs to go through a process of translation to unveil its value. All the organizations involved in knowledge exchange—beyond university Technology Transfer Offices—act both as boundary-spanners and as translators of new knowledge. In some cases (e.g. where knowledge has high levels of novelty), knowledge requires transforming in order to be shared and accessed across boundaries. This typically involves long-term interactions between actors.

To address these shortcomings, the new concept of knowledge transfer (KT) has been put forward over the years. KT is similar to TT but emphasizes a broader role for knowledge, also encompassing non-technical STEM knowledge and paying attention to contents from the social sciences and humanities. KT also sheds light on broader aspects of knowledge, including tacit components, know-how and all those parts that cannot be embodied in a patent (i.e. non-IP-based knowledge) but still represent important components of the IP of universities and PROs.

However, the term 'knowledge transfer' still has some limitations, specifically:

- The word 'transfer' conveys an idea of mono-directionality in the flow of knowledge from a sender to a recipient.
- KT is based on the idea of a dyad, where some IP based knowledge content is transferred between two entities.

To address these shortcomings, the new concept of knowledge exchange (KE) was introduced. The word 'exchange' conveys the idea of a bidirectional flow of knowledge and also implies giving something away to get something back. 'Exchange' also allows for more players in the equation, introducing the idea of multisourced knowledge. There is co-creation involving both the sender(s) of knowledge and the recipient(s), which attempts to address the objectives/goals of the collaboration that have been set up *ex ante*.

While the concept of KE overcomes some of the limitations of TT, we believe that it still has some shortcomings, specifically:

– It emphasizes deliberate (intentional) flows of knowledge and what is planned at inception (entailing an effort to codify and define upfront all the possible outcomes of the collaboration/exchange).
– It does not pay attention to the social process through which knowledge flows. Several different actors (some of which may be unknown at the beginning because they only get involved at a later stage) can come into play during the process (not point to point, and not necessarily with the same objectives), and they can be unintended beneficiaries of this flow at different temporal moments, even beyond the terms and scope of the initial exchange and collaboration.

This is where the idea of KS comes in. We see KS as the last stage of an evolutionary process (Fig. 1.4).

The concept of KS, in our view, overcomes the limitations of previous concepts and offers a more comprehensive description of how knowledge flows. In addition to previous concepts, it encompasses situations in which there are unintentional flows of knowledge (externalities) stemming from the sharing. These unintentional

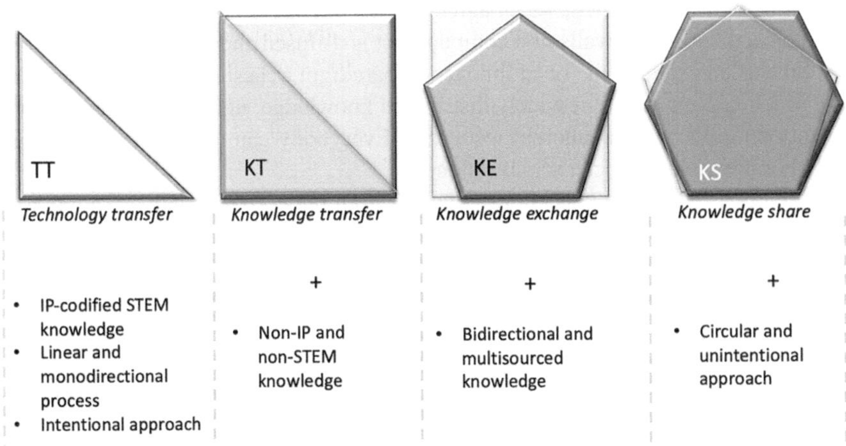

Fig. 1.4 Knowledge share evolution process

flows find their rationale in the fact that not all activities can be planned upfront. Externalities may emerge during the collaboration in a spontaneous way.

Moreover, KS emphasizes the socialization process (i.e. sharing your knowledge to let others be part of it), and the fact that knowledge that originally comes from a given source can be enriched throughout the process via a circular approach and can have diverse applications/uses for the different actors involved in the sharing, intentionally or unintentionally, for different reasons and with different objectives.

We believe that the term 'knowledge share' is better suited to represent the plethora of situations and mechanisms through which knowledge flows in our society nowadays. Hayter et al. (2020) call for a broader conceptualization that includes the transfer, translation and transformation of knowledge. This view underlies a necessary conceptual shift from formal TT to a more comprehensive conception of pathways for knowledge exchange.

Furthermore, KS is better suited to embrace knowledge produced within humanities and social sciences disciplines, which is difficult to predict upfront and traditionally emerges through formal and informal interactions and collaborations.

We see KS as an umbrella concept that overcomes some of the limitations of the other definitions and at the same time embraces all of them.

KS also embraces a more comprehensive definition of impact by taking into account different dimensions of impact at the same time. We will address these aspects below.

1.3 Why Should We Pay Attention to Knowledge Share?

Why is KS so important? The easiest and quickest answer is: because sharing knowledge is important for any organization to proliferate and grow in a fast-changing world and in knowledge-based economies.

Regardless of whether the organization is public or private, small or big, or where it is geographically located, we all agree that knowledge is not locally concentrated or enclosed within the walls of a company but is diffused and distributed.

Take as an example the open innovation paradigm (Chesbrough, 2003), according to which, in a world of widely distributed knowledge, innovators cannot afford to rely entirely on their internal resources. Everybody can achieve more through collaboration than they can achieve alone.

The open innovation concept originates within the corporate field. It refers to a business management model of innovation that fosters collaboration with people and organizations outside the company. Open innovation challenges introduce cultural divergence from the mentality of isolation, protection and secrecy that is traditionally associated with corporate research and development culture. This innovation model becomes viable when organizations acknowledge that there are many bright professionals and greater knowledge outside their walls. Private companies implement open innovation practices in different ways, through collaborations with other companies, researchers at universities, crowdsourcing competitions and exploiting innovation ecosystems. In all of these, KS is central. Such an open attitude to innovation pushes companies towards more active collaborations with universities and PROs.

In a similar manner, and also in response to more proactive corporate behaviours, universities and PROs have acknowledged the importance of external exposure and an outward-looking attitude and have become increasingly keen on external collaboration. On the one hand, they are incentivized to collaborate with companies in order to address the financial constraints that follow cuts in public expenditure on research and development. On the other hand, they may feel they can have a more proactive role in fostering the technological and economic development of their countries through engagement in TM activities, thus also generating social and environmental impact.

Finally, we should pay attention to KS from a strategic and also from an organizational perspective. The internal institutional organizational design of universities and PROs does not fit with what is required for new knowledge production and for having a broader impact on society. Universities often suffer from a formal separation between research and innovation activities, research and teaching, and, at individual level, between professors/researchers and students. Also, the role of administrative staff is often neglected.

This is not coherent with the KS domain. The way knowledge is produced and distributed nowadays requires new organizational forms within universities and PROs. Universities are the heart of knowledge production in contemporary societies, but in many cases they approach knowledge creation in traditional ways, ignoring the fact that, in the KS domain, knowledge is created in chaotic, diffuse and innovative ways, in which actors (e.g. professors, students, technicians, administrative staff) come together from different internal areas—as well as from outside—to work on time- and space-bounded projects, such as contests, bootcamps, maker and coworking spaces, open innovation programmes, fab labs, etc. These kinds of interstitial spaces have been shown to be fruitful places for innovation (Furnari, 2014), but they remain unexplored as ways for universities to valorize and enhance collaborative methods of knowledge creation.

Greater awareness of new organizational forms better suited to the KS domain on the part of universities and PROs can help them to position themselves better in the landscape of third mission in general.

1.4 Knowledge Share and the Third Mission of Universities and PROs

1.4.1 What Is the Third Mission?

The KS domain is key for universities' and PROs' TM activities. Scientific research does not end with the production of new knowledge and the validation of new theories. Scientific discoveries and new technologies are the outcome of research activities that have changed the world we live in and the ways in which we think and behave. Directly or indirectly, science is responsible for cultural, economic, social and environmental impacts; the results of research are relevant for humanity in general and are not limited to experts and scientists. Understanding how science impacts on society at large is the objective of university and PRO TM activities.

A general definition of TM is: *'The active engagement of universities and PROs in activities related to the valorization of knowledge produced via research and/or teaching that generate impact and value for a broader external community'.*

In line with this definition TM encompasses both initiatives/activities aimed at commercial exploitation of knowledge produced within universities and PROs (economic impact) and initiatives/activities aimed at generating public, social, environmental and cultural impact for a broader non-academic community.

TM has been defined as the openness of the university to the socio-economic context through the valorization and transfer of knowledge. TM represents the economic and social mission of the university and its contributions to communities and territories (Compagnucci & Spigarelli, 2020). TM defines additional functions for universities in the context of a knowledge society. Universities are not only responsible for qualifying human capital (education) and for producing new knowledge (research); they should also engage with societal needs and market demands by linking their activities with the socio-economic context. Today, most universities develop their strategies around the three missions: education, research and TM.

More generally speaking, TM accounts for different dimensions (Fig. 1.5), including:

- Elaboration of policies and strategies (TM objectives)
- Creation of incentives for engaging the academic community in TM activities and actions

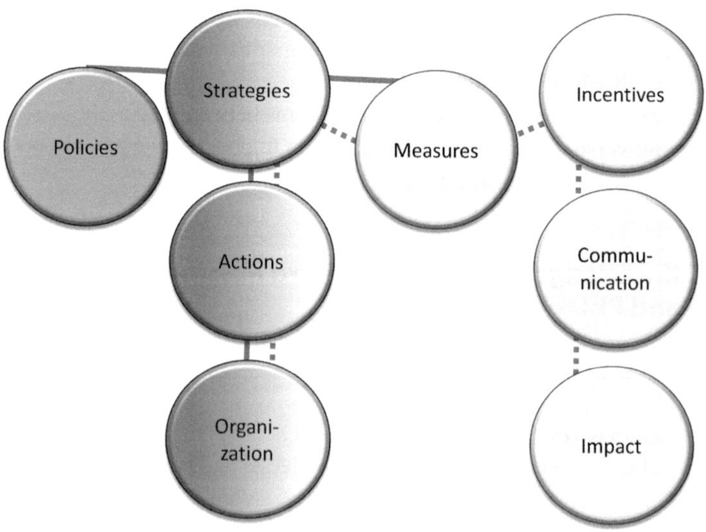

Fig. 1.5 Third mission dimensions

- Designing TM actions (e.g. spin-offs, disclosures, licences, research contracts, consultancy activities, other activities of public engagement)
- Organization of TM actions themselves
- Communication of TM actions and their results
- Assessment and measurement of observable TM outcomes in terms of TM metrics (e.g. number of spin-offs, number of disclosures, number of public engagement events)
- Measurement of the overall impact generated by TM actions (e.g. jobs created; products on the market; internal cultural change; economic, societal, cultural, educational and environmental benefits)

The last two activities are particularly relevant, as we often tend to misunderstand TM outcomes, assimilating the metrics that measure the size or magnitude of the actions (e.g. number of spin-offs, patents) with indicators of the impact (e.g. number of jobs created, number of innovative products launched).

In Italy, the National Agency for the Evaluation of the University System and Research (ANVUR), classifies TM activities in two main areas: 'commercial valorization of research results' and 'production of public goods'. The former includes Intellectual Property management, academic entrepreneurship (spin-off companies), research on behalf of others, intermediary management and support structures (scientific parks, incubator, technological transfer office, placement office). The latter accounts for cultural heritage production and management (museums, archaeological excavations, and historic buildings), clinical trials, research infrastructures and medical training (health protection), lifelong learning, and public engagement.

The ANVUR evaluation methodology[2] has been defined in a specific document published by ANVUR (Manual for the Evaluation of Third Mission) with criteria, indicators and evaluation questions. In this way, ANVUR has set up an information system together with the Italian Ministry of Education, University and Research, to collect standardized and comparable data on all the universities and PROs involved in the evaluation.

1.4.2 Importance of the Third Mission for Universities

Why has third mission become so important for universities and PROs? Why do universities and PROs increasingly invest in it? There are several explanations.

First, they want to be key actors generating impact through the valorization of their research results and contributing to the scientific, technological, economic, social and cultural development of their countries.

Second, they wish to attract additional resources from the private sector. This is a more selfish driver, which is important for universities in a world of declining public resources and increasing competition between higher education institutions. In many disciplines, particularly technology-related fields (Perkmann et al., 2011),

[2] https://stip.oecd.org/assets/TKKT/CaseStudies/11.pdf

collaborations with private companies are instrumental for providing resources and funding to feed into the research system. Often, collaboration with industrial partners is required to participate in public calls for granting public money. In many countries, public science funding entities encourage academic researchers to seek matching funding from commercial organizations (Behrens & Gray, 2001; D'Este & Patel, 2007). Overall, the evidence indicates that many academic researchers seek to attract industry funding to increase the overall resources available to them for research.

Third, they are looking for partners for the implementation of their inventions, to test them, gain feedback to nurture further research and trigger learning that will open up new research avenues and better teaching.

Fourth, they are looking for other non-financial benefits, such as increasing their reputation or attracting international students or top scientists. Higher education institutions are assessed on the impact that they have on society at large. Perkmann et al. (2011) show that, in technology-oriented disciplines, there is considerable academic value in engaging with industry. In addition to providing complementarities with academic research, working with industry will, in many cases, enhance scientists' resource position.

Finally, they are looking to attract students for exchange programmes or international degrees, and such students are increasingly interested in courses in entrepreneurship that have a strong impact and that provide the possibility to engage with innovation and hands-on, transversal activities in collaboration with companies. The attraction (and retention) of international faculty and visiting professors from abroad is also a driver. For many star scientists (Zucker & Darby, 2009), finding opportunities to monetize their scientific eminence and excellence is very attractive, so universities that offer this possibility via third mission are more attractive than those that don't.

These reasons explain the increasing orientation of universities and PROs towards science and research valorization. Understanding these drivers is important for gaining a better understanding of the associated KS activities.

1.4.3 Actions Performed as Part of the Third Mission

What are the specific actions that universities and PROs perform as part of third mission?

There are several taxonomies that can be used to describe TM actions, clustered around different bases (e.g. generating financial/economic benefits vs. production of public goods; targeting private companies vs. targeting a larger external audience; being run internally vs. being outsourced to external organizations).

Below we present them by distinguishing between those that are intentionally designed or planned as TM actions with clear indicators and expected results (in universities' and PROs' strategic plans), and those that are not intentionally designed or planned as TM activities, though they fall within current institutional actions and as such have indicators and results related to institutional objectives (e.g. education, research or both).

The reason why we think this in an interesting criterion for clustering TM actions is that many universities are not aware of the externalities in terms of third mission that they generate every day through their institutional duties, even when they do not fall within formally designed TM activities.

Both categories of TM actions (intentionally designed and non-intentionally designed) are relevant in terms of KS and impact.

The first are TM-related actions that are formalized into strategic objectives, that appear in TM strategic plans with specific TM indicators that have associated TM-related metrics (e.g. number of patents, spin-offs, events) and that generate TM-related impact (e.g. unemployment, new products, social impact).

The second, while not formalized as TM-related actions—as they fall within research or education and appear as such within strategic plans with research- and education-related indicators (and associated metrics)—can also generate TM-related impact.

As an example, consider Table 1.1. Patents are intentional TM actions. They fall within the TM strategic area, have a related objective in the strategic plan (e.g. increase by X% the number of new filings in a given number of years) and have an associated metric (e.g. number of new patents filed). They also generate TM-related impact (e.g. new products, process innovations). Student internships are non-intentional TM actions, as they fall within the education strategic area, have a related objective in the strategic plan (e.g. increase by X% the number of internships with companies in a given number of years) and have an associated metric (e.g. number of internships). They also generate education-related impact (e.g. open-minded students) as well as TM-related impact (e.g. development of new IP and innovative solutions).

We believe that this distinction is particularly interesting because it highlights that universities do more than they think in terms of generating TM impact, and it is

Table 1.1 Example of intentional and non-intentional third mission actions

IP Protection process			
Institutional action	Strategic area	Strategic plan objective	Outcome
Intentional TM action			TM metrics and impact
Patent	Third Mission	Increase by X% the number of new filings	Number of new IPs Number of new products and/or process innovations
Non-intentional TM action			Education metrics and TM impact
Student internship with company	Education	Increase by X% the number of internships with companies	Number of interships Open-minded students New IP and innovation in products and/or processes

important for them to know this. Of course, it is not easy to identify the potential impact that non-intentional TM actions can generate.

Table 1.2 describes traditional, intentional TM-related activities. We rely on the ANVUR classification illustrated above (see note 2 in this chapter). Table 1.3 introduces examples of non-intentional TM-related activities, for which we provide realistic examples of TM externalities that they could generate.

Table 1.2 Intentional third mission actions and their impact

IP Protection process		
Action	Description	TM impact
Patents and IP-related activities	Valorization of IP or industrial property, including industrial property rights and any other forms of IP, in particular copyright Industrial property rights include both those subject to patenting and those subject to registration (trademarks and other distinctive signs, designs and models, topographies of semiconductor products)	Impacts on commerce and economy Impacts on production
New ventures in the form of science-based spin-offs or student start-ups	Valorization of research results in order to develop innovative products and/or services in the form of spin-offs and start-ups (including student entrepreneurship)	Impacts on commerce and the economy Impacts on production
University–industry collaboration	Valorization of research results via contract research with third parties (mainly innovative companies)	Impacts on commerce and the economy Impacts on the environment
Executive and professional education	Valorization of research results and academic knowledge can also take the form of education programmes that are offered to companies (can be customized on the basis of their requirements) to favour advancement of competencies and continuous learning for their employees (reskilling and upskilling) Permanent training and open education means activities carried out by institutions and/or in collaboration and agreement with external organizations aimed at non-traditional users	Impacts on commerce and the economy Impacts on practitioners and delivery of professional services, enhanced performance or ethical practice
Intermediary structures (e.g. incubators, KTOs)	Valorization of research results (IP- and non-IP-based) can happen via activities and actions put in place by intermediary organizations with the primary objective of bridging the gap between universities and industry/markets	Impacts on creativity, culture and society Impacts on social welfare Impacts on practitioners and delivery of professional services, enhanced performance or ethical practice

(continued)

Table 1.2 (continued)

IP Protection process		
Action	Description	TM impact
Public engagement	Valorization of research results can take different forms, including: • Cultural activities of public utility (e.g. concerts, theatrical performances, film reviews, sporting events, exhibitions and other events open to the community) • Scientific dissemination (e.g. publications dedicated to the non-academic public at large) • Initiatives to involve citizens in research (e.g. debates, scientific festivals, etc.)	Impacts on creativity, culture and society Impacts on social welfare Impacts on the environment
Cultural heritage	The production and management of artistic and cultural assets, meaning the protection, management, use and enhancement of archaeological excavations, museums, historic buildings, libraries, newspaper libraries and historical archives, theatres and sports facilities, as well as other musical and performative arts	Impacts on understanding, learning and participation Impacts on creativity, culture and society
Clinical trials	Clinical trials and health-protection initiatives (e.g. clinical trials, medical device studies, non-interventional studies, biobanks, patient empowerment, veterinary clinics, information and prevention, screening and awareness campaigns) are a series of research actions characterized by wide transversality and that therefore produce significant externalities in the economic sphere, as well as social and cultural impacts	Impacts on the health and well-being of people and animal welfare Impacts on practitioners and delivery of professional services, enhanced performance or ethical practice

For TM impact, we rely on a report published in 2021 by the UK REF (Research Excellence Framework, 2021), which, among other things, gives examples of research impact. Specifically, nine areas of impact are identified:

1. The health and well-being of people and animal welfare
2. Creativity, culture and society
3. Social welfare
4. Commerce and the economy
5. Public policy, law and services
6. Production
7. Practitioners and delivery of professional services, enhanced performance or ethical practice
8. The environment
9. Understanding, learning and participation.

The Research Excellence Framework report highlights that these areas are indicative only: in practise, much impact will cross boundaries between areas or go beyond them.

It is worth highlighting that, in the specific domain of university–industry interactions, there are several formal and informal mechanisms of collaboration, not listed here in our tables. Specifically, many firms and universities have increasingly turned to open science strategies, whereby new knowledge is published instead of patented (Friesike et al., 2015; Hayter & Link, 2018) through open data partnerships between firms and universities (Perkmann & Schildt, 2015). According to Franzoni and Sauermann (2014), an increasing number of actors dispersed across multiple locations can be engaged in research activities, such as crowd science. Stanko and Henard (2016) highlight the importance of crowdfunding not only as a mechanism for collecting additional resources for research, but also to have a better understanding of end-users' needs through their feedback, turning this into more effective KS.

In Table 1.3 we list some non-intentional TM actions and highlight the impact they are likely to generate in terms of third mission. The list is not exhaustive; it is supposed to shed light on institutional actions and initiatives that are generally not traced in relation to third mission and that underestimate its potential.

Table 1.3 Non-intentional third mission actions and their impact

IP Protection process		
Action	Description	TM impact
Joint publications with industry and collaborative research	Joint university–industry publications are the outcome of collaborative research through which there is a bidirectional share of knowledge (both tacit and explicit). These activities and their related impact are normally accounted for within research outcomes	Impacts on understanding, learning and participation Impacts on creativity, culture and society
Research workshop and conferences	Participation in conferences where there is a joint discussion and debate engaging people from academia and industry represents an informal outlet for sharing knowledge. These activities and their related impact are normally accounted for within research outcomes	Impacts on practitioners and delivery of professional services, enhanced performance or ethical practice
Internships of students supervised by faculty members	Through internships and stages, students and PhD scholars carry out external, third-party (mainly in a company) training activities, working in close collaboration with non-academic people and supervised by academic professors. Through such activities, there is a bidirectional flow of knowledge. These activities and their related impacts are normally accounted for within teaching and education outcomes	Impacts on understanding, learning and participation

(continued)

Table 1.3 (continued)

IP Protection process		
Action	Description	TM impact
Researcher and student mobility	Through mobility programmes, students and scholars move to different academic institutions and organizations, thus fostering informal knowledge exchange, on top of creating useful networks for KS. These activities and their related impacts are normally accounted for within international research and teaching outcomes	Impacts on social welfare
Thesis	Theses represent vehicles for transferring academic knowledge to the outside. These are not traced as publications but are additional channels of KS. On top of the final documents, the entire process through which theses are produced offers several occasions for students to share knowledge. These activities and their related impacts are normally accounted for within teaching and education outcomes	Impacts on understanding, learning and participation
Industry speeches in teaching	On many courses, entrepreneurs, managers and people from industry are invited to give a speech in class. This represents a moment to share knowledge, the related impact of which is normally accounted for within teaching and education outcomes	Impacts on understanding, learning and participation
University-industry joint projects or events (e.g. placements, dissemination, corporate social responsibility)	Valorization of research results via informal collaborations and projects with companies. These activities and their related impact are normally accounted for within research and students services outcomes.	Impacts on commerce and the economy Impacts on practitioners and delivery of professional services, enhanced performance or ethical practice
Training programmes for faculty members (and mobility training programmes)	These are actions meant to update and teach new approaches through exposure to international best practices. They represent occasions to share knowledge, the related impact of which is normally accounted for within teaching and education outcomes	Impacts on understanding, learning and participation
Alumni-related actions	Many universities have formal alumni associations that are vital for their academic communities. Their stories, narratives and carriers can open up opportunities for students as well as scholars. These activities and their related impacts are normally accounted for within research and student services outcomes	Impacts on understanding, learning and participation Impacts on practitioners and delivery of professional services, enhanced performance or ethical practice

With the non-intentional TM actions, we wish to raise awareness among policy- and decision-makers about the fact that TM impact may be generated in unintentional ways, through other activities. Often universities and PROs do more than they think they do in terms of third mission (and they do not know they're doing it!).

Being aware of this can help them to think about how to formalize, institutionalize and perhaps create internal organizational conditions that support these activities, and generate better TM impact. Take as an example the huge increase that we have witnessed over the last 20 years in transversal training programmes, hands-on teaching workshops and courses aimed at fostering an innovative mindset for academic communities at large (e.g. hackathons, calls for entrepreneurial projects, entrepreneurship courses). They have contributed to new methods of knowledge generation and sharing (ultimately producing TM impact), but in many universities these initiatives are not formalized and institutionalized. Their outcomes and TM impact could be of great benefit if they were formalized, given continuity and supported through organizational mechanisms to make them more effective. Organizational conditions for effective KS and TM will be explored in Chaps. 3 and 4.

1.4.4 The Relationship Between Third Mission and Knowledge Share

Now that we have talked extensively about third mission, we would like to reflect on the relationship between KS and the TM. KS is a key part of knowledge and research-based organizations like universities and PROs. As we mentioned above, KS takes place within research activities and research communities, as well as in education and teaching activities (inside and outside their boundaries, targeting student and faculty communities, as well as external trainees such as professionals and employees of private and public companies).

However, we believe that it is within the TM domain that KS finds its best application, for reasons that have to do with:

- the way KS is defined (proactive behaviour encompassing the distribution/socialization, connection and co-production of multi-sourced knowledge through a circular and multidirectional process that unfolds in both intentional and accidental ways)
- the opportunities offered by third mission to focus on broader communities of individuals outside universities
- the final goal of third mission itself in terms of the generation of impact (in different forms).

So, to finally address the question of the relationship between the TM and KS, we see KS as the procedural view of the TM. KS underpins different TM activities (e.g. strategies, incentives, organization, communication). KS permeates the TM as it applies to the production, transformation, socialization and valorization of knowledge. KS and the TM run in parallel and have the same final goal: generating impact.

In this book, while being aware that TM includes both the commercial valorization of research results and the production of public goods and aims at generating broad impact (e.g. economic, social, cultural, environmental), we focus mainly on KS with regards to activities supporting the commercial exploitation of research results.

1.5 A Holistic View of Knowledge Share

There are several factors that simultaneously come into play and affect the process though which knowledge is connected, co-produced and socialized/diffused. We propose a framework that identifies three categories of factors corresponding to three different levels of analysis (environmental; organizational; individual).

The framework is presented in Fig. 1.6. The three levels will be explored in this book and we will dedicate specific chapters to each one. The model is general enough to be applied in different contexts in order to better analyse and understand KS. Given this book's focus on universities and PROs, we will explore the three levels to understand how the potential for KS and engagement is affected by:

1. Environmental dynamics (general trends external to universities and PROs and characteristics of the local context in which they are settled)
2. Organizational factors (strategic choices and organizational mechanisms implemented by universities and PROs)
3. Individual characteristics (roles of individuals within universities and PROs and outside).

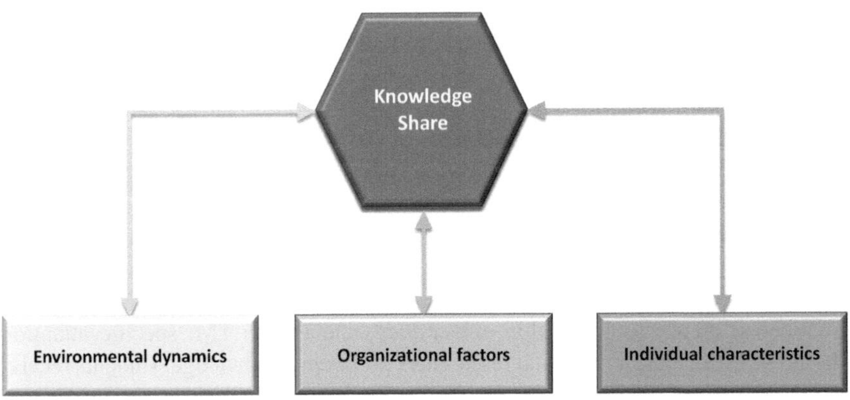

Fig. 1.6 Levels of analysis of knowledge share

1.5.1 Environmental Dynamics

Environmental dynamics include all the factors that are not directly related to individual features and to the organizational characteristics of the context in which individuals work, behave and move. Environmental dynamics include:

- General external macro trends that affect everybody's lives and every organization. Universities and PROs are open systems: they assimilate knowledge from the outside; elaborate, transform, and produce it; and finally give it back to the outside again. In this cycle, their activities are affected by technological evolution, demographic and social dynamics and economic factors, as well as political and legal changes.
- Physical characteristics of the local context (ecosystem) in which individuals and organizations happen to operate, which are key to explaining their performance.

These two categories of factors will be explored in Chap. 2.

1.5.2 Organizational Factors

Organizational factors are internal context features that characterize the settings in which knowledge with the potential to be shared is generated. Organizational factors include:

- The strategy that organizations (namely universities and PROs) have in relation to KS. If KS is important it has be translated in TM goals, with a clear strategic intent.
- The organization that is required to implement a given strategy in support of KS, in terms of resources, incentives and opportunities. Attention should be paid also to the activities to be performed, to partnerships and networks.
- Knowledge transfer offices' organizational design and their main processes.

These factors will be explored in Chaps. 3, 4 and 6.

1.5.3 Individual Characteristics

Individuals are the engine of every creative process. Based on their competencies, traits and networks, they continuously connect themselves with other sources of knowledge, produce new knowledge every day—in isolation or in collaboration with others (co-production)—and interact and socialize with others.

When it comes to KS within universities' and PROs' TM, specific attention should be given to: scientists and researchers producing knowledge; students receiving their professors' knowledge and elaborating it to generate their own competencies; and knowledge transfer office personnel with the knowledge to connect scientists to the outside and create the organizational conditions for KS to happen. Faculty participation will be influenced by perceptions of the competence and capabilities of the university's technology transfer office (Colyvas et al., 2002). These perceptions, in turn, are shaped by institutional history and the environment.

Among individuals, members of the governance also play a key role. Through their strategic decisions, they can profoundly affect and influence the breadth and depth of KS. Regardless of organizational design (following strategic and policy decisions), the attention that the governance pays to third mission in strategic plans and documents is relevant for its legitimization and for generating consensus and engaging the entire academic community.

Other individuals outside academic communities who are relevant to KS are those who work for entities in the local ecosystem (e.g. private companies, other research institutions, third parties, banks, financial institutions).

The role of different individuals in KS processes will be addressed in Chap. 5.

References

Azagra-Caro, J. M., Fernández-Mesa, A., & Robinson-García, N. (2020). 'Getting out of the closet': Scientific authorship of literary fiction and knowledge transfer. *The Journal of Technology Transfer, 45*(1), 56–85. https://doi.org/10.1007/s10961-018-9672-6

Behrens, T. R., & Gray, D. O. (2001). Unintended consequences of cooperative research: Impact of industry sponsorship on climate for academic freedom and other graduate student outcome. *Research Policy, 30*(2), 179–199. https://doi-org.ezproxy.unibo.it/10.1016/S0048-7333(99)00112-2

Bradley, S. R., Hayter, C. S., & Link, A. N. (2013). Proof of concept centers in the United States: An exploratory look. *The Journal of Technology Transfer, 38*(4), 349–381. https://doi.org/10.1007/s10961-013-9309-8

Carlile, P. R. (2004). Transferring, translating, and transforming: An integrative framework for managing knowledge across boundaries. *Organization Science, 15*(5), 555–568.

Chesbrough, H. W. (2003). *Open innovation: The new imperative for creating and profiting from technology*. Harvard Business Press.

Colyvas, J., Crow, M., Gelijns, A., Mazzoleni, R., Nelson, R. R., Rosenberg, N., & Sampat, B. N. (2002). How do university inventions get into practice? *Management Science, 48*(1), 61–72. https://doi.org/10.1287/mnsc.48.1.61.14272

Compagnucci, L., & Spigarelli, F. (2020). The Third Mission of the university: A systematic literature review on potentials and constraints. *Technological Forecasting and Social Change, 161*, 120284. https://doi.org/10.1016/j.techfore.2020.120284

D'Este, P., & Patel, P. (2007). University–industry linkages in the UK: What are the factors underlying the variety of interactions with industry? *Research Policy, 36*(9), 1295–1313. https://doi.org/10.1016/j.respol.2007.05.002

Drucker, P. F. (1993). The rise of the knowledge society. *The Wilson Quarterly, 17*(2), 52–72.

Franzoni, C., & Sauermann, H. (2014). Crowd science: The organization of scientific research in open collaborative projects. *Research Policy, 43*(1), 1–20. https://doi.org/10.1016/j.respol.2013.07.005

Friedman, J., & Silberman, J. (2003). University technology transfer: Do incentives, management, and location matter? *The Journal of Technology Transfer, 28*(1), 17–30. https://doi.org/10.1023/A:1021674618658

Friesike, S., Widenmayer, B., Gassmann, O., & Schildhauer, T. (2015). Opening science: Towards an agenda of open science in academia and industry. *The Journal of Technology Transfer, 40*(4), 581–601. https://doi.org/10.1007/s10961-014-9375-6

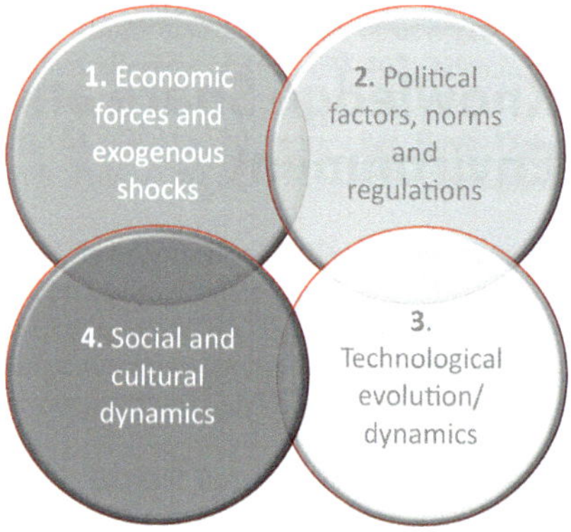

Fig. 2.2 General external trends in four clusters

2.1 General External Trends

General external trends refer to environmental macro-dynamics that affect the way in which KS takes place within universities' and PROs' TM activities. General external trends can influence everything. In Fig. 2.2 we introduce a non-exhaustive list of factors that are likely to influence the innovation potential of countries, regions, organizations and individuals.

We have gathered these general external trends into four clusters: economic forces and exogenous shocks; political factors, norms and regulations; technological evolution/dynamics; and social and cultural dynamics. Some of them overlap, as there are mutual influences and interrelations.

2.1.1 Economic Forces and Exogenous Shocks

The state of the economy can influence economic and technological progress and is therefore relevant for KS dynamics. Economic forces at large include variations in interest rates, recession, inflation, taxes, demand/supply and unemployment. We know that all these factors may influence organizations' investments in research and innovation in different ways, and therefore the production of knowledge, its contents, applications and flow. They also influence individuals' willingness and proactiveness in partaking in new knowledge production.

It is easy to understand that the overall state of an economy is likely to influence the progress and development of countries and organizations and, as such, their ability to move forward with the production and sharing of new knowledge.

On top of general economic conditions (and also related to them), there could be exogenous shocks such as wars, crises and epidemics. All of these can interfere with a country's progress, development and economy.

Exogenous shocks can include external changes, which are difficult to see and forecast in advance. Consider the Covid-19 experience, which slowed the economy of the entire world. While we all hope that we will never face such a pandemic again, it is important to point to some positive externalities of the Covid-19 pandemic in terms of KS and knowledge exchange dynamics. All over the world, Covid-19 has accelerated—and in many cases triggered—digital transformation processes (which were already in place in many countries, specifically in the private sector) that will be beneficial to public and private organizations in the future. While many businesses had to shut down, we have seen a surge in new start-ups offering solutions to pandemic-related problems, and many existing companies have invested in the requalification of their plants to address contingencies and demands for new products and services. The intensive use of remote working has severely affected KS processes.

A study by Yang et al. (2022) analysed email, calendar, instant message, video/audio call and workweek hours data from 61,182 US Microsoft employees over the first six months of 2020 and estimated the causal effects of firm-wide remote working on collaboration and communication. The results of the study show that firm-wide remote working led to workers' collaboration networks becoming more static and siloed, with fewer bridges between disparate parts. Furthermore, there was a decrease in synchronous communication and an increase in asynchronous communication and KS.

During the pandemic, the public sector also witnessed an increase in investment in technologies and digitalization. In terms of research activities at universities and PROs, workshops and conferences have moved online, resulting in an increase in the number of participants; in terms of the TM mission, most universities and PROs have continued their activities through these platforms. For many universities and PROs, online platforms and digital tools have offered the chance to reach out to other communities of scholars, students and civil society at large. Because of the ease with which these platforms can reach academic and non-academic communities, many universities and PROs have witnessed an increase in their international activities, which has had an impact on international KS.

2.1.2 Political Factors, Norms, Regulations

The breadth and depth of KS (both intra- and interorganizational) are influenced by policies and norms. Laws and policies within nations create frames that legitimate, promote or hinder KS and hence affect the incentives and motivation for organizations to partake in active engagement.

We have selected below a few examples of laws, schemes and policy interventions that are well known in the domain of TM activities. Although we often provide examples of international policies and support schemes, it is important to highlight that country-based and regional policies and norms are significantly affecting the research and innovation potential of universities, PROs and private companies, and therefore the opportunities for collaboration, knowledge exploitation and KS. Often these local policies and norms are a direct consequence of international actions and part of broader international frameworks implemented locally. In other cases, countries and regions, in their autonomy, can put forward local policies and norms to support the innovation potential of universities, PROs and private companies and the related KS.

2.1.2.1 Bayh–Dole Act

One of the most cited policies in the domain of technology transfer (TT) is the Bayh–Dole act. The Bayh–Dole Act was introduced at the beginning of the 1980s to enhance incentives for firms and universities to commercialize university-based technologies. Specifically, this legislation instituted a uniform patent policy across federal agencies and removed many restrictions on licensing.

The law allowed universities to own the patents arising from federal research grants. The Bayh–Dole Act also stipulated that researchers working on a federal research grant were required to disclose their inventions to the technology licensing office (Berman, 2008; Mowery & Sampat, 2004). The Bayh–Dole Act, by granting universities the rights to patent inventions funded by federal agencies, challenged the traditional approach of not giving universities direct involvement in the commercialization of research results, and therefore encouraged universities to participate in TT activities (Mowery et al., 2001; Mowery & Sampat, 2004; Baldini et al., 2006).

Several other countries (Wright et al., 2008) adopted similar legislation. Outside the USA, changes in university commercialization were the result of more general reforms (Geuna & Rossi, 2011), such as the reform of the entire academic system of the UK and the Netherlands during the 1990s, in France in 1999, efforts by the Swedish government to promote university technology commercialization since the beginning of the 1980s, and the transfer of several powers from the central government to universities in Italy (Baldini et al., 2006). Denmark, Germany, Austria and Norway reformed their intellectual property (IP) laws to grant IP rights to universities, in a similar manner to the Bayh–Dole Act. Other countries in Europe implemented similar reforms, except for Italy and Sweden, which implemented the 'professor's privilege' (Baldini et al., 2006), granting IP rights to individual scientists and not to the institutions to which they belong.

Kenney and Patton (2011) have criticized the university ownership model in the USA and suggest an alternative model based on inventor ownership. Based on empirical analysis comparing Canadian and US universities, they show that inventor ownership has a bigger impact on entrepreneurship. There is an ongoing debate in the literature (Kenney & Patton, 2009) relating to the pros and cons of Bayh–Dole-type institutional change, which we will not go into detail about here.

We want to draw attention, instead, to the significant impact the passage of this act had on knowledge circulation. The rationale behind Bayh–Dole Act was to enhance public–private research interactions and university patenting and, more generally, to increase awareness of the opportunities for the commercialization of research. More generally speaking, the intention was to shed light on the role that universities could play in the commercialization of the knowledge they produced, enhancing innovation and impact. The enactment of the Bayh–Dole Act in the USA resulted in nearly all major research universities establishing a technology/knowledge transfer office, with increasing attention being given to academic patents and licensing research results (Siegel et al., 2003).

Moreover, Bayh–Dole-like policies have created incentives for universities to elaborate their own specific internal regulations and implement mechanisms supporting academic entrepreneurship at large, including student entrepreneurship. Although at first attention was devoted to the commercial exploitation of research results and the appropriation of these results, universities later introduced other mechanism/channels through which they could valorise the knowledge they produced, including university–industry agreements, continuous education and student entrepreneurship. In fact, the multidimensional activities of university–industry linkages include a portfolio of mechanisms in which knowledge and resources are exchanged and co-created between universities and industry without any IP disclosure through formal systems.

Many universities in Europe have moved away from professor's privilege in the hope of facilitating the commercialization of research results. Specifically, firms and universities have started thinking more seriously about the implications of IP rights management and have started devoting time and attention internally through ad hoc regulations and more attentive negotiations with other public and private collaborating entities. Universities have started to pay more attention to codifying KT and KS processes, requesting clarity *ex ante* on IP rights in collaborative research, which in turn has smoothed the process, made it faster and reduced the costs of negotiation.

These efforts have contributed to speeding up collaboration and, more generally, have had a positive effect on universities' outward-looking attitudes and on the implementation of internal actions (starting from the establishment of knowledge transfer offices) in support of innovation, entrepreneurship and third mission in general.

Before concluding, we wish to make a quick note on the situation in Italy. As we mentioned, Italy has had professor's privilege in place since 2001. While we write this book a new law, abolishing professor's privilege is close to be finalized. The presence of professor's privilege in the past, in our view, has often caused complexities and inefficiencies on the university and the PRO side in the management of internal relations, and uncertainty and difficulties in external relations, especially with companies. The uncertainty in the ownership of patents deriving from inventions has slowed down the process of TT overall. The possibility for scientific inventors to access the increasing number of public–private funding resources in the seed or proof-of-concept phase is often not favoured by the uncertainty of ownership and the management of material rights to research results.

This uncertainty is even greater in the presence of numerous different entities and organizations (as in the case of KS processes) collaborating and developing joint activities. The involvement of students in knowledge exchange and KS activities adds an additional element of complexity and uncertainty that universities are trying to solve *ex ante* by introducing lump-sum rights regulation systems that are easier, more deterministic and faster. In fact, one of the main barriers to public–private collaboration in research is still the management of IP and contracting times.

2.1.2.2 The European Green Deal

The European Green Deal is a set of policy initiatives put in place by the European Commission with the aim of making Europe the first climate-neutral continent by 2050, by reducing greenhouse gas emissions to net zero.

The European Green Deal is an example of a policy intervention at the EU level that offers a road map for making the EU's economy sustainable, based on the idea of turning climate and environmental challenges into opportunities to learn, grow and progress across all policy areas. It also introduces concepts of justice and inclusion, to the extent that the transition talks to everybody and has to generate impact for everybody. The European Green Deal covers all sectors of the economy, including transport, energy, agriculture and construction, and industries such as steel, cement, ICT, textiles and chemicals.

The execution of Green Deal policies is relevant for KS and is likely to change the way knowledge is exchanged and shared. It calls for increased public research and development spending, better IP protection laws, government investment, programmes, incentives, public procurement, clean energy standards and, most importantly for KS, collaboration across different organizations. Specifically, it is important to implement more public–private partnerships and university–industry collaborations, investing at the same time in smart specialization strategies and the implementation of EU cohesion policies.

There are specific organizations at the EU level that are working in this direction and are key for KS.

The European Institute of Innovation and Technology (EIT) is an independent body that was created in 2008 with the specific mission to strengthen Europe's ability to innovate. Specifically, it supports the development of partnerships among companies, research labs and universities across Europe (Knowledge and Innovation Communities [KICs]). Each KIC is designed to find solutions to specific global challenges, and almost all of them are relevant in the context of green industrial policies.

Green transition is inevitable, and it has become an imperative for public and private organizations, forcing them to rethink their actions, strategies and the processes they have in place. It may require the development of new competencies, new technologies and calls for new knowledge to be shared and absorbed. It also calls for new knowledge to be produced and for new alliances and forms of collaboration to be set up.

In a recent European Commission Joint Research Centre report (Vysonka et al., 2021) attention was devoted to the process of TT of green technologies from public research organizations to the market, and to the factors that may facilitate or hinder that process. Among the most important concerns are regulatory uncertainty and a lack of clear political commitment to green technologies that can represent a substantial barrier to the commercialization of new green technologies and to the related sharing of knowledge.

Both investors and innovators need regulatory certainty and coherent and coordinated policy choices. A fragmented regulatory framework and uncoordinated national approach risks hindering the exploitation of cross-border synergies in the

EU. The authors of the report (Vysonka et al., 2021) conclude that policy should adopt a holistic, integrated approach along the entire value chain, from the preliminary phases of research up to the development of mature technologies, which reflects the need for green technologies with a systemic reach. Specifically, it is important for research and innovation policies, industrial and environmental policies and their respective tools and objectives not to act in isolation, but to be joined up into an integrated public policy approach.

2.1.2.3 Open Science

Open science policies are a set of strategies and actions aimed at promoting open science principles and acknowledging open science practices. In general, these policies are established by research institutions, including universities and PROs. The original goal of these polices was to foster open dissemination of research results based on the idea that results achieved by publicly funded research should be available to the public without any restrictions. Nowadays the scope of these policies has grown, and it is possible to find national policies fostering open science practices at any level of research.

Open science has important implications for KS. It stimulates open and collaborative ways of producing and sharing knowledge and data as early as possible in the research process, and for communicating and sharing results. This new approach affects research institutions and science practices by bringing about new ways of funding, evaluating and rewarding researchers. Open science can increase the quality and impact of science by fostering reproducibility and interdisciplinarity and by making science more efficient, reliable and responsive to society's needs.

Open science policies aim at making scientific knowledge, methods, data and empirical evidence freely available and accessible for everyone, thus increasing scientific collaboration and sharing information for the benefit of science and society. They also aim to open up the process of scientific knowledge creation and circulation to societal actors beyond the institutionalized scientific community. This is why open science is so important for KS. The expectation is that universal access to scientific knowledge, regardless of geography, gender, political boundaries, ethnicity or economic or technological barriers is a necessary condition for progress, growth, human development and sustainability.

The core concept of open science comes from the idea of openness itself, which applies not only to science but also to more downstream innovative practices in which universities and PROs are increasingly investing within their open innovation practices.

With specific regard to universities' and PROs' KS, we believe that open science prompts a more open circulation of ideas, which can make it easier for individuals and organizations to access knowledge, can create more and better flow of ideas with commercial potential and can foster the emergence of innovative solutions that are made possible by the combination of diversity and heterogeneity.

One challenge for the future will be the ability to select. The greater the volume of information and data available, the harder it will be to sort, analyse and identify high-potential technologies.

Within Horizon Europe (see Sect. 2.1.2.4), open science obligations are not a general obligation to disseminate all research results. They are even less an obligation to surrender IP rights, and for this reason they should not be construed as being in opposition to IP protection. The dissemination of Horizon results can be postponed, allowing for the appropriate protection of results beforehand. Therefore, it is possible for fellows and beneficiaries to protect their results first (e.g. via a patent filing), while ensuring compliance with the obligation to protect the project's results.

A final thought relates to how the idea of openness (both in science and, even more, in downstream innovation activities) combines with IP rights management and the ability of research and development institutions to appropriate the results of their efforts and investments to generate benefits. Is there a tension/paradox between managing IP rights and engaging in open science and open innovation? What are the implications for KS and knowledge exchange?

Our personal view is that there is no paradox, as the protection of intangible assets by any organization is a prerequisite for sharing and collaborating, especially when we talk about TT as part of KS. The increased attention being paid to IP management and the increased skill with which it is managed by companies has assisted them in developing open innovation strategies. Open innovation is based on the need to access resources from a variety of partners and to ensure the necessary compatibility of a firm's products with those of others. IP ownership enables firms to conduct the trade in technology that accompanies an open innovation strategy, without destroying any competitive advantage they might have.

Effective collaboration and the consequent KS require an upfront definition of the right to create incentives to invest and then to benefit individuals and organizations. The higher the clarity *ex ante*, the higher the chances of stipulating agreements and collaborations, and the greater the incentive to share and open up to the outside and benefit from this openness.

2.1.2.4 Horizon Europe

Horizon 2020 supports Europe's scientific excellence with a new, mission-oriented approach, with the aim of achieving wider social, environmental, technological, cultural, educational and economic impact. Specifically, the programme has diverse objectives and all of them have implications for KS. The most relevant are:

- To strengthen excellent basic and frontier research, including by fostering wider participation of citizens throughout the Union, reinforcing the link between research, innovation and education.
- To support the implementation of Union policy priorities and tackle global challenges, applying policies aligned to the Sustainable Development Goals (Agenda 2030).
- To increase collaboration links in European research and innovation (R&I) and across sectors and disciplines, strengthening international cooperation and attracting high-skilled research through mobility.

- To develop competitive research infrastructures across the European Research Area to foster easier open access and ensure visibility to the public and open access to scientific publications and research data.
- To encourage exploitation of R&I results and actively disseminate and exploit results, in particular for the leveraging of private investments and policy development.
- To deliver on ambitious goals through R&I missions, to stimulate R&I activities in small and medium-sized enterprises and to create and scale up innovative companies.
- To accelerate industrial transformation, to foster the EU's industrial competitiveness and innovation performance and to support market-creating innovation, including through improving skills for innovation and access to risk finance.

On top of this, the European Innovation Council (EIC), a programme established under Horizon Europe to identify, develop and scale up breakthrough technologies and game-changing innovations, shall stimulate all forms of innovation, ranging from incremental to breakthrough and disruptive innovations, and especially targeting market-creating innovations. Through its instruments—Pathfinder and Accelerator—the European Innovation Council aims to identify, develop and deploy all kinds of high-risk innovations.

All of these initiatives will have significant implications for KS, offering concrete incentives to scholars to engage in the valorization of research results and to collaborate with other research institutions and the private sector. The great challenge for higher education institutions will be to stick to their institutional mission and leverage on their excellence, and at the same time to embrace different institutional logics to meet societal challenges and develop frontier research. These measures, coupled with other support mechanisms, such as the European Innovation Ecosystems, will enhance the European potential for the exploitation of research results towards knowledge sharing and impact generation.

In this regard, the new framework programme pays more attention to impact with regard to engagement with companies and joint investment in the industrial system, in order to set a central role for Europe in basic technologies and innovations. It also provides better support for TT, entrepreneurship and 'unicorn' scouting (through the European Innovation Council), as well as attracting and retaining talent. Last but not least, the KS logic is enhanced by the KICs, that were created precisely to bring together players from research–education–market, to find solutions to specific global challenges.

2.1.2.5 University-Level Norms and Regulations

Following worldwide legislative reforms in the 1980s and 1990s (among which was the Bayh–Dole Act) favouring the valorization of research results, Italian universities also introduced internal mechanisms—such as organizational procedures, incentives and regulations—to foster and support academic entrepreneurship in its different forms (Baldini et al., 2006; Geuna & Rossi, 2011). The creation and diffusion of university regulations to incentivize academic entrepreneurship has promoted new approaches that focus on knowledge disclosure, patent activities, academic spin-offs and research collaboration with industry as being legitimate and desirable (AUTM, 2006). The enactment of organizational-level regulations (e.g. patents, IP, spin-offs) is important for creating a framework to legitimize researchers' and scholars' engagement with third mission.

The introduction of university regulations has contributed to the professionalization of activities that support the exploitation of research results in various forms (Meyer, 2003; Siegel et al., 2003). University regulations have raised awareness that universities can play an active role in TT, including licensing, patents, university–industry collaboration, the pursuit of research contracts with companies and academic spin-offs (Mowery & Sampat, 2004; Walter et al., 2016). Accordingly, over the last 30 years, universities have reshaped their role, becoming not only generators of new knowledge but also engines of innovation and sources of new ventures (Bolzani et al., 2021).

However, the effect of university-level regulations should be analysed in relation to other organizational-level mechanisms put in place to foster KS, the TM and academic entrepreneurship. In fact, it is difficult to isolate a policy's influence on KS from other contextual dynamics at play that are favourable to KS and the TM. The process by which individuals engage in entrepreneurial activities is influenced by the heterogeneous and multilevel nature of the context in which they work (Zahra & Wright, 2011). Organizational features of universities (at different levels) can affect scholars' engagement in entrepreneurship. Among these, at least two should be considered: scientific discipline and departmental characteristics and dynamics (Bercovitz & Feldman, 2008; Kenney & Goe, 2004; Perkmann et al., 2013; Rasmussen et al., 2014). Moreover, there are other organizational factors relating to resources, objectives and policies, which we will discuss in the next chapters.

The most important regulations that universities and PROs should have in place to support TT and entrepreneurship include (see Chap. 4):

- IP norms regulating IP for students, professors, administrators and PhD students, taking into consideration the variety of research activities they can engage in (autonomous, cooperative and contract research) and norms regulating out-licensing
- Spin-off and start-up norms regulating the process through which new ventures are established by the academic community and formally recognized as university spin-offs or start-ups
- Norms regulating academics' engagement in extra activities (conflicts of interest and non-compatibility).

All of these norms should be thought about and designed to incentivize academics' engagement, to make it easier and to clarify the process, to make individuals aware of and create an internal culture for academic engagement and KS, as well as to create a legal framework in line with the mission, vision and strategic objectives of the organization.

These regulations should be written so as to push KS further, defining the steps and the formal procedure, with the aim of facilitating individuals and not hindering them or creating boundaries. Regulations should contain and illustrate the main principles and be simple and easy to understand. They should clarify roles, positions, modalities and timelines. They can be accompanied by guidelines with the aim of integrating and explaining activities that are allowed and those that are not-with examples.

Within the new contexts of open science and open innovation, and with regard to the KS concept, the regulations mentioned above should be revised. The challenge is to create a set of rules that includes all types and forms of engagement and the implementation of activities that bring together many different actors. National laws do not provide specific guidelines for different entities to apply. For instance, some universities give students the status of researcher in order to dispose of their IP *ex ante*, before entering into agreements with companies. In other cases, the ownership of all forms of activity carried out by students remains with the students. This uncertain scenario does not incentivize collaboration with companies. Clearly, the difficulty of managing jointly owned inventions between natural and legal persons, students and researchers remains in a context that has become hyper-regulated. In practice, contractual forms have developed that overcome regulatory gaps and bypass excess regulation. These are forms of incentives linked to *ex ante* sales with lump-sum remuneration formulas. Once again, the accounting/financial management of royalties over medium-term horizons is not particularly appreciated by companies that prefer to pay once and in one solution a fair premium deriving from the enhancement of inventions and patents.

Therefore, as previously mentioned, the topic of IP becomes even more central in the context of open innovation and KS activities. The same challenges launched in the form of a hackathon or group work underlie careful agreements for defining pre-existing know-how and for managing what will arise instead (i.e. foreground).

2.1.3 Technological Evolution/Dynamics

2.1.3.1 Digital Technologies

KS has also received a boost thanks to the recent rapid advances in the power of computing technologies, along with the decrease in their cost. Technology has always been important to enable KS. Technological advancement can be very fast, and this pushes many organizations to try to catch up with it and stay at the forefront of knowledge, to access knowledge from the outside, stay connected and collaborate. Therefore, KS is vital. Digital transformation, with its 'enabling' functions, is part of this broader technological evolution. Digital transformation, broadly speaking, refers to the integration of digital technologies into all areas of organizations, fundamentally changing how they operate. It's also a cultural change that requires organizations to continually challenge the status quo.

When it comes to private companies, the integration of new technologies into business models is vital for them to be successful, innovative and to remain competitive. Digital transformation, defined as the integration of new technologies into any process or activity of an organization, is essential to generate new opportunities.

Digital transformation is driven by diverse technological evolutions, the most important of which are: the Internet of Things (IoT), AI (artificial intelligence) and big data analysis. The alliance of IoT, AI and big data analysis encourage organizations to make informed decisions through gathering, understanding and recognizing patterns from collected data. With these high volumes of data and their analysis, organizations could learn from the past behaviours of individuals (e.g. employees, clients, entities they interact with), their interests and problems and act accordingly.

Let us consider AI. AI-based machines may introduce changes in many domains of human labour, influencing the reorganization of supply chains, fostering platform economics and redefining the role of economic actors in the value chain. The recent development of ChatGPT by OpenAI exemplifies the impact that AI can have on our lifes. (Digital) Knowledge and data complement capital, labour and natural resources as major economic variables. The basic intent of AI is to enable computers to perform tasks that normally require human intelligence. AI provides machines with tools that make them learn. AI allows machines to acquire, process and use knowledge to perform tasks and to unlock knowledge that can be delivered to humans to improve the decision-making process.

AI technologies and the exposure to big data affect behavioural and cognitive processes at the individual level and at the social and organizational levels (groups of individuals). They have implications for how individuals think, design, act, collaborate, share and exchange.

Hence, there is a strict relationship between digital technologies and KS. KS allows the flow of knowledge to occur (according to our definition, KS encompasses the distribution, connection and co-production of knowledge), while IoT, AI and big data analysis provide the capabilities to expand, use and create knowledge in novel ways, including new systems that enable organizations to efficiently manage their knowledge, as well as possibly collect new knowledge.

IoT, AI and big data analysis also require organizational employees to acquire new knowledge and skills (reskilling and upskilling) in order to stay and to become competent at performing tasks and activities (Nyikes, 2018). Virtual and augmented reality are also increasingly being used in education programmes, given their potential for educating individuals and thus expanding their knowledge and disseminating the overall knowledge gathered by the organization.

The advent of digital technologies created important implications for universities and PROs and their KS activities, in terms of both research and the production of new content/research results, and in terms of education (e.g. transferring new technologies and new approaches) to train students and external actors to meet new challenges. Universities have new educational needs that can be addressed through technology, which has led to the emergence of new educational approaches and methodologies (e.g. open innovation projects, hackathons, design-thinking-based workshops), leveraging on interdisciplinarity and group thinking, and favouring KS and the emergence of new, innovative solutions.

With specific regard to TT and KS, there are attempts to automatize the TT process through digital twin solutions. Overall, we believe that the automatization of information systems in TT processes—the creation, management, and consultation of large databases (with information on competence, research results, patents, industrial needs, start-ups, multinational expectations, etc.)—may be highly desirable and introduce great benefits. However, this is not going to replace the human component. The obvious benefits will be the reduction of information asymmetries and the speeding up of matching processes. In fact, very important activities in the old TT processes—such as scouting on the business side and marketing on the university/research side—will become real time, automatic and much more effective. That will work well for more traditional TT, but in the KS domain, which is characterized by the distribution, connection and co-production of knowledge through a circular, multisourced and multidirectional process (both intentional and unintentional), a continuous, fast innovation system generating new solutions to emerging problems is needed. Matching solutions to problems will be anticipated and will take place, to an increasing extent, before the filing of a patent and with the creative participation in the co-creation process of a KS domain involving many different actors. The human component and relationships among individuals are and will remain key to creating and delivering value in KS.

2.1.3.2 Deep Tech

Innovations are increasingly the result of the convergence between digital technologies and scientific fields, leading to 'deep-tech' innovations. There is no formal boundary between digital technologies and deep tech. In general, 'digital technologies' refers to new technological knowledge with advanced features and capabilities, generally with a focus on business and industry. Digital technologies enable changes and innovations in core processes and business models, and in societal behaviours around existing services, products and ways of life.

Deep tech addresses mankind's problems by tackling societal and environmental issues by means of often revolutionary and disruptive approaches that take a long time to reach the market (Gourevitch et al., 2021). It requires large capital investment and its success depends on the availability of technical and business expertise that can support the considerable amount of research and development required. Deep tech is deeply rooted in advanced research and has to do with the development of frontier knowledge that can eventually turn into applications addressing big societal and environmental issues. Deep tech is having a profound impact on segments such as autonomous systems, robotics, smart homes/cities, medical devices, clean tech, energy efficiency and many more developing and emerging areas of application.

Deep tech can be defined as technologies based on tangible engineering innovations or scientific advances and discoveries, bringing together many technological areas and having diverse applications. These can include innovations in processing and computing architecture, advances in semiconductors and electronic systems, power electronics, vision and speech algorithms and techniques, AI and machine learning.

Its potential is already clear, and in some ways, it has begun to bear fruit. According to a Boston Consulting Group report[1] (Deep Tech and the Great Wave of Innovation) investments in deep tech have gone from $15 billion in 2016 to over $60 billion in 2020, and estimates are predicted to triple by 2025, reaching $200 billion. Deep tech is today's choice of value for governments, investors and corporations, and investments in it have grown significantly from 2016 to 2021. Corporate investments in deep tech have increased by almost twice the average for corporate venture capital.

Deep tech will be central to future industrial challenges, including the green sustainability of economic and social systems, the early diagnosis of diseases, personalized therapies, and the ability to extract value from the large amount of data we will be able to record thanks to the ever-increasing diffusion of IoT and the paradigms of Industry 4.0 and smart cities.

Deep tech is relevant for university–industry collaborations, TT and KS. While different verticals have different specificities, there are some elements that unite these types of projects and give universities and PROs a key role. These include a significant component of basic research, the large size of investments and, as we mentioned, more time to bring solutions to the market, compared to 'purely' digital projects. In such a context, the public contribution to development that can be offered by universities and PROs is extremely important, at least in the initial phase where the project risk is still too high to attract private capital. Historically, these risky, early-stage big-volume investments, in Italy have been realized through programmes financed at the local, national and European level. Over recent years, these efforts have been increasing thanks to new forms of public–private collaboration, such as the launch of various investment funds by the European Innovation Fund and the Cassa Depositi e Prestiti (CdP), or the Italian Recovery Plan's focus on these issues.

Deep-tech projects represent a great opportunity for venture capital investors. All the actors involved, from investors to scientists to potential clients, are aware that, to grow these initiatives and capture the opportunities they offer, it is important to be patient and participate with an entrepreneurial spirit, as they are characterized by an above-average level of risk. In fact, these projects require more time to mature, and often also more rounds of financing as a function of the progressive achievement of developmental milestones.

The opportunities for universities and PROs in terms of TT and exchange, collaboration with other parties on complex projects, co-production and sharing of knowledge, specifically for leading research institutions, and the production of frontier research have been growing and will continue to grow in the future.

2.1.4 Social and Cultural Dynamics

Technological evolution is intertwined with social change—they influence each other. Over the last thirty years we have seen major changes in the ways we interact,

[1] https://www.bcg.com/it-it/publications/2021/deep-tech-innovation

connect with others and share knowledge. Most of these changes have been made possible by technological evolution, and specifically by digital transformation.

Social and cultural dynamics include:

- Increasing diversity in the workforce
- Increasing interest in healthy foods and green products
- New forms of music and entertainment
- Increasing focus on healthcare, fitness and wellness
- Emphasis on alternative forms of energy
- Increasing access to digital technologies.

We could take as an example the sharing economy, which has seen a rise in new businesses based on the idea of sharing assets and not owning them. This has lot to do with new ways of sharing knowledge, bringing together different individuals and organizations and giving rise to new forms of innovation that deliver value to end users in a novel way. The outcomes of the sharing economy are driven by technological forces, such as the development of the Internet and the spread of digitalization. These technologies facilitate sharing of not just digital but also non-digital, tangible things.

Another reason might be demographic in nature. In many countries, a generation of young people is moving to big cities, renting apartments, and finding that they can rely on public transportation, as well as other public assets. They don't want to own cars, but if they can go online and hire a car, that is more convenient. This generation is driving a lot of the sharing that is taking place.

The third reason is environmental: people are realizing that it is wasteful to have duplicate possessions, particularly of those items that are rarely used but that it's nice to use occasionally.

Also, social media technologies play a key role. Social media generally refers to 'collaborative online applications and technologies that enable and encourage participation, conversation, openness, creation and socialization among a community of users' (Bowley, 2009). They are web-based tools and practices that enable participation and collaboration based on individuals' activities (Storey et al., 2010).

According to Surowiecki (2005), social media should make use of the 'wisdom of the crowd'. A group of 'selected' people is better at problem-solving and decision-making than the individuals are alone.

Vuori (2011) characterizes social media by considering the extent to which it supports communication, collaboration, connection, completion and combination (the five Cs) (Jalonen, 2014). Social media seems to be a good way to share knowledge and promote learning in networks, because social activities contribute to the learning process.

The words 'social media' have a very clear connotation: this is a medium that is all about social activities. Social media users create their own content (known as user-generated content), which can easily be made available to others, who can build on the initial contents to generate new knowledge. This interaction not only leads to new knowledge, it can also ensure that ties with others strengthen or weaken

(Sie et al., 2012). Interaction takes place through commenting, tagging, rating, blogging and liking.

Social media tools are powerful building blocks that can transform the way we enable learning, through knowledge sharing and growth. They foster a new culture of sharing, one in which content is contributed and distributed with few restrictions and costs. According to Bingham and Conner (2010), the potential benefits are evident:

- Easier horizontal networking
- Wider networks of relationships with diverse actors (e.g. scientists, entrepreneurs, people from industry, associations, students, politicians) and more frequent interactions
- The possibility of reaching out to larger audiences through platform-based events or massive open online courses
- More effective connections and management of relationships.

Other social dynamics—such as increasing diversity in the workplace, the orientation towards multi-disciplinarity and heterogeneity, the proliferation of digital media, mobile phones and digital devices, and new forms of entertainment (e.g. video games)—all affect the contents and modes of KS.

2.2 Local Context Characteristics

The local context in which universities and research organizations operate can offer threats and opportunities to their KS activities and the impact that they generate. Knowledge is an intangible asset and, as such, it can easily move around. This could suggest that knowledge flows do not depend on physical proximity—for instance, knowledge can flow via digital devices. Yet, the impact that KS can generate depends very much on the physical characteristics of the recipient organization, the work setting and, more generally, the external context. There is extensive literature (Feldman et al., 2006; Grimaldi et al., 2021) highlighting the importance of local context characteristics for effective TT, KS and innovation to take place.

The business environment within which universities operate can provide important resources for them to valorize research results. Local contexts may offer a set of competencies and resources that are both tangible (e.g. physical infrastructure, corporate physical assets and research and development laboratories) and intangible (e.g. human capital, routines). Local contexts might develop and offer specific support services directly targeted towards facilitating TT, KS, the valorization of research results, new venture creation and university–industry collaboration.

In addition to support mechanisms specifically targeted at supporting TT and KS (e.g. knowledge transfer offices, agencies for university–industry collaboration), there are other factors that may contribute to the creation of an environment supportive to innovation at large.

First, different studies show that the level of financial development makes growth and expansion possible, and that these effects are particularly relevant for small, young firms (Beck et al., 2005; Love, 2003). Venture capital plays a critical role in both the direct financial support that is provided by capital investments and the additional support that is typically attached to early-stage investments. There is consensus that venture capitalists are critical for establishing connections with potential suppliers and customers, increasing the managerial competencies of the founding team and recruiting additional managerial resources (Fini et al., 2011). Other financing institutions, like business angels and banks, are important as well. Many banks have become very active, providing services to scout out and support new entrepreneurial ideas and offer them services for growth.

The characteristics of the industries present in the local context can also determine significant business opportunities (Klepper, 2007). The existence of companies that operate in the same or related sectors promotes the natural exchange of ideas through formal and informal networks among organizations. Closer interactions among companies help to create a social environment that allows and encourages individuals to share knowledge and ideas. Deeds et al. (1998) showed that firms located in a geographical area with a high concentration of similar firms have access to information, personnel and support structures, and enjoy benefits from their proximity. Additionally, Friedman and Silberman (2003) found that universities in locations that are characterized by a relatively high concentration of technology firms generate more licences and licence income.

There is evidence that universities and society at large can benefit from the commercialization of advanced knowledge only when the local context in which they are settled is 'fertile' enough to leverage academic resources (Florida, 1999). The key argument is that communities surrounding universities must have the capability to absorb and exploit the science and knowledge that the universities generate. Even if new knowledge is generated in many places, it is only those regions that can absorb and apply the ideas that are able to turn it into economic wealth.

Florida (1999), for example, argues that Stanford did not turn Silicon Valley into a high-tech powerhouse on its own, but that regional actors built the local infrastructure that the economy needed. The same happened elsewhere (e.g. Boston, Austin), where regional leaders undertook measures to create local opportunities for the commercial exploitation of academic knowledge, ranging from incubator facilities to venture capital and outdoor amenities to attract and retain knowledge workers, and to facilitate knowledge and experience sharing. Accordingly, it is in situations in which local contexts are well developed and rich in opportunities that universities are more likely to turn their knowledge into economic wealth (Degroof & Roberts, 2004; Roberts & Malone, 1996).

In line with this reasoning, the idea of innovation ecosystems has received increasing attention. An ecosystem is a set of interconnected business actors, business organizations, universities, public sector agencies, large and small businesses, financial bodies, etc. Successful innovative ecosystems include the contexts of Israel, Berlin, London, Silicon Valley, etc. These all have different characteristics; there is no recipe for the ideal ecosystem that works for everyone. The ecosystem that works is also the result of the history, tradition, culture, behaviours and values of a territory.

The availability within a given boundary of private companies, universities and other research organizations and bridging institutions promotes collaboration and therefore supports KS. The interrelations of these diverse actors in a specific physical context (with its own stories, traditions, values, etc.) generate idiosyncrasies that turn out to be intrinsic characteristics of ecosystems that influence the ways in which they work, generate and assimilate knowledge and grow. In recent times, characterized by fast connections and rapid technological evolution, the physical characteristics of territories and the connections and networks between actors are even more relevant.

There are different models of ecosystems: business ecosystems, digital ecosystems, platform ecosystems, service ecosystems and also knowledge and innovation ecosystems, in which activities and relationships are measured according to the growth capacity of innovative services, competitive companies and knowledge creation. Knowledge and innovation ecosystems can be defined as geographically co-located hotspots, in which local universities and public research organizations are typically the central actors (Clarysse et al., 2014), and where the key activity of knowledge exploration is accomplished through collaborative research work (Valkokari, 2015).

Knowledge and innovation ecosystems are key in the KS domain. The approaches used by different actors interacting in these knowledge ecosystems influence the type of knowledge that is shared. In this regard, 'the definition of joint objectives (i.e. to facilitate and legitimize interactions and collaborations) and collective, coordinated and synchronized actions towards that goal, should be part of an approach aimed at the maximization of joint benefits' (Ostrom, 1990).

Knowledge ecosystems are relevant in the KS domain from both an input and an output perspective. In fact, they are an important precondition for KS to happen, and at the same time their features and dynamics are affected by the type of knowledge that is generated. The availability of universities and research centres specializing in each vertical domain can affect the nature of knowledge that is produced and shared and can favour the gathering of private companies of other entities/institutions operating within industries thus contributing to the creation of clusters.

Knowledge production, co-production and sharing depend on the active participation of multiple actors. Participation in the knowledge ecosystem can vary in terms of openness (e.g. Gulati et al., 2012). Also, not all actors in a knowledge ecosystem are equally active all the time (Davis & Eisenhardt, 2011) or simultaneously (Davis, 2016). Coordination across knowledge boundaries, domains of expertise and organizational boundaries is required. According to Järvi and colleagues (2018), knowledge ecosystems of various kinds can be understood as meta-organizations (Ahrne & Brunsson, 2005; Gulati et al., 2012), in which autonomous individual and organizational actors come together to reach system-level goals of exploring and creating knowledge, in a more flexible way, while preserving a high level of autonomy for the actors (Felin & Zenger, 2014). While they remain independent entities (Järvi et al., 2018), actors who participate in knowledge ecosystems are expected to 'organize' collectively, which requires relevant organizing elements.

We will go back to ecosystems in Chap. 6, highlighting their role for entrepreneurial universities to be at place.

2.3 Policy Implications for Effective Knowledge Share

What is the relationship between general external trends and local context characteristics? The 'former' are more abstract, dynamic patterns (some are international, others are country- or region-based) that land in the 'latter', in specific local contexts (e.g. countries, regions, cities, organizations) thus becoming embedded into them and shaping local knowledge ecosystems.

This is to say that local context characteristics, including innovation ecosystems, are affected by external dynamics: they assimilate, absorb, and incorporate them and in turn produce outcomes that are given back to the broader external environment, ultimately affecting and influencing its evolution.

Take as an example the evolution of policies and norms that we illustrated above. The introduction of the Bayh–Dole Act and the subsequent proliferation of knowledge transfer offices triggered the emergence of a plethora of specialized players (e.g. local agencies in support of knowledge transfer, business angel communities) wanting to interact with universities to contribute to the valorization of research results. It enhanced and gave rise in many situations to the development of local knowledge ecosystems. Also, localized clusters of spin-off companies have contributed to creating pools of specialized competencies anchored in specific locations. Companies in the local context have created better linkages with universities in an attempt to access research results with commercialization potential. Such local knowledge ecosystems have in turn inspired policymakers to come up with new laws/norms to attract talent, new companies, people exchange and mobility, as well as new funding opportunities for universities and PROs dedicated to TM activities.

So, there are mutual influences between general external trends and local context characteristics. These mutual influences also suggest that the effectiveness of policy intervention depends to a great extent on the characteristics of the local context.

The same policies and rules/norms when applied in different ecosystems can produce different results in terms of KS and impact. Therefore, while it is great to get to know successful policies and to be inspired and to emulate other best practices, and to pay attention to what goes on in other Countries, we recommend that attention be devoted to the specificities of the local context that might affect the ultimate success of policy intervention.

References

Ahrne, G., & Brunsson, N. (2005). Organizations and meta-organizations. *Scandinavian Journal of Management, 21*(4), 429–449. https://doi.org/10.1016/j.scaman.2005.09.005

AUTM. U.S. Licensing Activity Survey (2006) http://autm.net/events/file/AUTM_06_US%20LSS_FNL.pdf

Baldini, N., Grimaldi, R., & Sobrero, M. (2006). Institutional changes and the commercialization of academic knowledge: A study of Italian universities' patenting activities between 1965 and 2002. *Research Policy, 35*(4), 518–532. https://doi.org/10.1016/j.respol.2006.01.004

Beck, T., Demirguc-Kunt, A., & Levine, R. (2005). SMEs, growth, and poverty: Cross-country evidence. *Journal of Economic Growth, 10*(3), 199–229. https://doi.org/10.1007/s10887-005-3533-5

Bercovitz, J., & Feldman, M. (2008). Academic entrepreneurs: Organizational change at the individual level. *Organization Science, 19*(1), 69–89. https://doi.org/10.1287/orsc.1070.0295

Berman, E. P. (2008). Why did universities start patenting? Institution-building and the road to the Bayh-Dole Act. *Social Studies of Science, 38*(6), 835–871. https://doi.org/10.1177/0306312708098605

Bingham, T., & Conner, M. (2010). *The new social learning: A guide to transforming organizations through social media*. Berrett-Koehler Publishers.

Bolzani, D., Munari, F., Rasmussen, E. & al. (2021). Technology transfer offices as providers of science and technology entrepreneurship education. Journal of Technology Transfer, 46, 335–365. https://doi.org/10.1007/s10961-020-09788-4

Bowley, R. C. (2009). *A comparative case study: Examining the organizational use of social networking sites*. Doctoral dissertation, The University of Waikato.

Clarysse, B., Wright, M., Bruneel, J., & Mahajan, A. (2014). Creating value in ecosystems: Crossing the chasm between knowledge and business ecosystems. *Research Policy, 43*(7), 1164–1176. https://doi.org/10.1016/j.respol.2014.04.014

Davis, J. P. (2016). The group dynamics of interorganizational relationships: Collaborating with multiple partners in innovation ecosystems. *Administrative Science Quarterly, 61*(4), 621–661. https://doi.org/10.1177/0001839216649350

Davis, J. P., & Eisenhardt, K. M. (2011). Rotating leadership and collaborative innovation: Recombination processes in symbiotic relationships. *Administrative Science Quarterly, 56*(2), 159–201. https://doi.org/10.1177/0001839211428131

Deeds, D. L., DeCarolis, D., & Coombs, J. E. (1998). Firm-specific resources and wealth creation in high-technology ventures: Evidence from newly public biotechnology firms. *Entrepreneurship Theory and Practice, 22*(3), 55–73. https://doi.org/10.1177/104225879802200303

Degroof, J. J., & Roberts, E. B. (2004). Overcoming weak entrepreneurial infrastructures for academic spin-off ventures. *The Journal of Technology Transfer, 29*(3), 327–352. https://doi.org/10.1023/B:JOTT.0000034126.23592.23

Feldman, M., Gertler, M., & Wolfe, D. (2006). University technology transfer and national systems of innovation: Introduction to the special issue of industry and innovation. *Industry and Innovation, 13*(4), 359–370. https://doi.org/10.1080/13662710601035781

Felin, T., & Zenger, T. R. (2014). Closed or open innovation? Problem solving and the governance choice. *Research Policy, 43*(5), 914–925. https://doi.org/10.1016/j.respol.2013.09.006

Fini, R., Grimaldi, R., Santoni, S., & Sobrero, M. (2011). Complements or substitutes? The role of universities and local context in supporting the creation of academic spin-offs. *Research Policy, 40*(8), 1113–1127. https://doi.org/10.1016/j.respol.2011.05.013

Florida, R. (1999). The role of the university: Leveraging talent, not technology. *Issues in Science and Technology, 15*(4), 67–73.

Friedman, J., & Silberman, J. (2003). University technology transfer: Do incentives, management, and location matter? *The Journal of Technology Transfer, 28*(1), 17–30. https://doi.org/10.1023/A:1021674618658

Geuna, A., & Rossi, F. (2011). Changes to university IPR regulations in Europe and the impact on academic patenting. *Research Policy, 40*(8), 1068–1076. https://doi.org/10.1016/j.respol.2011.05.008

Gourevitch, A., Portincaso, M., De la Tour, A. & Goeldel, N. (2021). Deep Tech and the Great Wave of Innovation. BCG report. https://www.bcg.com/publications/2021/deep-tech-innovation

Grimaldi, R., Kenney, M., & Piccaluga, A. (2021). University technology transfer, regional specialization and local dynamics: Lessons from Italy. *The Journal of Technology Transfer, 46*(4), 855–865. https://doi.org/10.1007/s10961-020-09804-7

Gulati, R., Puranam, P., & Tushman, M. (2012). Meta-organization design: Rethinking design in interorganizational and community contexts. *Strategic Management Journal, 33*(6), 571–586. https://doi.org/10.1002/smj.1975

Jalonen, H. (2014). Social media and emotions in organisational knowledge creation. In *2014 Federated conference on computer science and information systems* (pp. 1371–1379). IEEE. https://doi.org/10.15439/2014F39

Järvi, K., Almpanopoulou, A., & Ritala, P. (2018). Organization of knowledge ecosystems: Prefigurative and partial forms. *Research Policy, 47*(8), 1523–1537. https://doi.org/10.1016/j.respol.2018.05.007

Kenney, M., & Goe, W. R. (2004). The role of social embeddedness in professorial entrepreneurship: A comparison of electrical engineering and computer science at UC Berkeley and Stanford. *Research Policy, 33*(5), 691–707. https://doi.org/10.1016/j.respol.2003.11.001

Kenney, M., & Patton, D. (2009). Reconsidering the Bayh-Dole Act and the current university invention ownership model. *Research Policy, 38*(9), 1407–1422. https://doi.org/10.1016/j.respol.2009.07.007

Kenney, M., & Patton, D. (2011). Does inventor ownership encourage university research-derived entrepreneurship? A six university comparison. *Research Policy, 40*(8), 1100–1112. https://doi.org/10.1016/j.respol.2011.05.012

Klepper, S. (2007). Disagreements, spinoffs, and the evolution of Detroit as the capital of the US automobile industry. *Management Science, 53*(4), 616–631. https://doi.org/10.1287/mnsc.1060.0683

Love, I. (2003). Financial development and financing constraints: International evidence from the structural investment model. *The Review of Financial Studies, 16*(3), 765–791. https://doi.org/10.1093/rfs/hhg013

Meyer, M. (2003). Academic patents as an indicator of useful research? A new approach to measure academic inventiveness. *Research Evaluation, 12*(1), 17–27. https://doi.org/10.3152/147154403781776735

Mowery, D. C., Nelson, R. R., Sampat, B. N., & Ziedonis, A. A. (2001). The growth of patenting and licensing by US universities: An assessment of the effects of the Bayh–Dole act of 1980. *Research Policy, 30*(1), 99–119. https://doi.org/10.1016/S0048-7333(99)00100-6

Mowery, D. C., & Sampat, B. N. (2004). The Bayh-Dole Act of 1980 and university–industry technology transfer: A model for other OECD governments? *The Journal of Technology Transfer, 30*(1), 115–127. https://doi.org/10.1007/s10961-004-4361-z

Nyikes, Z. (2018). Digital competence and the safety awareness base on the assessments results of the Middle East-European generations. *Procedia Manufacturing, 22*, 916–922. https://doi.org/10.1016/j.promfg.2018.03.130

Ostrom, E. (1990). *Governing the commons: The evolution of institutions for collective action.* Cambridge University Press.

Perkmann, M., Tartari, V., McKelvey, M., Autio, E., Broström, A., D'este, P., et al. (2013). Academic engagement and commercialisation: A review of the literature on university–industry relations. *Research Policy, 42*(2), 423–442. https://doi.org/10.1016/j.respol.2012.09.007

Rasmussen, E., Mosey, S., & Wright, M. (2014). The influence of university departments on the evolution of entrepreneurial competencies in spin-off ventures. *Research Policy, 43*(1), 92–106. https://doi.org/10.1016/j.respol.2013.06.007

Roberts, E. B., & Malone, D. E. (1996). Policies and structures for spinning off new companies from research and development organizations. *R&D Management, 26*(1), 17–48. https://doi.org/10.1111/j.1467-9310.1996.tb00927.x

Sie, R. L., Ullmann, T. D., Rajagopal, K., Cela, K., Bitter-Rijpkema, M., & Sloep, P. B. (2012). Social network analysis for technology-enhanced learning: Review and future directions. *International Journal of Technology Enhanced Learning, 4*(3–4), 172–190. https://doi.org/10.1504/IJTEL.2012.051582

Siegel, D. S., Waldman, D. A., Atwater, L. E., & Link, A. N. (2003). Commercial knowledge transfers from universities to firms: Improving the effectiveness of university–industry collaboration. *The Journal of High Technology Management Research, 14*(1), 111–133. https://doi.org/10.1016/S1047-8310(03)00007-5

Storey, M. A., Treude, C., van Deursen, A., & Cheng, L. T. (2010). The impact of social media on software engineering practices and tools. In *Proceedings of the FSE/SDP workshop on Future of software engineering research* (pp. 359–364). https://doi.org/10.1145/1882362.1882435.

Surowiecki, J. (2005). *The wisdom of crowds*. Anchor.

Valkokari, K. (2015). Business, innovation, and knowledge ecosystems: How they differ and how to survive and thrive within them. *Technology Innovation Management Review, 5*(8) https://timreview.ca/article/919

Vuori, V. (2011). *Social media changing the competitive intelligence process: Elicitation of employees' competitive knowledge*. Doctoral dissertation, University of Technology, Tampere.

Vysonka, L., Dorr, R., Sarris, S., & Gathy, G. (2021). Technology transfer and commercialisation for the European green deal, Fazio, A. editor(s), EUR 30694 EN, *Publications Office of the European Union*, Luxembourg, 2021, ISBN 978-92-76-37536-4 (online), https://doi.org/10.2760/918801 (online), JRC124354.

Walter, S. G., Schmidt, A., & Walter, A. (2016). Patenting rationales of academic entrepreneurs in weak and strong organizational regimes. *Research Policy, 45*(2), 533–545. https://doi.org/10.1016/j.respol.2015.11.008

Wright, M., Clarysse, B., Lockett, A., & Knockaert, M. (2008). Mid-range universities' linkages with industry: Knowledge types and the role of intermediaries. *Research Policy, 37*(8), 1205–1223. https://doi.org/10.1016/j.respol.2008.04.021

Yang, L., Holtz, D., Jaffe, S., Suri, S., Sinha, S., Weston, J., Joyce, C., Shah, N., Hecht, B., & Teevan, J. (2022). The effects of remote work on collaboration among information workers. *Nature Human Behaviour, 6*(1), 43–54. https://doi.org/10.1038/s41562-021-01196-4

Zahra, S. A., & Wright, M. (2011). Entrepreneurship's next act. *Academy of Management Perspectives, 25*(4), 67–83. https://doi.org/10.5465/amp.2010.0149

Knowledge Share Within Research Organizations

3

This chapter is devoted to illustrating the characteristics that are relevant for research organizations willing to engage in knowledge share (KS).

There are two main dimensions that are likely to affect KS within universities: strategy, dealing with defining long-term goals, and organizational design, encompassing the procedures and organizational choices and mechanisms implemented to support the achievement of strategic goals.

In this chapter, strategic and organizational design factors will be addressed from a hands-on perspective, with concrete examples of strategies and organizational mechanisms to support KS. In adopting this practical approach, the authors rely on their past professional experience (as Deputy Rector for entrepreneurship and Head of the knowledge transfer office at the University of Bologna) and present the case of the University of Bologna (Alma Mater Studiorum). The strategy, actions and a coherent organizational architecture in support of the strategy were designed by the two authors in a joint effort with other colleagues from within the governance and KTO division. We believe that the case of the University of Bologna can represent a source of inspiration for other universities. It is not meant to be exhaustive, as other universities might have additional actions and services in place. Moreover, the description of the University of Bologna strategy that we present here refers to the period 2015–2021 and does not consider its evolution from 2022 onwards, following a change of the governance. Also, it is not meant to be generalized. On the contrary: we encourage universities to leverage their own specificities to work out strategies and models that will suit their stories, locations and values.

G. Conti, R. Grimaldi, *Knowledge Share: the (R)evolution of Technology Transfer*, SxI - Springer for Innovation / SxI - Springer per l'Innovazione 16,
https://doi.org/10.1007/978-3-031-51384-8_3

3.1 Entrepreneurship Strategy: The Case of the University of Bologna

A strategy in support of entrepreneurship will be, for most universities, part of broader strategies around the third mission. We argue that the design and implementation of entrepreneurial actions aimed at fostering entrepreneurial behaviour are core components of universities' KS dynamics. In many universities the development of an entrepreneurship strategy can be tricky, as it can require important changes, such as overcoming internal resistance, looking for external support and building a clear positioning in the eyes of the surrounding external ecosystem. For this reason, we have decided to focus on entrepreneurship strategy within the broader concept of KS.

A strategy in support of entrepreneurship should be detailed in two main documents: a more general document called the Strategic Plan, and a more specific document called the technology transfer Plan. The first describes the vision and mission of the university/public research organization (PRO), illustrating technology transfer initiatives and setting up expected results and key performance indicators (KPIs) to measure outcomes and their impact. The second takes into account specific investments and changes in organizational structures, internal regulations and processes. We start with a quote from the Strategic Plan of the University of Bologna for the period 2015–2021 as a concrete example.

"Alma Mater is a large community of men and women who, with different roles and competences, strive to transmit knowledge, experiment with techniques, and develop the ideas that will address the transformations of our time. Building on centuries of history and fuelled by an inexorable drive to innovate, the vocation of the University for education and research is rooted at the very heart of our life and autonomy. These pillars are accompanied by a third mission: the maintenance of dynamic relations and exchanges with society as a whole and the world of work."

The strategic road map related to third mission at the University of Bologna (following the Strategic Plan) builds on two main blocks: innovation and dissemination.

The first accounts for: improving the transfer of technologies and knowledge in favour of social and economic impact; promoting entrepreneurship and relationships with businesses; enabling professional training and lifelong learning; and supporting development and cooperation.

The second is about socializing the research results and generating impact for society by promoting cultural initiatives (and their wider opening to citizens), favouring the dissemination, promotion and co-production of knowledge and supporting alumni network initiatives.

Within these two blocks, specific strategic goals have been set up and monitored by several indicators, as illustrated in Table 3.1.

In line with the Strategic Plan, a specific strategy in support of entrepreneurship has been elaborated. At the heart of this strategy there are clear vision and mission statements (Table 3.2) that explicitly focus on spin-off and start-up creation. A

Table 3.1 Third mission goals and indicators at the University of Bologna

Third Mission goals and indicators at the University of Bologna	
Goal	Indicators
1. Strengthen the social and economic impact at a regional, national and international level via entrepreneurship projects and university business initiatives	Number of patents, trademarks, vegetable varieties Number of accredited/active spin-offs and start-ups Turnover of commissioned commercial and scientific activities
2. Strengthen cooperation in the areas of economic, social and cultural development	Number of cooperative projects

Table 3.2 Vision and mission of the University of Bologna entrepreneurship strategy

Vision and mission at the University of Bologna	
Vision	Mission
Leveraging the entrepreneurial potential of students and faculty to generate impact	Fostering the diffusion of entrepreneurial culture within the university community Promoting the commercial exploitation of university research results through the creation of spin-offs Encouraging the creation of student-based start-ups

spin-off company is defined as a research-based company formed around knowledge developed within the university, both intellectual property (IP)- and non-IP-based, with the involvement of at least one person from the research community (e.g. professor, research fellow, PhD student). A start-up is conceived as a company started by students (e.g. undergraduate and master's students) and 'fresh' graduates, based on the skills, know-how and experiences they developed during their training at and with the support of the university.

The 2015–2021 entrepreneurship strategy at the University of Bologna builds on five pillars (Fig. 3.1) that represent the steps of a process the university invests in to promote entrepreneurship, from the initial emergence of an idea worth exploiting, all the way through to the establishment of a new company and the provision of support for their growth.

Pillar 1: Entrepreneurial Culture Creation
Actions within this pillar are intended to generate an entrepreneurial culture and raise entrepreneurial awareness within the entire University of Bologna community.

Pillar 2: Ideas Scouting
Actions within this pillar are meant to foster the identification of business opportunities, targeting scholars and faculty and encouraging them to disclose their ideas and share them within the broader University of Bologna community.

Fig. 3.1 The five-pillar strategy in support of entrepreneurship at the University of Bologna

Pillar 3: Business Development

Business development activities are thought to help would-be entrepreneurs assess the viability of their ideas, create prototypes, and develop a proper business plan through ad hoc training, so they can contact experts, industry players, mentors and institutional investors.

Pillar 4: Incubation

Incubation activities are meant to offer support to companies as they establish themselves and run their businesses. Logistics services and legal and accounting advice are offered to entrepreneurial teams. More traditional ‘pre-incubation’ services, including support with business plan development and team-building, are provided to aspiring entrepreneurs, both students and faculty, as well as to inventors.

Pillar 5: Growth and Scale-Up

The growth of spin-off and start-up companies requires connections to networks of players who can offer the capital and expertise to turn start-up companies into high-flyers. The University of Bologna leverages formal and informal relationships with regional, national and international players (e.g. foundations, business angels, venture capitalists, banks, regional schemes and initiatives, and other private and public organizations supporting entrepreneurship) to create the conditions for successful companies to grow and scale up.

Across the five pillars, two different sets of support actions are designed (two lines in Fig. 3.2) that address two targets: researchers, willing to engage in the creation of spin-offs, and students, exploring the possibility of establishing a start-up.

These two targets need similar, though different, actions. While most individuals go through the same phases of the entrepreneurial process (from idea definition to new venture creation), researchers (scholars, faculty members, professors, PhD students) and students (mainly undergraduates) have different experiences, different levels of seniority and maturity and different networks. Moreover, they rely on different knowledge bases (more research based for founders of academic spin-offs) and are moved by different drivers.

Figure 3.2 illustrates the diversity of mechanisms for the two targets alongside the five pillars. In the upper part of the figure there are actions targeting researchers and aimed at generating research-based spin-offs. In the lower part there are actions targeting students and aimed at generating students’ start-ups. Below, we provide a detailed description of each support mechanism.

3.1.1 Spin-Off Initiatives

3.1.1.1 Pillar 1: Entrepreneurial Culture

Entrepreneurship Club

This is an open community of academics interested in entrepreneurship that meet up to six times per year. The entrepreneurship club provides opportunities to socialize, share ideas and learn. Each event is organized to host an inspirational talk by an

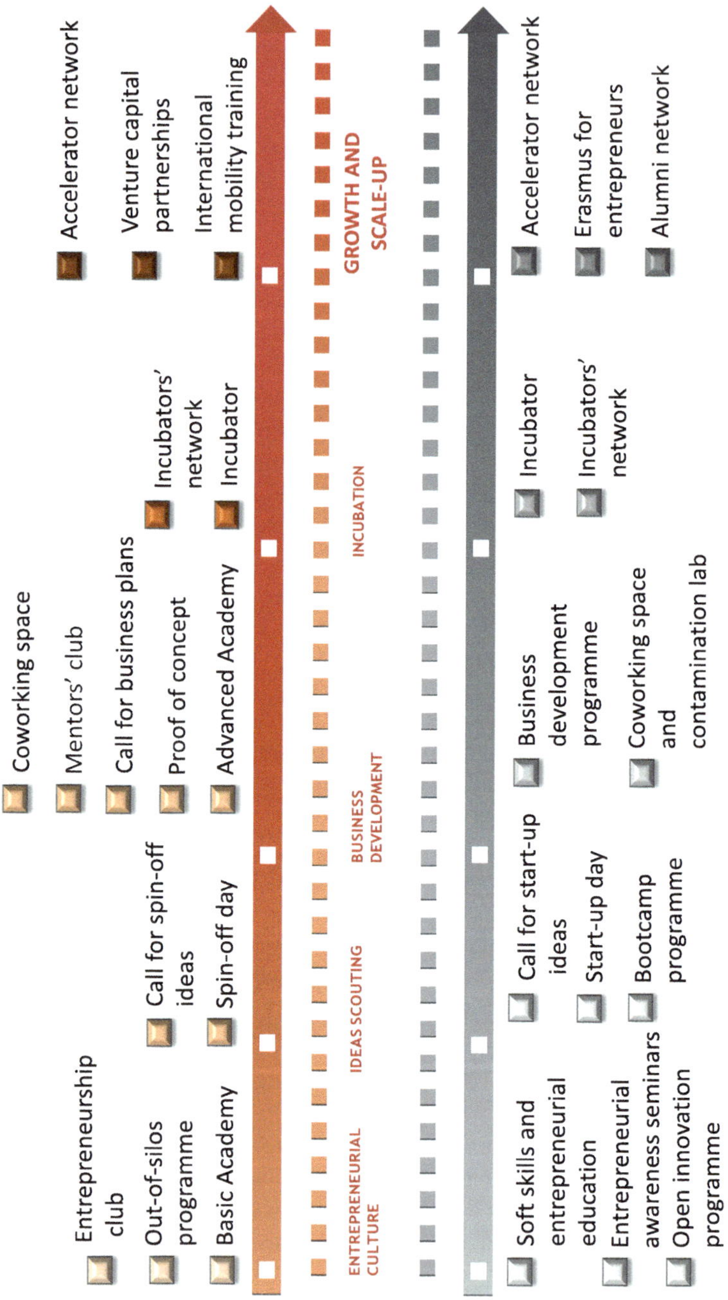

Fig. 3.2 Diversity of mechanisms for the two targets alongside the five pillars

influential person in the field of entrepreneurship/innovation and a focus group session aimed at collecting ideas from the research community on specific issues relating to how to turn the University of Bologna into an entrepreneurial university. Participants come from different departments with the aim to share their ideas and learn from others.

Key elements:
- *Continuity (a champion/manager is needed to keep the club alive)*
- *Incentives' scheme to maintain the community involved*
- *Heterogeneity of people and departments*
- *Involvement of the governance (participation to events).*

Out-of-Silos Programme

A programme targeting newly enrolled scholars (new employees of the university) and aimed at sharing the core values, disseminating information of the strategic projects, favouring socialization. Topics discussed include IP protection and exploitation and mechanisms to support participants along academic valorization of their research results.

Key elements:
- *Involvement of the governance*
- *Presence of technical people from the KTO*
- *Heterogeneity of people and departments.*

Basic Academy

A programme aimed to raise awareness about IP and entrepreneurship, targeting the entire research community. This training programme stimulates creativity through inspirational talks and provides information about support mechanisms available within the university and the basic tools to start developing entrepreneurial projects.

Key elements:
- *Involvement of the governance*
- *Presence of technical people from the KTO*
- *Heterogeneity of people and departments.*

3.1.1.2 Pillar 2: Ideas Scouting

Call for Spin-Off Ideas

A call for research-based ideas runs every year. The call targets the entire university research community (PhD students, faculty members, research fellows) and is meant to collect research-based ideas. The call is the start of a cycle/process through which ideas that show potential for commercial exploitation are selected first and then supported in their evolution into a business plan.

Key elements:
- *Strong promotion of the initiative to maximize ideas' collection*
- *Support from the KTO*
- *Simple procedures and tools to encourage participation.*

Spin-Off Day

Organized by the university in collaboration with its internal coworking space and incubator, this annual event targets the entire research community, from staff to PhD students (according to the chosen definition of a spin-off company, as mentioned above). It offers them the possibility to present their early-stage entrepreneurial ideas to the broader university community, business angels, investors and other potential stakeholders.

Key elements:
- *Strong promotion of the initiative to maximize ideas' collection*
- *Support from the KTO*
- *Easy and clear procedures and tools for participation*
- *Availability of financial resources to support early stage ideas*
- *Involvement of investors, both as speakers and as supporters/mentors.*

3.1.1.3 Pillar 3: Business Development

Proof of Concept

This tool is designed to foster the development of university-patented (IP-based) technologies, maximize their commercial exploitation (increasing technology readiness level) and help their inventors identify avenues for commercial exploitation through either out-licensing or the creation of spin-offs. The proof-of-concept (PoC) fund is financed by the university and can be supported (matched) by external private investors.

Key elements:
- *Strong promotion of the initiative to maximize proposals' collection*
- *Support from the KTO*
- *Easy and clear procedures and tools for participation*
- *Availability of financial resources to enhance inventions' potential*
- *Involvement of investors within the internal selecting committee assigning the grants.*

Co-working Space

A physical location offering opportunities to meet, discuss ideas, develop entrepreneurial projects, access instruments and tools and receive technical support for prototyping. The coworking space also has a prototyping area (maker space) equipped with a laser cutter, 3D printers and other digital tools.

Key elements:

- *Easy and clear procedures and tools for participation*
- *Availability of financial resources*
- *Heterogeneity of the people involved*
- *Availability of a critical mass of researchers, ideas and supporting people.*

Advanced Academy

This training programme targets researchers who already have feasible ideas (many of them selected through the call for spin-off ideas) and provides customized support (both specific and vertical expertise) to further develop their businesses through the involvement of experienced faculty members, external experts and industry mentors.

Key elements:

- *Focus on specific contents of every idea through one-to-one meeting*
- *Availability of financial resources to support ideas' development*
- *Hands-on training modules aimed at shaping single ideas.*

Call for Business Plans

A call for business plans runs every year to select viable business plans that leverage and exploit the results of university research. The call provides awards (including scholarships for international training, seed money investments, grants to invest in human capital to work on ideas, etc.) to teams that are close to setting up new ventures. The call can be offered in addition to other training programmes and PoC initiatives.

Key elements:

- *Strong promotion of the initiative*
- *Support from the KTO*
- *Easy and clear procedures and tools for participation*
- *Availability of financial resources to support business plan evolution.*

Mentors' Club

A community of (up to) 30–40 faculty member entrepreneurs (involved in spin-off companies), alumni entrepreneurs and non-university (external) entrepreneurs offering support and expertise and willing to champion business ideas from the university community. Mentors are involved as coaches and investors in specific sessions of the advanced entrepreneurship training programme, but also in internal committees like IP and PoC committees/boards.

Key elements:

- *Strong promotion of the initiative*
- *Support from the KTO*

- *Continuity (a dedicated manager is required to keep the club alive)*
- *Incentives' scheme for mentors' involved*
- *Heterogeneity of technical competencies.*

3.1.1.4 Pillar 4: Incubation

Incubator (and Incubators' Network)

The incubator of the University of Bologna is a public–private joint venture between the *Confindustria Emilia Area Centro* and the university itself. It offers support for the university's entrepreneurial strategy in different ways, including support for spin-off companies. It provides legal and administrative services to establish spin-off companies, as well as physical locations (offices). It helps spin-offs to access financial resources.

Key elements:

- *Support from the KTO to the incubators' network*
  - *Clear goals (and KPIs)*
  - *Incentives' scheme for people running incubators.*

3.1.1.5 Pillar 5: Growth and Scale-Up

Accelerator Network

To foster the growth of its affiliated companies, the University of Bologna has created partnerships with other institutions, organizations, programmes, and key players that might be interested in supporting new ventures through acceleration programmes. The main strategic partners include embassies, local communities, alumni chapter communities, banks and accelerators. The aim is to expose spin-off companies to different ecosystems providing complementary resources/technologies to boost their market penetration growth.

Key elements:

- *Strong endorsement, visibility of partners, and win–win partnerships*
  - *Support from the KTO and internal incubators to move forward*
  - *Putting strong relationships in place.*

Venture Capital Partnerships

The possibility of getting financial resources and mentors from the pre-seed phase to scale-up can make a difference during a spin-off company's first years. Partnerships with venture capitalists can be set up based on specific agreements or programmes (e.g. management of an internal venture capital fund).

Key elements:

- *Availability of deal flow*
  - *Strong relationships (both institutional and personal) between the KTO and venture capitalists based on trust and track record.*

International Mobility Training

To promote the sharing of best practices, to gain international exposure and to access international markets, it is important to foster the mobility of scholars and PhD students with entrepreneurial ideas by inviting scholars from other countries to join the University of Bologna entrepreneurship programmes, and vice versa. Specific partnerships with international universities and other organizations investing in entrepreneurship can be set up.

Key elements:

- *Strong endorsement network of international accelerators, programs and investors*
- *International promotion of the entrepreneurial programmes and strategies.*

3.1.2 Start-Up Initiatives

3.1.2.1 Pillar 1: Entrepreneurial Culture

Soft Skills and Entrepreneurial Education

Soft skills and entrepreneurship courses are put in place to allow students in all degree programmes, disciplines, and curricula to gain basic training in entrepreneurship and to learn the foundations of business management.

Key elements:

- *Work out entrepreneurial contents that can be accessible by different targets*
- *Incentives' scheme for instructors and students to be involved*
- *Strong promotion of the initiative*
- *Blended educational programs.*

Entrepreneurial Awareness Seminars

These events target different groups of students with the goal of raising awareness about entrepreneurship and encouraging entrepreneurial values. They target students in all disciplines: science, technology, engineering, mathematics, social sciences and humanities.

The main goal is to help students figure out how their knowledge and skills could be used to generate innovative ideas. Examples in Italy are "Aperitech" and "Aperiseed", which are organized by universities together with contamination labs, coworking spaces and incubators, and also involving external investors, business angels and all stakeholders with a specific interest in entrepreneurship.

Key elements:

- *Build strong stakeholders' network*
- *Continuity (ideally one short event every week)*
- *Dedicated spaces and resources*
- *Interdisciplinary and multidisciplinary approach.*

Open Innovation Programme

There are different ways to organize open innovation programmes, from one-day events built around company challenges, to more complex and structured events. During open innovation programmes, students experience real-world innovation challenges, working side by side with innovative companies to use design-thinking methods and tools. Some programmes are built around short-term goals based on problem-solving approaches; others aim to develop highly futuristic, technologically feasible ideas that have the potential to challenge the status quo on global issues.

Key elements:

- *Strong industrial networks*
- *Strong international networks*
- *Incentive scheme/credits to engage students.*

3.1.2.2 Pillar 2: Ideas Scouting

Call for Start-Up Ideas

A call for ideas from university students is issued every year, aimed at selecting the most promising ones. The call is the entry point to a process through which teams of students are supported in transforming their preliminary ideas into viable business plans.

Key elements:

- *Strong promotion of the initiative*
- *Support from the KTO and/or other stakeholders/partners*
- *Easy and clear procedures and tools for participation.*

Start-Up Day

This event is organized by the University in collaboration with other dedicated structures (e.g. contamination labs, coworking spaces, incubators) with the aim to offer students the chance to present their early-stage entrepreneurial ideas to a broader community (made up of business angels, investors and other potential stakeholders). Thanks to this event, students can validate their ideas and complement their teams with additional resources and competencies (e.g. look for other students willing to engage).

Key elements:

- *Strong promotion of the initiative (and support from media partners)*
- *Support from the KTO and/or other stakeholders/partners and volunteers*
- *Easy and clear procedures and tools for participation*
- *Availability of resources for investment (money, people, space).*

Bootcamp Programme

A bootcamp programme is generally a one-day event that engages students, encourages them to disclose their preliminary projects and offers them the possibility to test their project's technical and economic feasibility.

Key elements:
- *Support from the KTO and/or other stakeholders/partners*
- *Availability of resources for investment (money, people, space).*

3.1.2.3 Pillar 3: Business Development

Business Development Programme

This is a training programme that offers early-stage support to selected teams of students as they develop their ideas and businesses. Students from all disciplines are provided with basic tools and models (e.g. market analysis, SWOT analysis) to start crafting their ideas and turn them into viable business plans.

Key elements:
- *Strong promotion of the initiative (and support from media partners)*
- *Support from the KTO and/or other stakeholders/partners and volunteers*
- *Appropriate timeline for the programme (considering availability of students)*
- *Organization of one-to-one training sessions with specialized mentors.*

Coworking Space and Contamination Lab

A coworking space and a contamination lab are places where students with entrepreneurial ideas can meet to discuss their projects and receive support and advice to assess their viability.

It is also desirable to offer a maker space where students can use prototyping tools and receive technical support.

Key elements:
- *Strong endorsement from the governance*
- *Skilled employees and collaborators to deliver effective services*
- *Availability of resources for investment.*

3.1.2.4 Pillar 4: Incubation

Incubator (and Incubators' Network)

The incubator of the University of Bologna is a public–private joint venture between the Confindustria Emilia Area Centro and the university itself. It offers support for the university's entrepreneurial strategy in different ways, including support for start-up companies. It provides legal and administrative services for the establishment of both spin-offs and start-ups, as well as physical locations (offices). It helps newly established start-ups to access financial resources.

Key elements:

- *Strong endorsement (and control) of the initiative/structure*
  - *Support from the KTO and key people within the incubator governance*
  - *Clear goals (and KPIs) and design of complementarities between incubators and the KTO.*

3.1.2.5 Pillar 5: Growth and Scale-Up

Accelerator Network

The university leverages partnerships with national and international accelerators to offer additional funding and growth opportunities to its start-ups.

Private accelerators are linked to investment funds and/or big companies interested in the selected deal flow of existing start-ups. They can run training programmes and act as incubators for foreign start-ups, but most importantly they will boost access to markets and customers.

Key elements:

- *Strong endorsement from the governance*
  - *Critical mass on deal flow and track record*
  - *Brand visibility.*

Erasmus for Entrepreneurs

This is a European programme that fosters the mobility of student entrepreneurs (over 1–6 months) so they can be exposed to different ecosystems and international opportunities.

Key elements:

- *Strong promotion of the initiative*
  - *Well-established international network*
  - *Internal skills to manage procedures and projects.*

Alumni Network

A network of graduates from the university involved in supporting students' entrepreneurship in different ways. Alumni bring their unique insights to entrepreneurship events, sharing their experiences to inspire other students, provide support, guide aspiring entrepreneurs, and help students develop their ideas. The alumni network acts in relation to and in synergy with the mentors' club, being potentially both coaches and investors.

Key elements:

- *Strong endorsement from the governance*
  - *Skilled employees and collaborators to deliver effective services*
  - *Availability of resources for investment.*

3.2 Organizational Models

In the second part of this chapter, we will address how to design effective organization and efficient processes that are coherent with the strategy. The models that we describe here have been somehow put in place at the University of Bologna to implement the strategy described above. Though, here we present them as a general framework that can inspire and be applied also in other contexts.

Regardless of the type and size of universities and PROs, we think it is desirable to have in place an internal organizational area that we call the KS Area (made up of divisions, sectors and offices) that deals with the broad concept of KS and the valorization of knowledge and research results. KTOs would be part of this broad "umbrella" KS Area. Designing an effective macro-organization is important to create impact and exploit synergies across different divisions and activities. Such a design can rely on both internal and external resources. While it is desirable to externalize some services and/or create partnerships with other stakeholders, at the same time attention should be paid to maintaining ownership of core business activities, so as to guarantee strategic proprietary knowledge of those processes that are central to orchestrating external partnerships.

In our view, to create the conditions for KS to be deployed successfully, it is important to have in place (ideally within the same area/internal division) the following entities/factors (Fig. 3.3), including physical offices and spaces, activities and services:

1. KTO (IP, spin-off, start-up, PoC)
2. Fab lab, coworking space, incubator

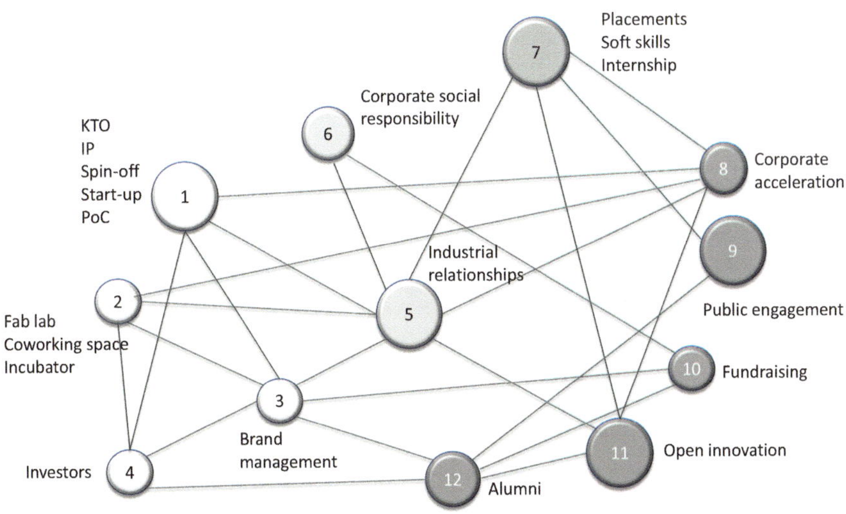

Fig. 3.3 Entities of the knowledge share macro-organization

3. Brand management
4. Investors
5. Industrial relationships
6. Corporate social responsibility
7. Placement, soft skills
8. Corporate acceleration
9. Public engagement
10. Fundraising
11. Open innovation
12. Alumni.

For an effective organization to be in place, it is important to bring together the right people, skills, data and tools and to manage all of them in line with strategic goals.

Following the evolution that we described in Chap. 1 (from TT to KT, KE and to KS), we will show a possible way to boost synergies between different offices, activities and services. We will describe how internal rules can influence activities, and the importance of having organizational processes designed to connect different players. Figure 3.3 illustrates the first core entities set up under the umbrella of TT. Below we describe each component of this system. Coherently Figs. 3.4, 3.5, and 3.6 describe the evolution of the core entities and their interactions, as we move from technology transfer, to knowledge transfer and then towards knowledge exchange, to end up with knowledge share.

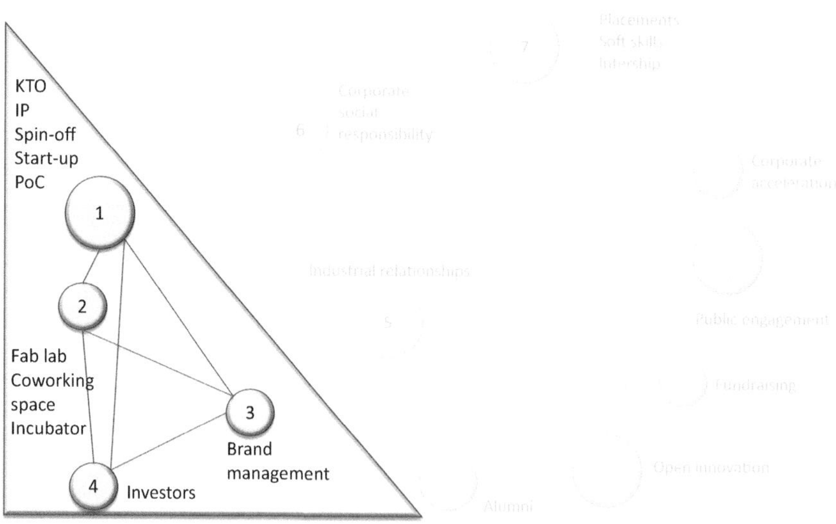

Fig. 3.4 Entities of knowledge share macro-organization (technology transfer)

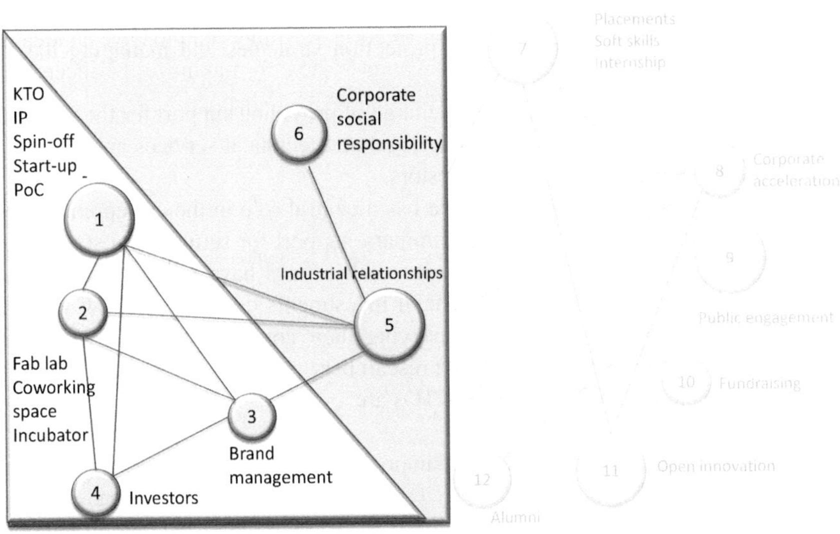

Fig. 3.5 Entities of knowledge share macro-organization (knowledge transfer)

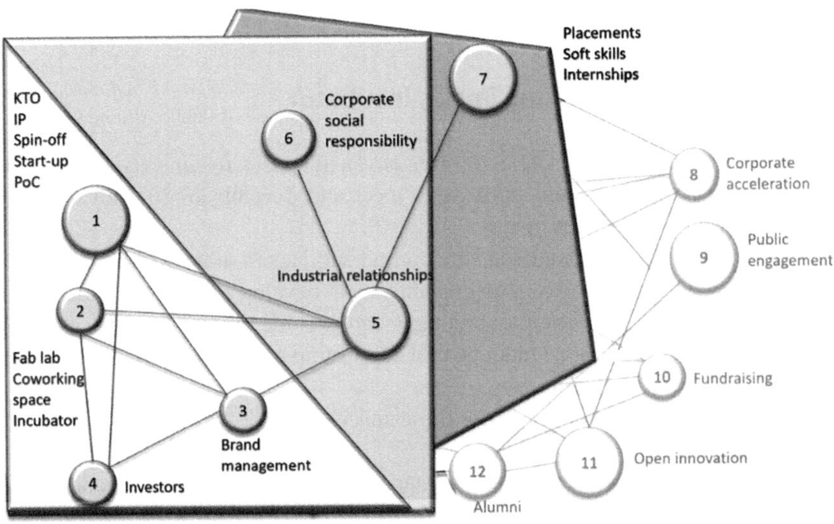

Fig. 3.6 Entities of knowledge share macro-organization (knowledge exchange)

3.2.1 KTO (IP, Spin-Off, Start-Up, PoC)

At the heart of the KS Area are KTOs, which, in line with the core processes, account for three main divisions/activities: KTO IP protection, KTO IP exploitation and KTO start-ups and spin-offs. These are three core processes of technology transfer activities and, at the same time, the foundation of KS activities.

The KTO IP protection office works on promoting IP culture and raising awareness about it, offering support for IP protection strategies and managing the IP portfolio.

The KTO IP exploitation office is in charge of providing support for the negotiation of IP licence agreements, providing legal and technical services and assisting spin-off companies in dealing with investors.

The KTO start-up and spin-off office has a central role in the entrepreneurship strategy illustrated above. It offers preliminary support for setting up a start-up or spin-off company. Over the last 10 years such offices have received significant attention following the growth of financial investments dedicated to new venture creation. These offices have been amplifying their competencies to become the 'counterpart' to investors and to support researchers.

Among the key success factors for KTOs are:

- Paying equal attention to the three main processes: IP protection, IP exploitation, and start-ups and spin-offs
- Having (and continuously updating) the appropriate competencies to support researchers
- Being the entry point to industry and investors
- Investing in continuous growth to offer accurate services to different departments.

3.2.2 Fab Lab, Coworking Space, Incubator

The main goal of these offices is to offer physical spaces for university and PRO employees, collaborators and students to meet and develop joint (innovative and entrepreneurial) ideas and projects.

These offices provide hands-on support and services to those within the university community who are looking for consultancy to develop a prototype or design an entrepreneurial project. Different structures can provide diverse services, but they should all be aligned with the main goal of supporting entrepreneurship, from training to testing and prototyping.

Among the key success factors for these spaces are:

- Making resources available to the start-up and for sustainable management of growth
- Showing continuity in offering activities to reach a minimum critical mass of involved people and stakeholders
- Developing strong links with the KTO and other offices within the KS Area.

3.2.3 Brand Management

Brand management is gaining increasing importance in the KS domain. Brand management is relevant for the valorization of spin-off and start-up companies, fab labs, coworking spaces and incubators, but also for single initiatives or events, in order to be positioned on entrepreneurial matters with a clear identity through which to convey specific messages (e.g. innovation days, graduation days, placement events, etc.).

The basic idea behind brand management is to protect identity and to create better conditions for brand to be valorized. It is therefore important to develop brand management services dealing with brand and trademark protection and exploitation.

A brand management office should work on the correct institutional use of brands and trademarks, both in terms of active licensing agreements and for infringement monitoring. Different channels (and ways to use the brand) should be considered (e.g. research contracts with industry, events and activities about placement, open innovation).

Among the key success factors for brand management are:

- Developing a strategy and guidelines for protecting brands
- Building a brand portfolio that supports identity.

3.2.4 Investors

As already mentioned, the numbers of investors, investments and stages of deals are increasing tremendously in Europe and in Italy. In this new 'golden age' the treasure is the research results (or, better, IP-protected research results), technically called 'IP deal flow'. For this reason, it is extremely important for universities and PROs to devote effort to promoting the scouting and selection of internal deal flow. The main goal of such services is to boost scouting activity and select a qualified deal flow to increase the likelihood of negotiating with investors.

This service should be able to run specific scouting activities dealing with different thematic investment funds. In close collaboration with KTO IP exploitation and KTO spin-off creation, it is important to engage investors from the beginning of internal cycles and processes related to spin-off creation.

Among the key success factors for investors' services are:

- Building strong skills for dealing with investors
- Focusing internal effort on generating a qualified deal flow
- Creating an internal pre-seed investment fund (alone or with other universities).

3.2.5 Industrial Relationships

In order to promote relationships with private companies, the first step is to make research more accessible, which means creating a central entry point that is visible and easily identifiable by industry. The creation of a dedicated central office goes in this direction. The goal of this office is to establish strong, long-term partnerships with companies on top of existing connections, and to promote brand new relationships.

This office can work with single researchers, with research centres and with all the research departments/divisions of the university/PRO. It is important to offer additional value-added services based on institutional and central strategies, and to avoid competing with single departments or other structures. Professionals involved in this office should work out framework agreements with the aim to increase the amount of collaborations with corporates but also to diversify the typologies of collaborations (e.g. not only research contracts, but also joint participation in competitive research projects, internships, PhD grants, open innovation initiatives, corporate social responsibility events, joint labs, etc.)

Among the key success factors for the industrial relationships office are:

- Starting with a clear strategy aligned (and not in competition) with departments' interests
- Focusing on 'target' companies (by size and/or industrial sectors)
- Working closely with other offices (e.g. the KTO, recruiting/placement)
- Monitoring activities and results with specific KPIs.

3.2.6 Corporate Social Responsibility

For many universities and PROs this is a new field still to be explored and designed from an organizational point of view. The concept of corporate social responsibility (CSR), in line with the idea of social impact, is growing fast and there are many opportunities to be taken, especially within a framework agreement or long-term partnership with companies, as mentioned before.

The aim of this service is to work with companies to launch joint initiatives aimed at generating social impact. The service can be provided by an already existing office, like the industrial relationships' office or the communication office.

Among the key success factors for the CSR service are:

- Starting with target companies and projects
- Focusing on the development of internal competencies.

3.2.7 Placements

Traditionally, especially in Italy, this service has been promoted within organizational structures devoted to education and/or student services, in parallel with the development of central offices dealing with companies. The importance of relationships with companies has also increased in education. There is a growing awareness that students can benefit from closer interactions with companies during their studies, and vice versa.

An office in charge of placement should work with companies to support them in recruiting graduate students. At the same time, it should continuously update

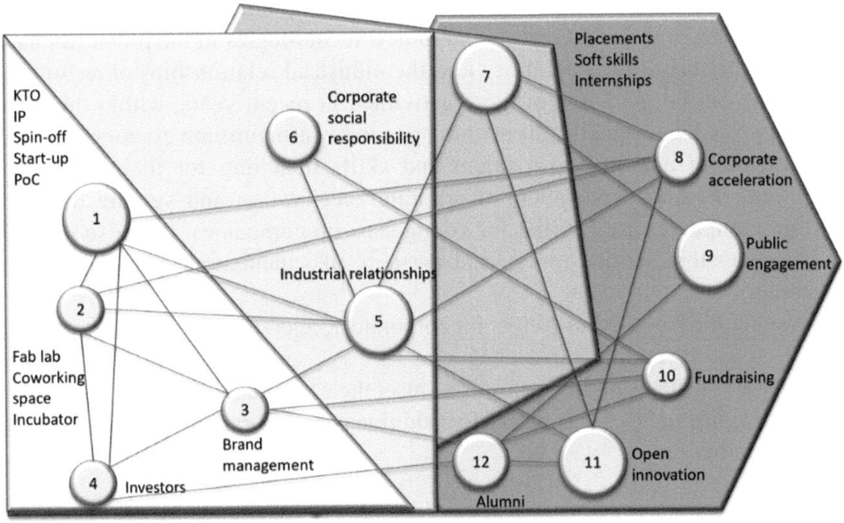

Fig. 3.7 Entities of knowledge share macro-organization (knowledge share)

students about companies' requirements and expectations to maximize their employability.

Companies (as well as start-ups and spin-offs) are increasingly interested in working with students (even before they are graduated) to expose them early to different and concrete approaches and methods to generate innovation.

This office is no longer dealing only with employability but is fully embedded in the process of KS. Professionals working within this office should be able to understand key concepts and processes of IP and TT, and also share data and industrial contacts with the KTO and industrial relationships office in order to increase connections and joint activities.

Among the key success factors for placement services are:

- Supporting the entrepreneurial mindset and employability of students
- Favouring data sharing across administration offices
- Engaging companies in education and open innovation committees and initiatives (Fig. 3.7).

3.2.8 Corporate Acceleration

Corporate acceleration services are becoming popular in response to an increasing need among companies to accelerate innovation rates. These services can be offered by universities and PROs to help companies find technologies (or more often patented research results) and/or spin-offs and start-ups to invest in.

Companies (mainly big and multinational companies) represent one of the main sources of financial investment in new technologies in the pre-seed phase. From an organizational point of view, the industrial relationships office or even the KTO can be in charge of these activities. In recent years, within the broad concept of KS and specifically within open innovation initiatives, companies are looking more and more for talent and skills matching for their innovation requirements and expectations. Corporate acceleration and venture divisions within companies are looking for young start-up companies. It is also possible to delegate this service to external partners like incubators or other external agencies.

Among the key success factors for corporate acceleration there are:

- Supporting start-ups and spin-offs to meet their first customers and investors
- Leveraging industrial contacts for additional collaboration opportunities with universities.

3.2.9 Public Engagement

A service or division in charge of public engagement should work with most of the offices within the KS area and with all external stakeholders, with the aim of amplifying the knowledge and awareness of all activities and results of KS.

A public engagement service can be organized by setting up a central communication office (for the university but also dedicated to the KS Area) or by exploiting specific skills available in other offices, such as fundraising. It is extremely important to have an internal system and process to monitor KS activities for several reasons (and for different stakeholders), including: internal governance and internal departments (to show results on investments); external partners (to clarify goals and the role of the university/KS Area); and external stakeholders (to provide accountability in terms of generated impact).

Among the key success factors for public engagement are:

- Investing resources to support other offices and monitor results
- Facilitating communication among different offices.

3.2.10 Fundraising

Fundraising is key to managing activities related to financial campaigns designed to support the research of KS initiatives, even or especially with social impact.

This service is strictly connected to other offices like the KTO, the industrial relationships office, the CSR office and the alumni and communication office. Fundraising is based on single campaigns and events, but it is also a long-term approach with everybody who is in some way connected with the university (i.e. alumni or key players within companies).

Among the key success factors for fundraising are:

- Having a long-term structured approach
- Focusing on specific campaigns to provide activities with continuity
- Hiring and developing vertical skills.

3.2.11 Open Innovation

According to the initiatives we previously described, the goal of this office would be to manage open innovation activities in order to boost opportunities to find solutions to challenges, to create and invent new products, processes or business methods and to set up new start-up companies.

This service is based on: collecting the needs of the market, coming from society and companies; and stimulating the creation of solutions starting from available technologies, and in coherence with market needs. Many different players will be involved simultaneously. The method for finding an idea or solution is itself innovative (i.e. the design-thinking method). In our experience, the concept and value of KS is fully exploited here. Bringing together students and young researchers from different disciplines is the key to generate innovative ideas. Having companies involved in the process from the injection is ideal to access and generate new ideas as quickly as possible.

Among the key success factors for open innovation activities are:

- Collecting a large portfolio of companies and listening to their needs
- Setting up incentives for engaging different players
- Creating internal incentives to have a variety of students and scholars involved
- Setting up and managing a community of coaches and professional people to run these initiatives.

3.2.12 Alumni

The aim of services for alumni is to set up and manage a strong network, or a community of graduate students who are willing to contribute in some way to their university.

This service is devoted to setting up the alumni community and keeping it alive and engaged. The potential of alumni networks is explosive. Alumni can support most of the activities and actions of a university KS strategy, both directly and indirectly. They can act as mentor, coach, investor or partner within different types of knowledge process.

Among the key success factors for alumni actions are:

- Having a long-term strategy for engaging alumni
- Having adequate resources and skilled people to manage alumni networks
- Satisfying alumni needs in terms of visibility and gratitude.

3.3 Normative Approach

In this section we illustrate how internal norms can affect some of the core activities described above and influence the effectiveness of KS activities.

According to the '*Proposal for a Council Recommendation on the guiding principles for knowledge valorisation*' adopted by the European Commission in August 2022,[1] the normative approach, guidelines and internal system of rules about IP can play a central role in KS activities in order to:

- Ensure that policies and practices for intellectual asset management are defined, implemented and publicized in all organizations involved in knowledge valorization
- Raise awareness among universities, research organizations, public authorities and businesses of the importance of managing intellectual assets in an international environment
- Ensure that intellectual assets developed by publicly funded research and innovation activities in the EU are managed and controlled in such a way that the socio-economic benefits, including contributing to sustainability for the EU as a whole, are taken into account and maximized
- Increase awareness and uptake of intellectual asset management practices and tools in open science to facilitate the use of results and data for innovation
- Ensure that intellectual assets are efficiently managed in open innovation processes, e.g. by helping and supporting the management of web-platforms devoted to link and match offer and demand for intellectual assets.

For the reasons here described, and to ensure the correct valorization of intellectual assets, it is important to put at place a structured system of rules based on general IP regulations, that can define and describe the 'principles' of IP protection and exploitation. An IP rule should be clear in showing the rights and duties of the researchers and how they can be supported by the KTO, as well as which benefits and incentives they can have (not only bounds and constraints). It is important to provide guidelines and also offer a collection of cases/best practices in order to simplify the interpretation and application of the principles.

Below we define the main aspects of internal regulations, starting with IP that stems from autonomous research activities, moving to spin-off and start-up rules and ending with IP related to research cooperation activities.

As we can see from Fig. 3.8, the general rules for managing IP within different types of research activities involve many players (with different types of IP rights) and can be extremely useful. Originally, these rules were thought to address the core process of TT: IP protection and exploitation. However, during recent years, the growing number of players engaged in KS has amplified the effect and impact of these rules. Rules, by definition, should define what is allowed and what is not

[1] https://eur-lex.europa.eu/legal-content/EN/TXT/PDF/?uri=COM:2022:391:FIN

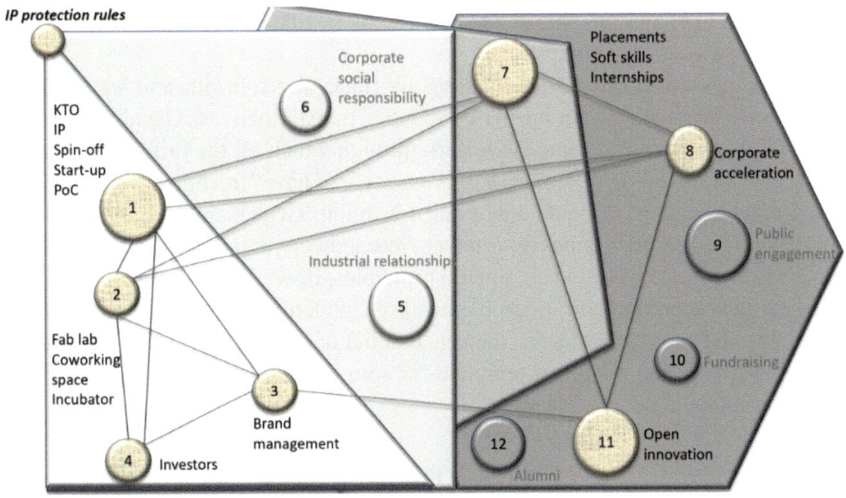

Fig. 3.8 Intellectual property protection rules

allowed. At the same time, they should leave room for individual and institutional interpretation of the law.

It would be useful to complement these rules with some additional guidelines and practical cases for guiding researchers and other individuals in their KS-related behaviours. Below we define a list of main elements to deal with managing IP from research results:

- Definitions of research activities, results, authors, inventors, IP rights, industrial property rights, researchers, students, non-employee workers, inventions and know-how
- Goals of the university in promoting and managing IP
- Goals for applying IP rule within the university and with all KS players
- Rights and obligations of the inventor (according to national laws around ownership, but also generic confidentiality and communication of research results)
- Registration procedure to file a patent (e.g. involving an internal patent committee)
- Rights for the university (e.g. ownership, pre-emptive rights)
- Access rights and share/percentage of income (with or without lump sums, down payments)
- Patent costs and maintenance fees
- Legal proceedings related to the patent/licence (e.g. rights to act).

Typically, an IP rule is addressed to university employees, but in the KS domain it would also be important to consider other scenarios, like inventions generated by non-employed workers or with other universities, institutions and industrial partners. It is important to deal with unconventional ways of using IP without commercial exploitation, and so on. This is why IP rules are so important and have an impact on so many initiatives.

As we can see in Fig. 3.9, regulations for managing spin-off (and start-up) processes have implications for most TT and KS actions/initiatives. The aim of internal regulation is to set up a legal framework through which all the different players in KS scenario, including potential entrepreneurs, can have ‘freedom to operate’. It is important to emphasize legal bounds and constraints (which are different in relation to different spin-off founders: students/researchers, employees/non-employees, etc.) and to have rules based on general principles. It would be useful, year by year, to write and keep updated a complementary ‘guidelines’ document with specific examples and cases (e.g. how to manage conflict of interest).

Below we define a general template for spin-off regulations, with a list of elements that should be considered:

- Definitions of researchers, students, professors, spin-off applicants, the entrepreneurial team, the entrepreneurial committee, intangible assets, IP rights, spin-offs, start-ups, affiliation procedures, administrative process owners and other offices/stakeholders involved in the process
- Administrative offices and committees devoted to support the administrative procedures
- Administrative procedures (e.g. requirements for the participation of researchers and employees, incompatibility, affiliation procedures)
- Relationships with the university (equity share, research contracts, access rights to facilities and laboratories, use of trademarks)
- Evaluation and monitoring procedure to maintain spin-off affiliation.

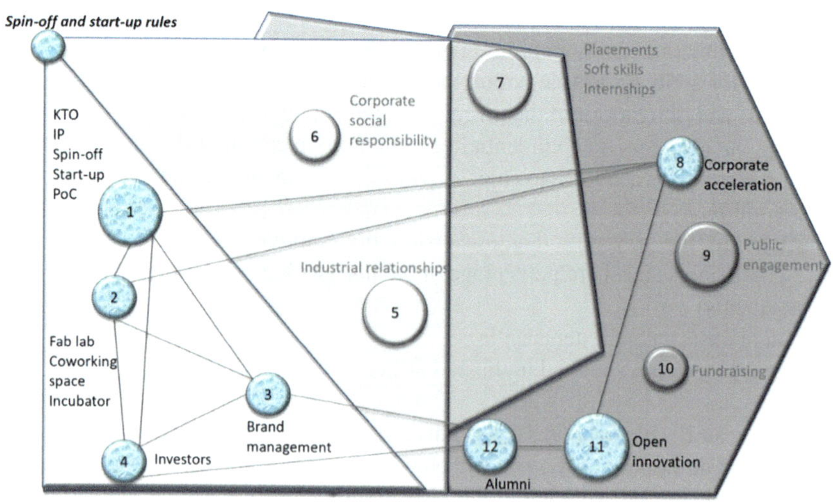

Fig. 3.9 Spin-off (and start-up) rules

As we can see from Fig. 3.10, regulations for managing IP within different types of collaborative research are embedded in several actions/initiatives and related organizational mechanisms and offices.

As we have previously seen, there is a growing number of interactions and ways to exchange knowledge among an increasing number of stakeholders. Differentiation also involves the IP rights of research results and innovations produced during these KS activities by different players (e.g. students, researchers, employees of companies). The management of IP requires simplicity and speed in achieving agreements in the management of joint activities.

Therefore, the goals of IP management regulation, in the various ways of interactions (commissioned, cooperative and collaborative research) are:

- Clarify *ex ante* and *ex post* IP rights produced by all players
- Set up clear and simple rules for the management of IP rights
- Introduce flexible rules to deal with companies
- Introduce adaptable rules to account for disciplines' specificities
- Maintain balance between different interests brought in by different stakeholders.

The evolution of the context should be taken into account for setting up IP rules with regard to:

- Open innovation approaches, which are becoming very popular in interactions with companies.
- The system of national regulations.
- The initiatives connected to the evaluation of universities' performance in research and innovation impact activities.

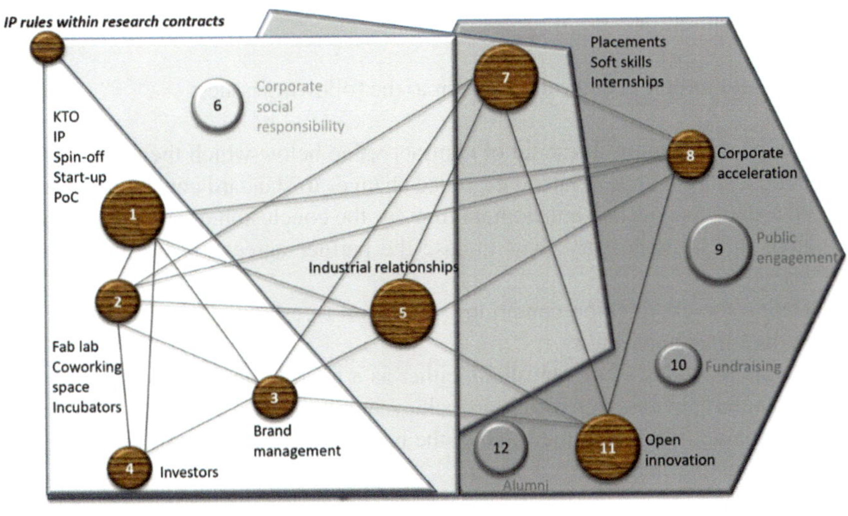

Fig. 3.10 Intellectual property rules within research contracts

Departmental structures (and research centres or laboratories) should be able to identify the clauses that are best applicable to a specific case, taking into consideration the type of activities commissioned, the expected results and discipline driven peculiarities. It is essential that researchers, who are the principal investigators of the research contracts, prepare technical documents with clear indications of the type of activities commissioned, the expected results and the opportunities for using and exploiting research results.

A proper framing of the rules relating to the management of IP from the results that will be generated within the framework of the collaboration is fundamental to foster the exploitation of these results by balancing the commercial interests of the companies with the university's interest in seeing the added value.

In most cases, the research team promotes the first (personal) contact with the contracting companies, negotiates and defines the technical and scientific aspects of the project, as well as the financial aspects and the contractual framework.

The principles of IP regulation in contract research are:

- Define and declare IP related to already existing knowledge and information (background)
- Protect IP related to new knowledge and information stemming from collaboration (foreground)
- Protect the confidentiality of exchanged information
- Define IP ownership/co-ownership
- Define access rights for IP exploitation by industrial partners
- Clarify conditions for researchers to publish research results
- Ensure the application of the regulation for university's brand
- Ensure the university's rights to access research results for teaching and internal research purposes
- Find a balance between the right to publish results and the commercial interests of companies.

It is also important to dedicate attention to the following issues:

- Define a minimum threshold of contract value below which the university will not consider it appropriate to negotiate changes to standard contractual models
- Introduce and declare a maximum time for the conclusion of contracts' negotiation; this must be very short in case the partner agrees on the standard contract terms
- Define the exploitation conditions: minimum thresholds for the transfer of IP, both *ex ante* and *ex post*
- Define the value of the threshold, either as a fixed lump sum if defined *ex ante* (i.e. before the research results are achieved or before the contract is concluded), or variable if linked to the value of the market and the economic benefit for the industrial partner.

A possible outline of the main aspects to be regulated with respect to the type of collaboration is illustrated in Fig. 3.11.

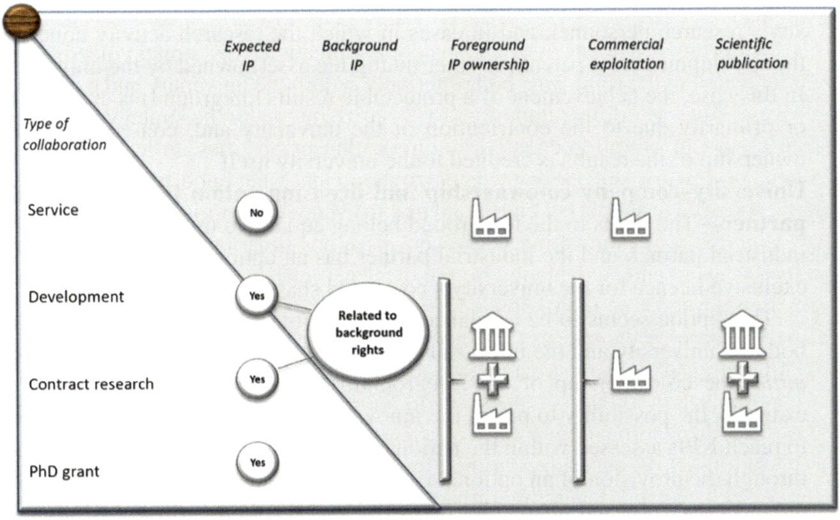

Fig. 3.11 Intellectual property rule scheme within research relationships

Below we provide a list of elements that should be considered for IP regulation within cooperative and commissioned research:

- Definitions (background, sideground and foreground)
- Parties and actors involved.
- Ownership and co-ownership of sideground and foreground
- Access rights of the parties to background, sideground and foreground
- IP rights vs. scientific publications and dissemination activities
- Patent filing procedure
- Confidentiality
- Use of the brand.

Ownership and co-ownership is one of the most crucial barriers in the relationship between university and industry. We suggest using a number of options, as tested at the University of Bologna, to account for different bargaining power and balance between the parties, but also to establish a fair return for the university.

3.3.1 Options for Managing IP Within Cooperative Research

Below, we show the different options for managing IP within cooperative research.

A. **University ownership and licensing options for an industrial partner**—The rights to the foreground belong to the university; the industrial partner has an optional right to acquire an exclusive or non-exclusive licence.

   This option should be chosen in all cases in which the contracted research activity is carried out with a key contribution from the university's background and thanks to the exclusive or prevalent intellectual contribution of the university's research personnel, and in cases in which the research activity concerns the development of a patent (or other intangible asset) owned by the university. In this case, the achievement of a protectable result (foreground) is exclusively or primarily due to the contribution of the university and, consequently, the ownership of the results is credited to the university itself.

B. **University–company co-ownership and licensing option for an industrial partner**—The rights to the foreground belong equally to the university and the industrial partner, and the industrial partner has an optional right to acquire an exclusive licence for the university's co-owned share.

   This option seems to be a balanced way to protect the different interests of both the university and the industrial partner. Both parties formally acquire, *ab initio*, the co-ownership of the foreground, thus granting the university, for example, the possibility to patent the innovation in order to be accountable and to reach KPIs assessed within the national evaluation system. At the same time, through the provision of an optional right for the acquisition of a licence on the university's co-owned share, the industrial partner secures the possibility to exclusively exploit the innovation and the related competitive advantage. When the granting of the optional right takes place through payment of a fee by the industrial partner, this also gives the university the opportunity to be formally acknowledged for its fundamental contribution to the innovation.

C. **University–company co-ownership and option for an industrial partner to acquire the university's share**—The rights to the foreground belong equally to the university and the industrial partner, and the partner is granted the option to assign the university's share of the co-ownership.

   This option is, in many ways, similar to option B. The difference is that the partner is not merely offered the option to acquire an exclusive licence from the university but is given a more substantial option to assign the co-ownership share of the foreground IP rights. This assignment, unlike the exclusive licence, allows the partner to distribute the property to the foreground as widely as possible and even to assign it to third parties. Obviously, in return for a larger concession by the university to the partner, higher fees are applied as compared to option B.

D. **University–company co-ownership and commitment by the university to the industrial partner to sell its share**—This option represents a simplification of the arrangement delineated in option C, in which the partner's benefit of the rights to commercial exploitation of the foreground is made more explicit from the moment in which the foreground is granted, without prejudice to the co-ownership of any patent applications. In fact, the optional right for the assignment of the university's share is eliminated, foreseeing the right to commercial exploitation by the partner as of now, but still requiring the filing of any patent applications in co-ownership, with the assignment of the university's share taking effect after publication of the title. The commitment to assign the foreground to the partner in co-ownership allows the partner to manage the foreground as widely as possible, so they will be able to benefit from a licence for the period prior to the assignment.

Obviously, in return for a larger concession by the university to the partner, a higher fee is envisaged than in option C. This option appears to be useful in the event that the university is seeking for a most certain economic return, while at the same time, the university is able to co-own the patented/registered foreground; moreover, it simplifies the administrative/managerial activity relating to the transfer of the foreground, since the contractual steps are already predetermined.

E. **Public body co-owner**—When the partner and co-owner is a public body (or in any case follows public interest), the rights to the foreground belong in equal part to the university and the partner, who will negotiate in a subsequent agreement the procedures for protecting and exploiting the foreground.

F. **No foreground expectation**—The results of the research solely involve scientific reports and are the property of the industrial partner. No results are expected to create foreground, but if they do, the parties shall agree in good faith in a separate agreement.

This option is preferred in cases where, in light of the technical scientific content of the research activity, it can be determined in advance that the research activity will not generate results that can be protected by proprietary rights, but only scientific reports.

In any event, the hypothesis must be safeguarded in the event that, unexpectedly, foreground is generated, by providing a reference to a subsequent agreement for the specific regulation of the ownership and rights to the use of such foreground.

G. **Divided foreground**—Research results, consisting of development of the partner's background or otherwise dependent on the partner's background, are the property of the industrial partner.

This arrangement allows the partner to have full ownership and consequent freedom to use the results of the research that are strictly connected to and dependent on its background, so as not to hinder the commercial exploitation of results connected to the company's business. At the same time, there are no disadvantages for the university as it can be the full owner of results that are not connected and linked to the background, or in any case not strictly connected to the partner's business, thus allowing them to pursue all possible strategies for research exploitation. If this option is used, it is highly recommended, if not mandatory, to specify the background of the partner and the university in the technical annex.

To conclude, we can summarize all these different options in a few key principles for achieving balance and success in public–private partnerships.

On the university side, it is important to take care of researchers' interests and to pay attention to the value of IP, reputation and fair returns.

From the industry perspective, we should be able to assure efficiency and effectiveness in the negotiation process and the possibility to exploit IP research results.

- Act as a bridge between the research community and external actors, including suppliers, partners and investors
- Promote and support student entrepreneurship and start-up and spin-off (research-based) creation
- Support grant offices within the university/PRO both with writing proposals (especially for impact sessions), managing and boosting the protection and exploitation of research results that stem from collaborative research projects
- Support offices/units in charge of managing intellectual property (IP) within commissioned research contracts (e.g. Industrial Liaison Offices)
- Support and act alongside other linked structures (e.g. contamination labs, coworking spaces, incubators, Industrial Liaison Offices) on open innovation initiatives.

All of these activities are relevant. In the face of increasing financial support for technology transfer processes, KTOs' scouting activities and the capacity to generate quality deal flow are going to be even more important. Those researchers active in technology transfer activities are still a small percentage of the total, so there is significant undiscovered potential still to dig out. Following this line of reasoning, to improve (in terms of both quantity and quality) the deal flow of ideas with market potential, it is crucial to improve collaboration between grant offices, supporting researchers in managing funded research projects, and KTOs.

The motivations for universities and PROs to invest in technology transfer have changed over the last 20 years. In the period between 2000 and 2010 the public research system has witnessed a decrease and a change in the nature of research funding, which has led them towards a more mission-oriented and performance-based management approach to research activities. They have become more sensitive to technology transfer related activities, as channels for accessing additional financial resources. In the same period, we have also seen increasing demand for research collaborations, particularly from large companies. More recently, we have been facing a moment of great change. Particularly in the European context, the implementation of the Recovery and Resilience Facility within the Next Generation EU plan will lead to the creation of large public resources dedicated to research, which could and should leverage other private resources.[1] In the face of these contextual changes, the role of KTOs (once TTOs) will become even more central as structures that ensure a steady flow of new inventions, preparing the ground for the management of all activities aimed at protecting and exploiting research results.

In the following sections we will define the role, positioning and organizational forms of KTOs. Only by looking at the variety of names used to address these offices (Technology Transfer Office, Liaison Office, University Industry Linkage, Contract Office, Patenting and Licensing Office, etc.), it is possible to understand the variety of priorities, objectives and processes that are put in place to support technology transfer. As we said before, KTO is nowadays the most widely used term, which also accounts for knowledge exchange activities, addressing

[1] https://ec.europa.eu/info/strategy/recovery-plan-europe_en

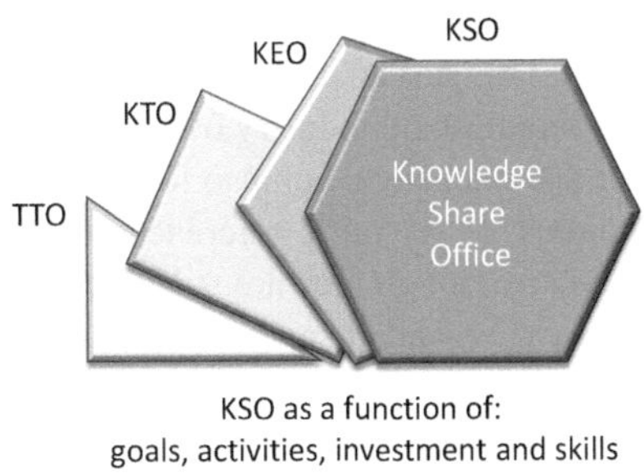

Fig. 4.1 The evolution of the technology transfer office

bi-directionality and dealing with different types of knowledge. In the future, the concept of Knowledge Exchange Office (KEO) could substitute KTO and, in some contexts, this is already happening. Though, what is desirable in our view is a future evolution towards the notion of KSO. Which we see as the ultimate evolution of these names, more in line with the KS domain. Figure 4.1 represents the evolution from TTO to KSO in line with the evolution from TT to KS (see Chap. 1).

How can traditional KTOs move towards becoming KSOs? First of all, KTOs should adopt a dynamic view and start working on designing dynamic goals (or at least realigning priorities among pre-defined goals), always taking into account emerging opportunities and new needs. The identification of new needs may come through all the stakeholders involved. At the same time, it is important to maintain the focus on the KTO's core business: IP and deal flow scouting.

Below we summarize KTOs' main goals, which we will address in details in the remaining part of the book:

- Supporting researchers
- Selecting IP deal flow
- Boosting IP and research exploitation
- Promoting and supporting research and student entrepreneurship
- Acting as a skilled and institutional interface for university stakeholders
- Promoting local/national impact.

4.2 The Role of KTOs

The flow from basic research to economic exploitation of research results is not without obstacles, as documented by the so-called European Paradox (Radicic & Pugh, 2017), which highlights how many European countries achieve excellence in scientific results and research activities (many indicators related to scientific publication show the highest performance in European countries), but at the same time these same results have a scant impact on markets and society and struggle to generate innovations. The non-linear, iterative nature of the innovation process is well known and extensively documented. Therefore, we should look at KTO operations from the perspectives of uncertainty and non-linearity that characterize innovation processes.

Recent studies (Campbell et al., 2020) using various key performance indicators (KPIs) suggest an intensification of the deep, knowledge-driven interactions between universities and industry over time. These interactions account for knowledge transfer and exchange, but also for the broader aspects of KS. There is evidence that the number of scientific references in corporate patents nearly tripled throughout the 1990s, although they are still highly concentrated within a limited number of patent classes. So-called science-based technologies (defined as fields that make frequent references to scientific knowledge) are biotechnology, information and communication technologies, nanotechnology, new materials' technology and optical technology. These science-based technologies are strong contributors to technological progress, as observed through the increasing share of patents in these fields.

Universities and PROs are now not only expected to produce research outcomes; they should also, if possible, consider these outcomes for their potential to be transferred into commercial applications and to generate impact. The surge in university patenting in the USA (as outlined in Chap. 1) is mostly attributed to the Bayh–Dole Act of 1980, which gave universities the right to keep ownership and to license inventions from federally funded research. On the demand side, companies are looking more extensively towards public science as one of the premier external sources of inventive and creative activity, allowing rapid and privileged access to new knowledge, especially in science-based domains. At the same time, there is an argument that PROs and universities in many countries are searching for new funding opportunities to compensate for the stringent budgets in public research and development funding.

For these reasons, all the players involved need multiple access to knowledge. The Recovery and Resilience Facility will increase the amount of money available both as grants and as loans. A direct consequence of this is that KTOs are expected to put more effort into discovering, protecting and valorizing future research results. They are going to have great responsibility in the face of greater challenges. To face these challenges, any KTO within a university or PRO should increase their interactions with companies and investors, and support the setting up of a new wave of research-based spin-off companies. The long-term sustainability of this huge amount of public investment is strongly related to universities' and PROs' (and their KTOs') ability to boost technology transfer and knowledge sharing.

Many stakeholders have 'apparently' divergent goals, though potentially complementary interests. Therefore, KTOs play a key role as bridges aimed at managing multi-partner relationships. Effective KTOs will be even more critical within the broad concept of third mission for the public higher education and research system. A clear strategy, an endorsement of political governance and the correct level of investment are necessary for effective KTOs to generate real impact.

Impact should be measured in the medium term (not less than 5 years, preferably 10 years) and from different points of view.

In the time frame of triple helix and open innovation (Leydesdorff & Etzkowitz, 1998), the role and activities of KTOs should evolve towards the KS domain, in line with the already cited evolution from technology transfer, to knowledge transfer, to knowledge exchange and finally to knowledge sharing (see Chap. 1). This evolution leads to a new concept of the modern KTO as a hub for serving the three different dimensions and institutional missions of modern universities: education, research and third mission. Here we put forward a few recommendations for designing effective, modern KTOs.

First, the university's leadership should provide a KTO with the necessary level of governance and financial autonomy within the university's structures (same for PROs).

Second, KTO functions should operate within an external environment that fully supports industry–academia links, including a proper legal framework—for instance, with simple, clear and transparent rules about IP ownership.

Third, KTOs should implement appropriate incentive schemes for the research community, but also a code of conduct to avoid the negative side effects of competition and conflicts of interest.

Fourth, the governance and leadership of universities (and PROs) should approve and apply a monitoring system to the activities and behaviours of the researchers.

Fifth, universities and PROs' strategic plan should include specific sections related to technology transfer, knowledge sharing and related KPI systems for monitoring and evaluating KTOs' activities.

Sixth, in order for KTOs to successfully interact in new ways with the academic community, and even more so with the student community, in line with the KS domain, it is important to have skilled KTO staff, able to master the academic institutional logic and, at the same time having deep (and vertical) understanding of the needs of industry and investors in order to speak the languages of both science and market commercialization. This is not easy and will require attention in the selection of KTO personnel and in their continuous training.

Last but not least, the professional development of KTO people, activities and functions should encompass 'continuous benchmarking', with top players learning and sharing best practices in line with the evolution of technology transfer towards the new KS domain. The modern KTO is based on experienced personnel and collaborators who are continuously trained in line with the evolution of policies, technologies, norms and regulations. In this regard, it is worth mentioning that both authors have contributed to designing and implementing, in collaboration with NETVAL, the first Italian edition of a master's programme targeting KTO personnel (more details on this will follow in Chap. 5). The main key words for knowledge share office operations are reported in Fig. 4.2.

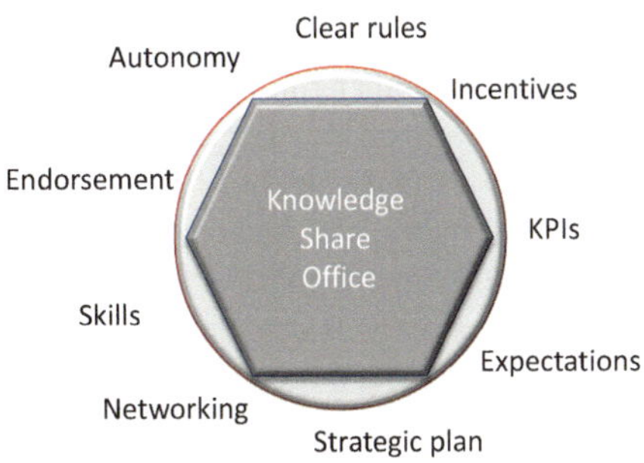

Fig. 4.2 Keywords for knowledge share office operations

4.3 KTO Goals

The majority of research universities around the world have created new organizational entities (KTOs) with the aim of managing their technology and knowledge transfer processes more effectively and efficiently (Siegel et al., 2004).

Defining, sharing and communicating clear objectives aligned with expectations and strategic goals is key for successful KTOs. These actions are not detached from the context and the territory in which a KTO and its parent organization (university or PRO) operate. Furthermore, it is appropriate to plan and structure a set of dynamic goals with respect to both endogenous variables and changes (i.e. governance) and exogenous ones (e.g. open innovation and the Next Generation EU plan).

The Italian NETVAL Survey Report (2020) shows an evolutionary trend regarding the goals of Italian KTOs over the last 15 years. These goals have influenced organizational design (e.g. internal and external organization), make-or-buy decisions and centralized and decentralized processes. In fact, different objectives/goals lead to different organizational models, process and service design, activities and hiring decisions in terms of the variety of skills and backgrounds required by personnel. The correct definition of goals can make a difference in terms of efficiency, effectiveness and, therefore, impact.

To this regard, the results of the NETVAL Survey Report (2020) in relation to the institutional goals of Italian KTOs show that the most frequent activity is the management of IP, which is indicated by more than 92% of respondents. This, in fact, represents the 'historical' and 'core' function of KTOs, along with offering support for the creation of spin-off companies (90.8%).

At the beginning of the 2000s Italian KTOs followed a natural evolutionary cycle with respect to technology and knowledge transfer processes, which is now out of date.

The first activities of KTOs were related to the protection of research results and the promotion and support of spin-off initiatives. Twenty years later, paying attention to IP protection and all its preparatory activities (among which are also those activities aimed at increasing the culture of IP management) is still very relevant in different types of research (e.g. autonomous, cooperative and commissioned research). Once this first basic goal of protecting research results has been achieved and a minimum critical mass of patents has been generated, the need to exploit the patents in the market becomes evident and necessary.

Many people still think of IP management as the primary goal of KTOs, but if we think more broadly about the rationale behind KTOs, it appears that their main goal is to 'enable' other functions, activities and relationships that will generate externalities, positive side effects and impact in the long run. This suggests that KTOs, like libraries and student offices, could be managed by universities and PROs as internal services, which need to be there, in the awareness that economic break-even is not be their main goal.

Of course, KTOs can generate direct economic returns. Yet, attention should be paid to generating these returns in a balanced way. KTOs should be given incentives to operate in consideration of broader, more general benefits for universities and

PROs, instead of being concerned, as often happens, with specific financial transactions. As an example, sometimes it is more convenient keep low the percentage rate of running royalties or the lump sum within a licence agreement if, in the negotiation, this brings to higher investments in research activities by the industrial partner, with better chances to develop and enhance the invention. Therefore, maximizing the profit or economic return from a single patent licensing transaction or agreement should not be a goal or a primary objective of KTOs; a patent licensing agreement could generate a research/development contract and long-term partnerships instead.

Another clear example of possible trade-offs within negotiation relates to situations in which there is a focus on getting money from an IP licence agreement instead of getting research contract funds and/or equity share in a new, IP-based spin-off company. The transition from a mere technology transfer logic towards a more articulated knowledge sharing domain should be accompanied by a change in the temporal perspective, introducing medium- to long-term objectives. In this vein, and in line with the new KS paradigm, we believe that more and better emphasis should be placed on long-term partnerships extended into multiple fields, opportunities and tools, in order to involve as many researchers and students belonging to different disciplines as possible, increase the potential for innovation and strengthen the relationships with all external stakeholders.

The NETVAL report highlights that almost all KTOs (about 80%) carry out licensing activities, which are complex and difficult tasks. KTOs could also activate collaborations with external entities. More than 76% of KTOs are involved in organizing matchmaking events and preparing digital tools for more effective valorization of research results. These activities are often carried out in collaboration with regional and national partners and can take the form of digital events and virtual fairs. 'Glocal' logic is also important as the majority of Italian KTOs aim at generating positive side effects for the regional economy and local territory in which they operate.

When it comes to goals, we should not forget the importance of defining and negotiating expected results in a correct and balanced way. Expected results depend on the resources that are invested, but also on the level of independence/dependence of the KTO with respect to governance. The extent to which the governance supports KTOs from a strategic, organizational and financial point of view, can make a difference. To maximize impact, KTOs should be able to act within the strategic plan and KPI framework, but also be free to make decisions on a day-by-day basis. KTOs should be able to plan ambitious and reachable goals, define clear results over the short and medium term and then make clear deals with the governance and their decision-makers to align expectations.

4.4 KTO Positioning

The starting point for KTO positioning is deciding how many activities should be carried out internally, how many externally, which activities should be outsourced and to whom. These choices are driven by the search for effectiveness and efficiency, as well as the necessity to comply with goals. The general 'inside or outside' positioning is affected by many context variables. Nevertheless, there are some key factors that are adaptable to different contexts and organizations.

It is not possible to outsource completely KTOs' services. One of the most important ingredients for effective technology transfer is the establishment of trust-based relationships between KTO professionals and the research community.

External organizations to which KTOs functions are outsourced—both those controlled by universities and PROs and those that are independent—will have their own goals, interests, expected results, KPIs and expected economic/financial returns. Sustainability is always key factor for everybody, even more imperative for external and independent organizations.

On the contrary, internal KTOs could be considered 'necessary costs' to run certain services. The trust between KTO personnel and researchers can be influenced by this logic, as it appears clear that there are no interests or expected results other than the benefits for the institution and the research community.

It is desirable to have KTOs that are close to the research community and to research laboratories. 'Close' refers to both geographical proximity and trust among individuals. We believe this is one of the key success factors (if not the most important) for technology and knowledge transfer processes. Closeness is a necessary but not sufficient condition.

In fact, a right mix of incentive schemes should be at place to boost activities and results. On the other hand, a series of internal system constraints and inefficiencies can push towards outsourcing parts of the process, such as out-licensing.

For universities or PROs, the issue of positioning their KTOs arises primarily in the choice between a centralized structure, within the general administration, or a decentralized one, distributed in research departments. There are several variables to consider, including age of KTOs (number of years of operations, since establishment, which affecting its scale of activities), the volume of research activities, heterogeneity of disciplines (Polytechnique vs. comprehensive universities, for example) and the quantity and types of skills available within the KTO itself.

In general, it would be better to set up a KTO with a centralized structure (one central division) during the initial development of a KTO and first years of investments by universities and PROs in KT. KTOs may evolve in the way they work throughout their life cycle, articulated through different phases.

In the first phase, they will work in 'pull mode' in relation to addressing researchers' requests, meaning that in the initial years KTOs will not have enough resources or a sufficient track record to scout among the entire universites/PROs. This means that KTOs have to initially invest in scouting and let the research community know about their activities and about the guide and support that they can offer to researchers. In this way they can build a first set of successful pilot cases.

After cumulating a certain number of successful pilot case studies/best practices, there is a track record to rely on which suggests it is time to move to a second phase, in which KTOs start planning new scouting initiatives, with a more 'aggressive' approach, becoming more proactive in the exploration and search for 'qualified' and better deal flow.

Only in the third and later 'mature' phase, when there is sufficient critical mass of skills and experience, KTOs can evolve towards a decentralized model, directly involving individual departments (or working in a coordinated way with them) in the scouting phase or even in the out-licensing phase. Decentralization has the advantage of further exploiting physical proximity with research groups, as well as benefits in terms of cognitive proximity, stemming from having within departments KTOs personnel with background and skills that are closer and more aligned to those of the researchers themselves and to their scientific disciplines.

When we talk about organizational models, it is worth pointing out that a decentralized model appears to be risky and potentially inefficient, given that activities may be duplicated, thus losing the advantage of economy of scale in terms of both protection and exploitation of IP. Moreover, more communication and coordination actions could be required in this model.

Being aware that there is no optimal or static solution in the choices between an internal or outsourced mode, or the centralization or decentralization of the activities of a KTO, an additional level of complexity should be taken into consideration: the direct relationships with other stakeholders in the process, such as incubators, business schools and foundations, to give an example.

The presence or availability of different actors who may be complementary to the KTO is now consolidated in the practices of many of the most important European research and university structures. These actors can be very important resources for developing and improving parts of the process or for highly specialized services. Attention should be paid to aligning goals, priorities, control, governance and communication mechanisms among these actors. While the advantages of simplification, speed and flexibility offered by these external structures are indisputable, possible misalignments of interests can create problems in relationships and disadvantages of a direct and indirect nature, economic or otherwise, in the medium term. Another issue could be represented by conflicts of interest: external KTOs may have income from directly managing research contracts and licensing agreements, and this will be reflected in the overheads they can ask for on a single contract/transaction. External KTOs naturally try to maximize profit related to the single deal, but this choice can go against the strategy and the benefit for the university/PRO in a long-term perspective.

Finally, as we have already said, KTOs create and maintain relationships with researchers and scholars by developing links based on trust, on the concrete value delivered through the skills of KTO personnel and on the complementary support offered for the protection and exploitation of research results, which is of utmost importance for scholars wanting to commercially valorize their research results.

The joint work between researcher and KTO manager is a necessary condition for successful TT and KS. The know-how component in any invention is a fundamental basis for the development and implementation of the patent. The collaborative approach and attitude towards potential licensee industrial partners are key to bringing patented inventions to the market and also for creating strong links and developing new collaborative research activities. The culture of disclosing starts any time a new research activity begins. That is when the possibility of inventing something innovative and original begins. KTOs should be able to evaluate and promote incentive schemes for researchers, to have them think not only about research impact in terms of scientific publications, but also about third mission impact indicators. Ideally, KTOs could receive a formal mandate from their research organizations to achieve this important goal.

In conclusion, while KTOs may adopt a variety of forms along their life cycle, there is no doubt that they support research organizations in achieving a very important objective: facilitating, enhancing and implementing the transfer of knowledge and technology, by translating the results of scientific activity into formats readily adoptable and absorbable by industry and commerce. KTOs deploy activities across three main business areas: (1) collaborative research with companies and provision of consultancy services; (2) patenting and licensing; and (3) development of spin-off companies.

Following the pandemic and the related Next Generation EU plan, the importance of moving from KTOs to KSOs mode should be even clearer. It is of the utmost importance to boost the capability to exploit, as much as possible, research results stemming from the great quantity of public investment. Consequently, we should work in a more inclusive way, with the aim to bring to the market new products, processes and services, reskill industrial employees and create new qualified job positions. This is possible only by carrying out technology and knowledge transfer activities and working with existing companies, institutional and private investors, banking institutions, non-profit foundations, and entities and, of course, local/regional/national government public bodies.

To conclude, we summarize the main aspects of KTOs positioning (Fig. 4.3):

- Correct positioning depends on the age of KTOs, their scale and cumulated experience
- Local proximity and cognitive proximity can make the difference
- It is important to have an internal KTO dealing with IP
- It is important to have an internal KTO acting as an entry point for companies, especially for dealing with IP issues within research collaborations.

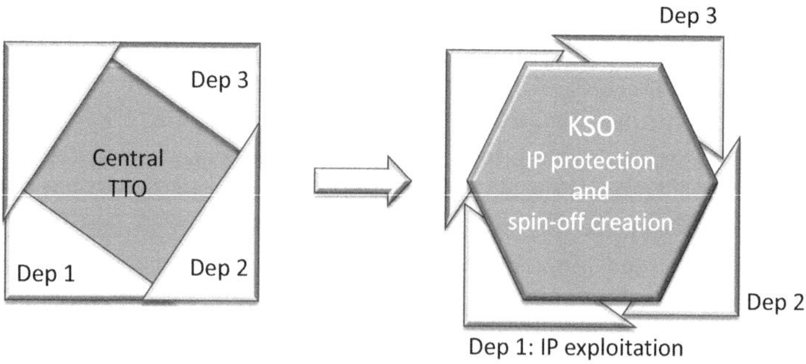

Fig. 4.3 The evolution of technology transfer office positioning

4.5 KTO Macro-Organizational Models

Since the design of an organization can affect the behaviour of its members and ultimately the success of any strategy, it is important for KTOs to investigate organizational models. We focus on organizational processes that enable the implementation of policies and higher-level strategies. We distinguish between macro- and micro-organization: the first is the outcome of make-or-buy decisions about processes and the relationships with external stakeholders; the second relates to implementing processes within the university/PRO and the relationships with internal departments.

Macro models have been already addressed in the extant literature by Brescia et al. (2016). Carlsson et al. (2008) analysed three different models by looking at the differences in IP management. The first level of classification concerns macro models. Three macro models have been identified and described: internal/integrated, external/collaborative and mixed, taking into account KTO's relationships with its own university/PRO. The second level of classification is related to the configuration model, which can be: single, multi, or joint. The third level of classification defines three types of university involvement and control: independent entity, participating entity, or wholly owned entity.

For each of these three models, we should also take into account the profit vs. non-profit dimension. Indeed, this is the fourth and final way to classify any possible future KTO/KSO configurations (Fig. 4.4) taking into account KTOs' models.

Figure 4.4 provides a comprehensive frame of different organizational models. Based on our experience, an appropriate structure should provide ad hoc incentives and organizational mechanisms to generate effective processes—i.e. the day-to-day operations of knowledge creation and innovation management within the academic environment. The organizational processes underpinning the management of university research and development for commercial exploitation include knowledge management, administrative project support and new spin-off company creation.

An appropriate structure needs to be embedded in a supportive context, and vice versa. Context accounts for the institutional and policy environment, the culture and the history of the university/PRO. It shapes and configures the rules, values, attitudes and behaviours of academic researchers towards combining 'curiosity-driven' research and actively seeking and supporting 'market-relevant' opportunities that originate from research. An appropriate organizational structure for the KTO should be coherent with the institutional context in which the KTO operates.

An important element to take in consideration is people. Human capital is core to any organizational structure, in terms of availability of internal competencies and effective procedures for training, recruiting and motivating employees and collaborators. As regard human capital, possible criticalities could be represented by low mobility between the public and private sector, low attractiveness of public organizations also because of the impossibility to implement effective incentive policies. In the face of these criticalities, it can be very difficult to recruit and retain the best people and to consolidate a core team that is fundamental for the efficient and effective management of highly complex TT and KS processes.

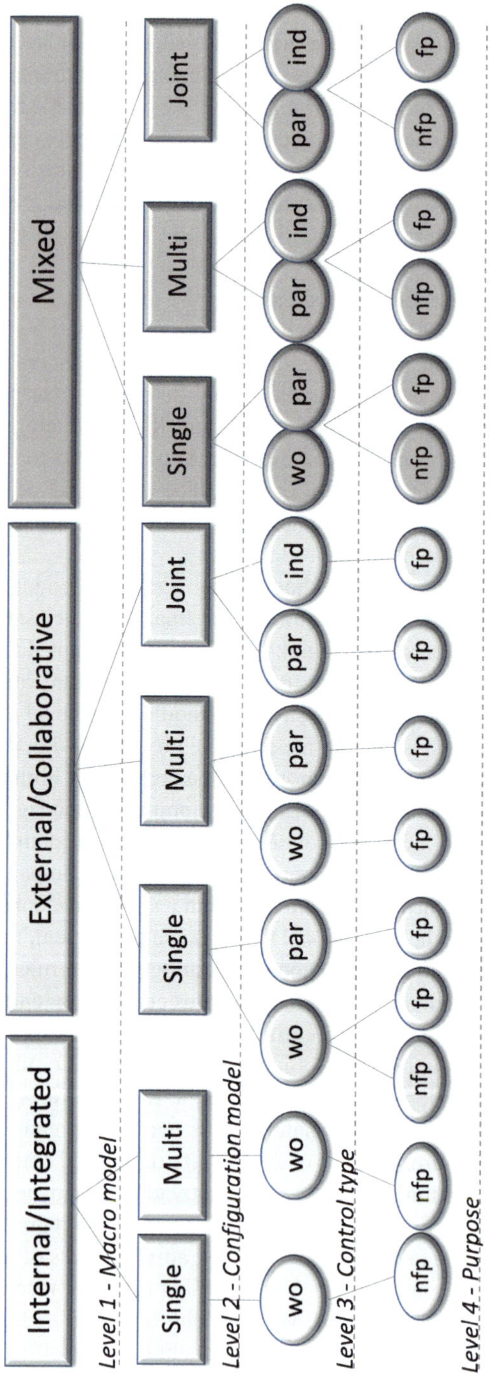

***Abbreviations:** fp, for profit; ind, independent; nfp, not for profit; par, participating; wo, wholly owned*

Fig. 4.4 Classification of possible knowledge share office configuration models

A second element deserving attention is the presence (and number) of other institutional, in-house, connected or controlled partners. As we have already mentioned in the previous chapter, forms of outsourcing might be inevitable and even desirable, as they are less expensive and more convenient, especially in the short term.

The ideal macro-organizational form should be designed based on the number and typology of players such as coworking spaces, incubators, university foundations, financial holdings, consortia. In this regard, solutions that are strongly unbalanced and too strongly relying on external partners could be risky because of: misalignment of objectives and expected results; competition between people operating within the KTO and those working for these other players; not clear positioning of the various players in the supply chain, in the processes and services provided.

A third factor to consider is represented by the characteristics of the external context, such as the external ecosystem within which KTOs operate—specifically, local or regional government; the presence, consistency, type and size of industrial actors; the availability (and proximity) of other research institutions like universities, PROs, etc. In order to reach a critical mass in the main KS processes, it could be desirable to set up joint KTOs between different universities and PROs localized in the same territory. Joint KTOs could give origin to initiatives within specific vertical fields (i.e. medical or engineering sectors) and be supported by regional policies. Figure 4.5 below illustrates KTO/KSO organizational models.

Another important factor to take in consideration is the extent to which KTOs are embedded within universities/PROs. Universities with a strong track record in science–business interaction most often opt for an integrated or internal TT model—i.e. professional KTO personnel are responsible for TT activities and operate in close proximity (managerial, physical and intellectual) to research groups, research departments and individual scientists. Such a model requires the KTO to offer adequate administrative support that will allow researchers to focus on their research and development efforts and the related knowledge exchange activities, leaving administrative and contractual issues associated with the transfer activities (e.g. legal agreements, financial management, personnel issues) to specialized KTO

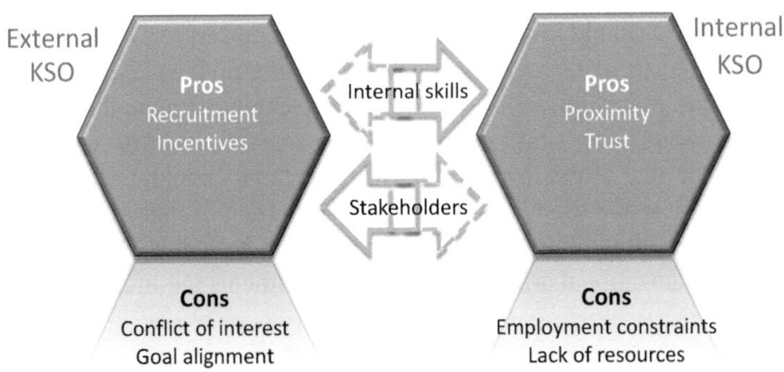

Fig. 4.5 Knowledge share office organizational models (internal vs. external)

functions. Furthermore, this specialized support function will include exploitation of research results via licensing and spin-off creation– areas in which specific legal and marketing know-how is needed.

Different modus operandi can be implemented depending on the specific characteristics of the universities and PROs: internal/integrated; external/collaborative or mixed. We will explore below three different models: internal/integrated, external/ collaborative and mixed.

Internal/Integrated Model

In the internal/integrated model, two elements are key for effective KTO operations. First, the availability of specialized, professional staff targeting the business and academic communities and transforming and translating scientific discoveries into a format that can be absorbed by industry. Second strong transversal support lines throughout the academic community are desirable.

The quality of KTO personnel will ultimately influence the quality and performance of the KTO's operations. KTO personnel should have experience with the business environment, thus facilitating the KTO's transformational role in making scientific discoveries 'ready to use' by industry and commerce.

As part of this model of KT, the KTO should have sufficient autonomy to develop relationships with business on behalf of the university's governance. Mediation by the KTO provides a good 'filter' against possible conflicts of interest between agenda skewed towards commercial exploitation and those embracing mainly research and teaching activities. Also, a significant degree of strategic, financial and managerial autonomy for the KTO facilitates relationships with third parties, such as venture capitalists, investment bankers and patent attorneys. This autonomy is one of the main success factors for determining effective KTO operations, plus the need for clear frameworks on IP rights and contractual arrangements.

In addition, the KTO is instrumental in reducing the problem of information asymmetry that is typically encountered in the market for scientific knowledge exchange. This can be a key point in the evolution of a KTO into a KSO. It is a new way to raise awareness about attitude, behaviour, language and risk approach, among all the different actors involved in the process.

Finally, a KTO should invest in vertical expertise to sort relevant inventions having the potential to generate impact. We name this process 'deal flow digging', which includes assessing and selecting deep-tech investment in the context of knowledge sharing. The 'sunk' costs to acquire and articulate this expertise can be overcome if the size of the invention portfolio is large enough to let KTOs exploit economies of scale and scope in sharing expertise. There is indeed an issue of scale, as smaller institutions often lack the resources and technical skills to effectively support the organizational arrangements and investments required to function at an optimal level.

External/Collaborative Model

A 'collaborative model' or 'wide area type' or 'network type' of KTO organization may offer a solution to scale-related problems. In fact, the other two models (internal and mixed) struggle to achieve sufficient critical mass. Scale can be a problem because small universities often lack the resources and skills to support core TT processes. According to Evans et al. (1999) KTOs tend to belong to a network of TT organizations that often act as gateways to areas of expertise. In our experience, the KS process is still based on a critical mass of inventions, IP, licence agreements and successful spin-off companies. It is well known that only a small percentage of the worldwide patent portfolio is used or transferred. So, from a quantitative point of view, to maximize the likelihood of success in TT, it is important to invest a lot, especially at the beginning. Being patient is important as well. KTO personnel should not be obsessed with the urge to produce economic results in the short term.

On the other hand, a key factor in setting up a strong patent portfolio could be to scout out and protect inventions that address the same or similar industrial needs. In this way it is possible to increase the probability of reaching successful licensing agreements with industries in the same sector. In a small geographical context with a significant presence of researchers and research activities, it is possible to set up a KTO that specializes in licensing in order to exploit IP clustering (high value generated by patents' pooling leveraging on a specific field of application). Another strength could be the possibility of hiring and concentrating specific skills focused on supporting institutions and researchers with legal issues and agreements. Litan et al. (2007) defined a regional alliance model in which multiple universities set up consortia to develop their commercialization mechanisms.

Mixed Model

In the mixed model, universities/PROs create an internal IP office or structure to concentrate their activities on digging out new inventions, plus another organizational unit, operating within the valorization phase: starting from IP exploitation and going through licensing for new company creation (based on protected research results), and also dealing with existing companies (e.g. collaborative programmes and research contracts).

This mix allows for the use of different incentive schemes, hiring different kinds of people on different wages, being more flexible in managing contracts. It is critical to maintain the right balance between the two structures (internal or external), to manage the flow of income, to remain close to researchers and to support them in the exploitation phase without conflict of interest. Finally, it is extremely important to pay attention to people, working with the same stakeholders, with the same or similar level of skills and expertise, but probably with different contracts/wages and incentives. Examples of mixed models are within the University of Tokyo and the University of Padova's UniSMART initiative. Examples in Italy include the U4I Foundation and the JOTTO TT network.[2]

Most Israeli KTOs are organized with external companies and wholly owned by their universities in a mixed or external/collaborative model. An example is the Yeda Research and Development Company Ltd.,[3] which is the commercial arm of the

[2] www.U4i.it and www.jointto.it

[3] https://www.yedarnd.com/

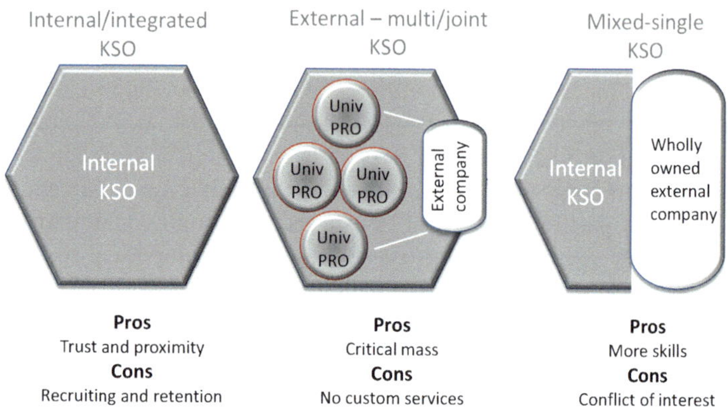

Fig. 4.6 Knowledge share office macro-organizational models

Weizmann Institute of Science. Yeda holds an exclusive agreement with the Weizmann Institute to commercialize the unique IP developed by its scientists. Other examples are: T3 (Technion Technology Transfer), Technion R&D Foundation Ltd.[4]; Yissum (the Technology Transfer company of The Hebrew University of Jerusalem[5]).

To conclude, we summarize the most important issues of different organizational models (internal/integrated, mixed-single, external-multi/joint) (Fig. 4.6):

- Strategy and goals determine the organizational model
- Geographical context influences the organizational model
- Outsourcing of activities may be more effective in later stages of the organizational evolution of a KTO.

4.6 KTO Phases

Historically, the set-up and growth of KTO functions, activities and models have evolved all over the world according to three stages or phases of development, reflecting evolution in environmental conditions, constraints, opportunities and incentives.

Before 1995, typically, KTOs operated in isolation within universities/PROs. TT was accepted, though it was far from central in the spectrum of academic activities. No well-grounded KTO business models existed and KTO activities were confined to the legal aspects of contract negotiation and monitoring. This first-stage mode of operation was in place until the mid-nineties, with differences across countries. KTOs' impact and visibility within universities were quite limited. Specifically in

[4] https://t3.technion.ac.il/

[5] https://www.yissum.co.il/

Italy, TT activities were barely visible and not recognized. Few senior researchers understood the importance of TT and probably started their own patents and spin-off companies. University and PRO governance were not familiar with the concept of TT, which did not appear in their Strategic Plans.

In 1995, the second stage in KTO development started. Rather than being situated at the periphery of academic activities, KTOs became core in the fulfilment of the university's so-called TM. KTO activities started to be deployed university-wide, and the professionalization of KTO operations spread rapidly and effectively. Integrated business models appeared, encompassing professional and university-wide IP management practices, the management of a complex and diverse contract portfolio (both bilateral and multilateral) and business development through spin-off creation, including a proactive stance marked by having an increasing impact on regional development. This second-stage mode of operation—also called the university-wide activity of the KTO—developed during the years 1995–2005 can still be observed at many universities. KTOs' impact and visibility increased rapidly during this second stage of development.

In Italy, we observed at least 10 years of delay. At the end of the nineties, our country started to set up the first KTOs and then moved quickly through this second phase, exploiting 'learning economies' to reach the first well-established KTO structures by looking at international KTOs in other countries.

In recent years, we have observed the development of another, more inclusive activity design of KTOs. This third-stage mode of operation can be summarized as 'inclusive KTO operations'. Rather than 'just' being the focus of the university's TM operations, KTO activities started to spread and became more robustly combined with the two core missions of education and research. The KTO has become fully embedded within the university, while TT activities generate a variety of relevant spillovers (cognitive and intellectual, as well as financial) for the education and research activities of the university. The broad presence of the KTO along the whole internal value chain of the university has turned into a fully inclusive activity. This third stage of KTO development is expected to take full effect in the decade to come. It will further heighten the impact and visibility of KTO operations in academia.

It is possible that a fourth stage, 'diffuse KTO operations', is about to come into existence. These stages are not separate steps; different countries have been moving through the stages at different speeds and with different levels of interpretation for each KTO mission. Customization is strictly related to the needs and expectations of the local context.

Below we summarize the most important elements of the KTO evolutionary phases:

- In the first phase, KTOs are 'isolated islands' with 'vertical missions' (science, technology, engineering and mathematics and IP-based)
- In the second phase, KTOs deal with the TM and 'horizontal missions' (wide IP and spin-offs)
- In the third phase, KTOs are inclusive with 'embedded missions' in the other two main missions—education and research

- In the fourth phase, KTOs become KSOs, in which engagement with all stakeholders and impact are the real missions.

4.7 KTO Governance

The literature highlights the differences between centralized and decentralized structures. Litan et al. (2007) noted a prevalent centralized model in US KTOs after the Bayh–Dole Act. Huyghe et al. (2014) studied the TTO model in Ghent and identified a combination of the traditional hierarchical structure at the central level and decentralized entities within departments.

In our experience, effective KTO governance requires a minimum amount of autonomy for the KTO's operations within the university. Before getting into the internal schemes of KTO organization, it is important to emphasize different attempts within the 'make-or-buy' logic (internal vs. external models), as mentioned above. Make-or-buy logic means the opportunity and capability to decide which type of services are provided within the university and which should be bought from external providers.

A possible intermediary solution for consolidating industry–science relations is to create a divisional structure, the mission of which is to exploit the university's know-how and IP (e.g. Oxford University Innovation,[6] Padova UniSMART[7]).

For many KTOs, this approach has resulted in setting up a dedicated division within the university for research exploitation, or even an autonomous holding structure (wholly owned or participated). This solution shows the strategic intent of the university to engage with industry and allows for the necessary economies of scale in its support services. The disadvantage, however, is that such a divisional structure is likely to create new boundaries within the institution, making it difficult to integrate basic research, education and exploitation of research at the level of the research groups.

In other words, divisional KTO structures, while demonstrating the institution's strategic intent towards commercial exploitation, may lack the proximity and incentive mechanisms that are required to engage and involve the researchers and their research groups as active partners in the exploitation process. It is possible that there will be a surge of internal competition to get research contracts or an application of overheads in licensing agreements.

A next step towards a professional KTO function is the creation of a transversal structure within the institution, alongside the central KTO operations. This approach allows research groups to be actively involved and engaged in the exploitation of their research findings. In this matrix-like structure, the activities of research exploitation are integrated within the research groups themselves. The central KTO experts assist the departmental organization with professional input and support,

[6] https://innovation.ox.ac.uk/

[7] www.unismart.it

such as IP management, contract drafting and negotiation, and business plan development for spin-off creation. They also take care of the financial and personnel management issues that occur when a local organization interacts with industry on projects, consortia and licensing schemes.

By adopting this transversal structure, the university assumes a strong orientation towards exploitation, since it not only commits resources to exploiting research findings (capitalizing on economies of scale and scope in support services), but also directly incentivizes its researchers and their groups to actively participate in the process. Indeed, in such a transversal structure, accountability (with respect to both revenues and expenses) is situated at the level of the research group, which should act as a direct incentive for the researchers to actively manage and grow their portfolio of explorative and exploitative research activities. The central support function of the KTO monitors these exploitation activities, thus avoiding potential conflicts of interest and commitment at its research base.

4.8 KTO Micro-Organization

The macro phases described above may have different steps which are not necessarily consecutive. In fact, we believe that in the start-up phase of new KTO structures, especially nowadays, it is advisable to work on different processes and activities in parallel. In the first decade of the 2000s in Italy, we witnessed some linear and sequential development phases of activities run by a KTO: patent and IP culture; the creation and management of a patent portfolio; the creation of the first spin-off companies; the valorization of IP; the management of IP in the form of commissioned and cooperative research; the growth of spin-offs and access to venture capital.

Today, the organization of KTOs on a sequential basis is no longer possible. The activities listed above should be managed in parallel. Indeed, conceiving new organizational forms for KSOs—in line with the KS domain and the challenges that it brings, and with the ability to be connected to and connect university structures and internal research departments—is key.

From the point of view of micro-organizational models, we can cluster the possible models or schemes into three main categories:

- Process-based models (IP protection, IP exploitation, spin-off creation, research contract negotiation, etc.)
- Discipline-based models (engineering, medical science, etc.)
- Matrix-based models (entirely centralized vs. hub and spoke).

Also in this case, and with regard to organizational models, the age of KTO, its critical mass and available resources are fundamental issues to be managed. At the same level, bounds and constraints, especially from the legal point of view, can affect organizational choices.

4.8.1 Process-Based Model

A new-born KTO can mainly work with the first of the three models, using a process logic by having personnel (one or more individuals) dedicated first of all to IP protection activities. In some ways, a KTO with a single professional figure can be set up by drawing on very different skills, technical and legal, concentrated in one person, without creating a multidisciplinary team (depending on the availability of people within the organization and/or the ability to recruit). Back in the early 2000s in Italy, the first KTOs spun off from legal offices.

As long as the KTO grows, still within the process-based model, it is important for KTO officers to have technical skills—they need to be able to understand the inventions and to speak the technical language of researchers, to support them with initial research activities around the state of the art, and to assist with filing patents or other forms of IP protection. In Italy some KTOs have not paid attention to the organization of skills necessary to operate in the exploitation of patents; some universities have for a long time only worked in the IP protection phase and not in the IP exploitation phase. As the size of the patent portfolio grows, the KTO's skills and human resources should increase almost proportionally. This organizational process-based model, which is desirable in the first phases of a KTO, has some drawbacks—e.g. the KTO personnel interacting with researchers may change at any time because one KTO manager is dedicated to the IP protection process and a second is dedicated to IP exploitation.

During the lifetime of a patent, researchers/inventors will contact different professionals within the KTO. Therefore, strong communication, data management systems and also relational abilities are required.

4.8.2 Discipline-Based Model

The second model, based on vertical subjects (discipline-based), compensates for the weaknesses listed above. However, it requires much more intensive and transversal training, and a critical mass of people with different technical skills who can be in charge of the management of the IP protection phase, or even the scouting phase. As mentioned above, the model—called 'from cradle to grave' in the USA—involves a preliminary phase of intensive training and learning-by-doing activities on the part of the KTO managers, who must acquire economic and legal competencies. In this model, in fact, a single person with a technical background is in charge of a given invention, staying close to the inventor throughout the TT process and through activities such as: researching patents' state of the art; providing support for dealing with patent attorneys in drafting the patent text and filing the legal title; searching for potential licensee companies; providing support in the negotiation phases and with the preparation of legal agreements (from the non-disclosure agreement to the licence agreement); providing support to the researcher for preparing funding applications (e.g. for ideas or Business Plan competition or proof-of-concept funding); and providing support for the management of investor relations for early-stage and pre-seed investment.

4.8.3 Matrix-Based Model

The third model can be considered an evolution of the second. It requires a critical mass of patents and, above all, professionals with different skills. Moreover, training and strong communication and coordination activities are necessary. In addition to the vertical technical disciplines that characterize the second model, there are more horizontal services in this model, such as legal support (especially for more complex cases) or support with communication and marketing activities. Finally, the administration and accounting activities must also be rethought, which, in this model and with the high number of cases to be managed, requires dedicated and professional support.

In addition to the models mentioned above, there are other mixed forms that include all organizational aspects, both macro and micro, as well as make-or-buy choices relating to internal development of activities vs. outsourcing.

More recently, hybrid solutions that outsource part of the process (e.g. out-licensing, incubation, holding companies to take equity in new spin-off or start-ups) are taking off. Outsourcing doesn't necessarily mean engaging external organizations. Different micro-organizational models have developed, including different thematic departments in specific processes (e.g. out-licensing).

It is clear that, with the growth and diversification of activities and cases to be managed, it is practically impossible to think of managing all TT and KS activities internally (and within a central KTO). It will be very important to focus on key activities, positioning upstream of the processes, close to the researchers. It will be equally important to establish partnerships with the various stakeholders and to exploit economies of scale and scope where possible and appropriate.

Finally, the governance of the KTO focuses on appropriate structures, processes and contexts within the university. An appropriate structure should provide adequately designed incentives and organizational mechanisms, to be translated into effective processes (i.e. day-to-day operations) for knowledge creation and innovation management within the academic environment.

In the face of so many different models, we may wonder whether one model is better than the others in the KS domain—more suited to addressing the challenges and more in line with the new concept of KSO.

We believe that the most suitable organizational structure will be an evolution of the matrix-based, "hub-and-spoke" model. This would be quite a complex evolution, taking into account a mixed system of both internal and external partners and stakeholders. A KTO is not only in charge of commercializing research results; it is involved in education and training activities as well. It promotes IP protection within all kinds of research projects (e.g. competitive calls, research contracts, cooperative agreements, joint labs, public–private partnerships, open innovation initiatives) and it manages different kinds of KS activities.

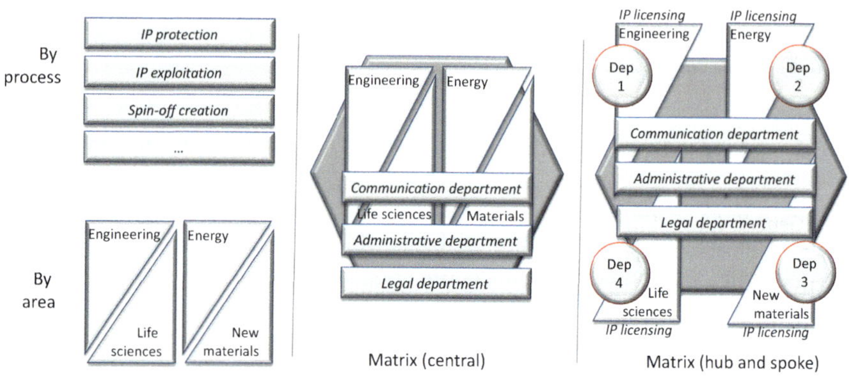

Fig. 4.7 Knowledge share office micro-organizational models

To conclude, we summarize the most important take-home messages regarding KTO micro-organizational models (Fig. 4.7):

- Process-based models characterize the initial stages of a newly established KTO, with few professionals involved and a small IP portfolio
- Discipline-based models are characterized by skilled professionals and a medium-sized IP portfolio
- Matrix-based (central) models are to be adopted in mature phases, with integrated core processes and horizontal supporting services
- Matrix-based (hub-and-spoke) models apply to KSOs in KS logic, with all stakeholders involved, from internal departments to external partners (e.g. foundations, incubators, venture capitalists).

4.9 KTO Processes

Having defined the strategies and objectives of the KTO in the field of TT and KS, and having described possible positioning in the value chain with related organizational forms—some internal and some external—in this section we analyse the main TT and KS processes managed by a KTO. We summarize possible evolutions of the processes within the micro-organizational models of the KTOs described above (process-based, area/discipline-based and matrix-based).

Typically, KTOs were born within universities/PROs (with few exceptions) and dealt with the fundamental processes of TT: IP protection, IP exploitation and the creation of spin-off companies. After preliminary experiences with the protection and exploitation of autonomous research results, the KTOs started to deal with the management of IP in the form of contracts and collaborative research. Finally, the process of creating research-based spin-off companies started almost immediately, targeting researchers with the aim of valorizing patents in the portfolio.

In a first moment, two important drawbacks emerged: poor targeted scouting (in fact, the KTOs were working in a 'pull' rather than a 'push' mode) and lack of attention and effort around the exploitation of generated IP. In fact, economic valorization of IP was very often not the outcome of a conscious process, but of the need to manage new activities with few resources and personnel.

Afterwards, with more mature and structured KTOs, we witnessed a strategic enlargement of the activities to be managed, in line with the logic of the TM and of KS. Management of IP activities was expanded, with a better focus on impact management.

At the European level, there was strong impetus in the Horizon 2020 framework programme towards new organizational forms and collaborations between KTOs and grant offices. The next Horizon Europe framework programme has a clear objective of increasing the impact of research (see Chap. 2). There are new tools and organizational initiatives, such as the European Innovation Council and forms of early-stage investment to exploit the research results of each technology readiness level (TRL).

Nowadays there is awareness that the process of protecting IP is no longer random, spontaneous or linked to the most active researchers. IP protection is more than protecting a knowledge and searching for the state of the art to assess the basic requirements. It builds on different typologies of protection rights to be applied to research results, from patents to plant varieties, from software to patent and biological databases. Attention is paid to exploiting the potential IP from the very beginning of the protection phase. The management of larger patent portfolios requires a clear strategy about where and when to apply for a patent application. Geographical expansion strategies for patent portfolios are turning to a more market-based approach—it would be better to start with a market analysis in order to plan whether or not to protect an invention in Europe instead of China or the USA.

The process of IP exploitation has become more continuous and structured and leveraging dedicated skilled professionals. In this context, goals, activities and efforts grow towards the creation of new spin-off companies, involving permanent researchers with the aim of bringing to market the patents in the portfolio.

At the same time there are emerging student entrepreneurship strategies and new initiatives to promote the creation of start-up companies by students and PhD students. In this context, training activities for students, initiatives to support student entrepreneurship and coworking structures (such as contamination labs, either in-house or connected to other universities) become popular and receive increasing attention. These new initiatives are the outcome of the evolution of TT towards KS. It is through these initiatives that students, researchers, companies and investors work together to address new issues and challenges where KS finds its place. It is in this mix of research, teaching and engagement that KS finds the greatest effectiveness and triggers TT processes, but also, above all, through people's know-how.

In order to promote and support these new models and initiatives, KTOs supplement their strategies with new activities and different people with specific competencies, and intensify their interactions with stakeholders in the various ecosystems, which are becoming increasingly numerous.

More structured relationships are created through framework agreements with external players, including companies and financial investors who are increasingly involved in the upstream stages, well before the formal creation of spin-offs and start-ups.

Nowadays, the scouting and protection of IP *ex ante* is the most important part of the process. Scouting should be proactive and selective. The possibility of clustering a patent pool increases the probability of success in the exploitation phase, as well as the value of the potential new spin-off company to be established. The search for the state of the art in patents does not only function to verify the patentability and defensibility of the invention, but it is meant to assess its commercialization potential. Doing business intelligence activities prior to filing is fundamental, as is being able to better write and protect the invention and to increase the probability of success in preparing a project in response to a competitive funding call.

A change of approach is taking place at the industrial as well as the economic level. After open innovation and the exploitation of intangibles that are more closely linked to data and data management, we are seeing an increasing emphasis by companies and investors on deep tech.

In this scenario, KTOs have to find their space, positioning and role. The new macro processes of KT and KS are developed along the first dimension of *research and experimentation*, the second dimension of PoC, the third dimension of *market entry* and the last dimension of *growth.* PoC is a formalized initiative and procedure devoted to developing a patented idea. With financial and technical/industrial support, an inventor can increase the TRL of its invention in order to reduce the gap of its inventions from the research laboratory to the market, turning an idea into a prototype.

KTOs find their ideal strategic positioning in the middle of these two dimensions. Training, stimulation and growth of awareness around the protection of research results are fundamental in all their forms, in all contexts (autonomous, collaborative and contract research). Scouting is strategic in order to increase unexpressed productivity and generate a greater deal flow of qualified (e.g. selected) inventions protected by IP rights.

The selection procedure is extremely important: first, there is self-selection by the researcher/inventor based on their competence and expertise. Then there is selection by the KTO. KTO personnel in this role should be trained in having dialogue with all stakeholders so they can be more supportive to the researcher in the protection of their know-how and research results. Finally, there is selection step by companies and investors. In the new deep-tech context, the involvement of investors in the PoC phase is very important (both in terms of internal initiatives and external investment measures). To reach the market with at least two rounds of investment, the KTO must train, assist and mentor the researcher (and potential future entrepreneurs of new spin-offs created ad hoc) in the phases of test-bed assessment, validation and engineering, design-driven innovation and use case and PoC validation.

To sum up, the most important processes to pay attention to come at the beginning of the TT pipeline include: training and scouting to generate qualified deal flow and to prepare the researcher for interaction with investors; managing inventions and patent portfolio; interacting with all potential investors and licensees.

The steps mentioned above are intertwined. For exploitation processes, as well as spin-off and start-up creation, it is possible to create partnerships with other stakeholders, also in the form of new participating companies created ad hoc.

As regards the different functions/processes carried out by Italian KTOs (which, as mentioned above, are not aligned with the three macro phases or cycles of KTOs at the global level), the NETVAL survey report (2020) shows that support for IP management is the main function of KTOs, followed closely by the creation of spin-off companies and licensing activities. Less important functions are the dissemination of information and calls for proposals, responses to requests for information and advice and management of research contracts and collaboration with industry. The management of seed capital funds has increased a lot over the last 10 years. Only a limited share of KTOs (between 10% and 25%) are involved in the management of science parks/incubators, the management of research funds and the provision of technical services.

To conclude, we summarize the main issues relating to KTO processes:

- Focus on a few processes and define priorities, taking into account the characteristics of the institution and the local context
- Hire the right people in order to support the main processes with the right skills
- Devote time and effort to IP protection and especially to ideas scouting.

We summarize the main KTO processes in Tables 4.1 and 4.2, providing information on the following:

- Phase/activity (divided into sequential steps)
- Players (divided into process owners and stakeholders)
- Timelines (when an activity starts and ends)
- Input (information, data and actions)
- Output (divided into activities and indicators)
- Tools/software (necessary for carrying out activities)
- Generated data/databases (where it is possible to find data).

Table 4.1 (continued)

Phase/activity	Players		Timeline		Input	Output		Tools/ software	Database
	Process owner	Other Stakeholders	Start	Stop		Activity	Indicators		
Geographical coverage	KTO	Inventor		Within 7 days	Choose IP rights/ tools	Choose territories of protection	N/A	IP research engines	Database inventions
Budget for IP protection	KTO	Inventor		Within 30 days	Type of IP rights and chosen territories	Estimated budget	N/A	Internal balance sheets	Database inventions
4.1 Economic evaluation									
4.1a Positive financial evaluation	*KTO*	*Inventor/ university*		*Within 60 days*	*Estimated budget for protection*	*Start filing procedure*	*N/A*	*N/A*	*Database inventions*
4.1b Negative financial evaluation	*KTO*	*Inventor/ university*		*1 day*	*Estimated budget for protection*	*Manage the end of the process*	*N/A*	*N/A*	*Database inventions*
Communication of negative evaluation	*KTO*	*Inventor/ university*		*1 day*	*End of the process*	*Conclusion and communcation*	*N/A*	*E-mail*	*Database inventions*
5. PATENT ATTORNEY									
Patent attorney research	KTO	Inventor		Within 60 days	Filing procedure begins	Analysis of the patent attorney	No. of patent attorneys selected	Web market research	Database patent attorneys
Patent attorney choice/mandate	KTO	Patent attorney		Within 10 days	Selection of patent attorney	Mandate to the patent attorney	N/A	E-mail	Database inventions
Disclosure form and other documents	KTO	Inventor/patent attorney		Within 7 days	Mandate to patent attorney	Transfer of documents	N/A	E-mail	Database inventions

Table 4.2 The spin-off set-up process

	Players		Timeline		Input	Output			
Phase/activity	Process owner	Other stakeholders	Start	Stop		Activity	Indicators	Tools/software	Database
SPIN OFF PROCESS									
The spin-off set-up process: Phases 1, 2 and 3									
1. RAISE AWARENESS									
Training	KTO	PhD students, researchers, professors	Jan	Feb	Design of training programme	Training modules	No. of training modules	E-learning platform	Database researchers
Feedback	KTO	PhD students, researchers, professors	Feb	Mar	Training modules	Evaluation test	Report	Google form	Database Researchers
2. IDEAS SCOUTING									
Scouting activity	KTO	PhD students, researchers, professors	AnyTime	Within 30 days	KTO contact/ researcher's request	Meetings with researchers	No. of meetings	E-mail	Database spin-off ideas
Selection of the filed IP	KTO	PhD students, researchers, professors	Any Time		KTO selected IP	Meetings with researchers	No. of´ meetings	E-mail	Database spin-off ideas
3. ADDITIONAL IP RIGHTS AND BUSINESS PLAN									
IP rights protection	KTO	Inventor/ spin-off promoter		Within 30 days	Analysis of IP rights related to business ideas	Selection of IP rights tools	Report		
Geographical coverage	KTO	Inventor/ spin-off promoter		Within 7 days	Choice of IP rights tools	Definition of countries to be covered	Report		

(continued)

Table 4.2 (continued)

	Players		Timeline		Input	Output			
Phase/activity	Process owner	Other stakeholders	Start	Stop		Activity	Indicators	Tools/software	Database
Budget/ investment	KTO	Inventor/ spin-off promoter		Within 30 days	Definition of set of territories	Budget planning	Report	IP DBs	
Business plan	Inventor/ spin-off promoter	KTO		Within 60 days	Estimated budget	Business plan	No. of BP versions	BP document template	Database spin-off BP
The spin-off set up process: Phase 4									
4. INVESTORS									
Investor research	KTO/spin-off promoter	KTO		Within 180 days	Business plan	Look for investors	No. of contacts	Websites, association,s networking	Database investors
Positive result	KTO/spin-off promoter	KTO		1 day	List of investors/ choosing investor	*Go to phase 4.1*	Report	E-mail	Database spin-off
Negative result	KTO/spin-off promoter	KTO		1 day	List of investors	Go to next activity	Report	E-mail	Database spin-off
Check for financial feasibility without investors	KTO/spin-off promoter	KTO		Within 30 days	No interested investors	Check for financial feasibility without investors	Report	XLS file template/BP sw creator	Database spin-off
Business plan review	KTO/spin-off promoter	KTO		Within 30 days	Investor search results	*Go to phase 4.1*	No. of BP document reviews	BP document template	Database spin-off
4.1 Economic evaluation									
Positive economic evaluation	*KTO/spin-off promoter*	*KTO*		*Within 30 days*	*Economic feasibility confirmed*	*Go to step 5*	*Report*		Database *spin-off*

Negative economic evaluation	*KTO/spin-off promoter*	*KTO*		*1 day*	*Estimated budget*	*End of the process*	*Report*		Database *spin-off*
Communication of negative result	*KTO/spin-off promoter*	*KTO*		*1 day*	*End of the process*	*Conclusion to communication*	*N/A*	*E-mail*	Database *spin-off*
The spin-off set up process: phase 5									
5. SPIN-OFF SET-UP									
Business plan development	Promoter/ shareholder	KTO		Within 60 days	Economic feasibility analysis	Final version of business plan	No. of BP document versions	BP document template	Database spin-off
Definition of the spin-off team	Promoter/ shareholder			Within 30 days	Final version of business plan	Definition of the team and shareholders	N/A		
Definition of places	Promoter/ shareholder			Within 90 days	Final definition of activities	Definition of places and headquarters	N/A		
Definition of company type	Promoter/ shareholder	KTO		Within30 days	Definition of headquarter and production sites	Definition of company type	N/A		
Spin-off set-up	Promoter/ shareholder	KTO		Within 120 days	Selection of notary and legal attorney	Set-up and start-up of the new company	N/A	Legal templates	Database legal attorneys Database spin-off

4.10 Spin-Off and Start-Up Cycles

In this section we focus on spin-offs and start-ups. As we mentioned, supporting new venture creation is an important element of modern KTOs. Unlike the processes of IP protection and valorization, where each individual case has its own life and history, spin-off and start-up processes can be described through cycles of subsequent activities (see Figs. 4.8 and 4.9).

While spin-off and start-up cycles share a common structure and follow similar paths of development, the support mechanisms for the two target companies can be different, considering the different natures of spin-offs (more grounded in research) and start-ups (usually more digital-based, app-related and less research-based) and

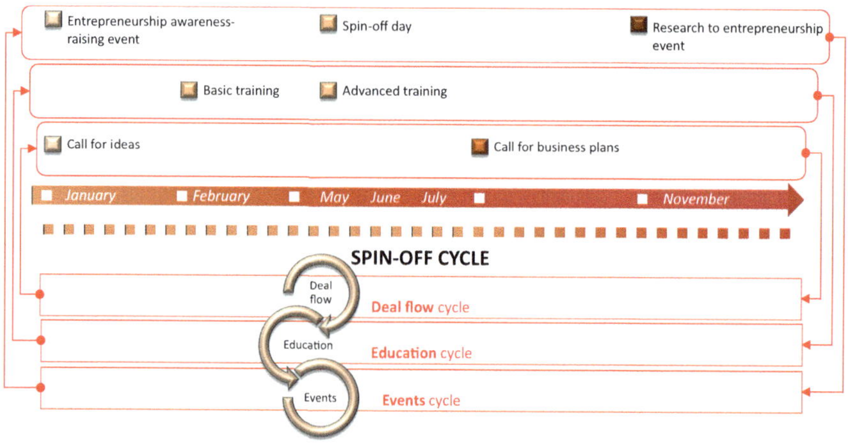

Fig. 4.8 The spin-off cycle

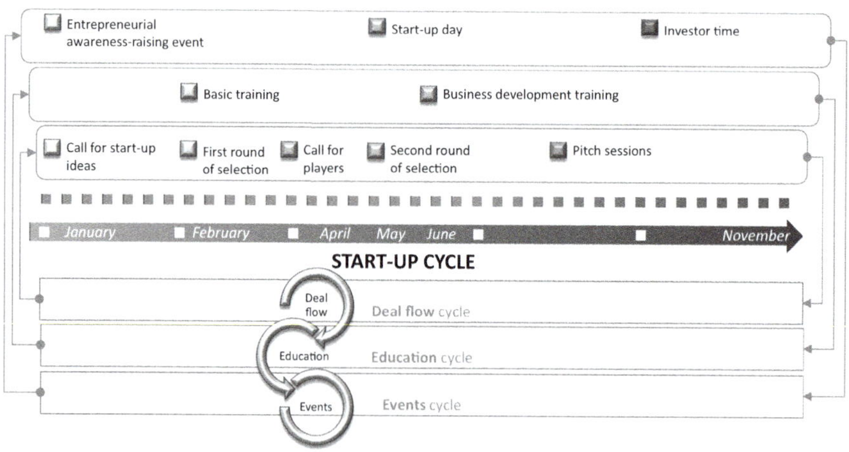

Fig. 4.9 The start-up cycle

the different levels of seniority and experience among the founders (researchers vs. students). Spin-off founders bring in more vertical expertise, struggle to understand the market potential of the inventions from their research results, and rely on external partnerships (e.g. experts, private companies) to complement the knowledge they're missing for new venture establishment.

Students have less vertical knowledge and are more willing to invest in learning and developing the missing competencies, so they appear to be more flexible and open-minded.

It is possible to identify three main clusters of activities (which we believe are necessary to support spin-off and start-up creation) within the cycles that are in some way connected and dependent: training, organizing events and generating deal flow. Ideally a structured training programme should be organized with different modules for different targets. The organization of social events is also important to keep alive different communities and stakeholders. Both training and events are useful for digging out new inventions and business ideas. Generation of deal flow is important not only for promoting technology and knowledge transfer via outlicensing, but also through the creation of independent ventures, in situations where IP based technologies can be used to sell products and/or services.

4.11 KTO Tools

In this section we present examples of tools that are relevant to core processes, both for TT and KS. To be effective in scouting new ideas, it is important to develop awareness of market needs and, at the same time, to be knowledgeable about research activities carried out within the institution and to select the best research results. The *disclosure form* (see below) is the tool to be used for this purpose. Within the IP exploitation process, it is important to develop PoC initiatives/tools to be repeated every year to provide additional benefits to aspiring academic founders. Reiterated PoC initiatives can prove useful for boosting scouting activities and for improving technology readiness levels (trl). PoC tools developed within the university can be combined with external PoC provided by venture capitalist and investment funds.

Another tool that can help in the IP exploitation process is an IP platform that acts as a matchmaking website space. The platform supports universities and PROs in showing their patented technologies to facilitate licensee access and promote licensing deals.

The success of this type of platform comes not only from its user-friendliness or the amount of content it has, but also from the fact that the database is continuously updated and attracts companies and investors. As an example, we suggest the Italian IP platform called the Knowledge Share Platform (see Sect. 4.11.2).

4.11.1 Disclosure Form

Aimed at boosting the performance of the scouting phase, it is useful to set up a simple tool/document called the *disclosure form*. This is recommended for describing new ideas, research results and potential inventions in a structured way. A disclosure form is a document that collects all the information declared by the inventors that is necessary to file a new patent application and it is useful for designing the first IP exploitation strategy.

A disclosure form template should contain the following sections:

- Personal contact details and qualifications of the inventors
- Title of the invention
- Source of the invention (autonomous or funded research, research projects or contracts)
- Teams of inventors, organization of affiliation
- Co-ownership
- Description of the invention (function, problem solved by the invention, differences from existing technologies, advantages for the state of the art, type of invention, main features, innovative technical features, areas of application, development status)
- Development of the invention (actors and resources needed for the development of the invention, existing companies and/or investors interested in exploiting the invention, potential joint development)
- Potential market (useful for identifying the correct geographical coverage of the IP)
- State of the art and prior art (existing patents, known and public publications)
- Confidentiality agreement.

4.11.2 Italian Knowledge Share Platform

The Italian Knowledge Share Platform (KSP) is one of the most promising IP marketplaces and national matchmaking systems available today.[8] It is a free-to-access, multisided platform that was launched in 2019 by NETVAL (the Italian Network for Research Valorisation) in collaboration with the Ministry of Economic Development and the Italian Patent and Trademark Office, and with the support of the Politecnico di Torino.

KSP is an online 'meeting point' for Italian universities, research hospitals and PROs to showcase their technologies and seek commercialization partnerships. KSP welcomes those involved in technology development and innovation scouting, such as innovation and technology managers/teams, external and academic collaboration liaisons, business development managers and angel and venture capital

[8] www.knowledge-share.eu

investors, to explore the technological opportunities available, connect with the academic network and catalyse the world of innovation.

Currently, KSP hosts more than 2000 technologies and works closely with 90% of Italian public research bodies; it has facilitated more than 350 connections. In addition to the patent portfolios, KSP 2.0 will showcase spin-offs and early-stage projects seeking financial investment and/or expertise. KSP is also about to scale up its offering at an international level, to house projects and patents with oversees collaborators.

Access to KSP is open to Italian and international companies looking for new technologies and research discoveries to translate into practical applications. Universities are eligible for a free account, which they can use to manage and promote their patent portfolio to prospective industrial partners. The content uploaded onto the platform undergoes a stringent review process by the KSP/NETVAL team, who ensure that patent descriptors follow the platform's 'total quality' communication standards.

Upon subscribing to the platform, users receive individual login details, giving them full access to the patent portfolios. Users can then navigate the platform and search for inventions that best meet their interests or needs by filtering them according to 'owner' or 'technology sector'.

It is important to be aware of the following factors that affect the success of this tool:

- Partnering with institutional partners: through relations with the Italian Patent and Trademark Office, KSP has institutional support and offers incentives to upload and update content for joining universities and PROs.
- Accessing national networking hubs: NETVAL, which made KSP one of its flagship projects, guarantees the continuous engagement of the entire Italian TT community.
- Guaranteeing free use: KSP supports the idea that knowledge shared by academic institutes with the industrial world must be free from any barriers that could undermine potential new collaborations.
- Supporting cooperation with international TT hubs: Collaborations with similar international networks grow the TT ecosystem and improve the dissemination of knowledge.
- Enhancing total content quality: Each tech brief is reviewed by the team so that its editorial style remains robust over time and its contents are aligned to KSP's standards. Each contact generated by the platform is in charge of the owner's TTO, but the KSP team follows each step of the process in order to continue to deliver value.

4.12 KTO Competencies, Individuals and Relationships

The skills that should be in place and orchestrated within KTOs are strongly linked to strategies, organizational models and context. The age of KTO (date of establishment and phase of development) is another determining factor in the skills mix of

KTO competencies. Traditionally, KTOs in Italy were born from a strong legal imprint, or from technical figures who eventually acquired new competencies in the economic and legal fields.

Italian KTOs have remained small for a long period of time and this has led to more horizontal professionalization, unlike in US KTOs (i.e. the internal organizational model 'from cradle to grave') where individuals with technical skills completed their training with a Master degree in Business Administration (MBA) or with legal specializations.

From the point of view of individuals, incentive systems and the recognition of the professional role of the KTO manager may push young people towards this new career path. In Italy, a lack of professional recognition has made the growth of KTOs more difficult and slower. Another weakness is the recruitment of people from outside the university/PRO or from the private world. All policies that aim to foster private–public mobility can be useful for improving the acquisition of different skills, approaches and behaviours.

However, the need to open up and connect to different actors (e.g. companies, investors, intermediaries and external participating or controlling structures such as business incubators and foundations) has led to growth and diversification of the competencies within the KTO.

The expansion of TT in the KS domain, and also the different interpretations of TT in KS, have led to the development of new professional roles both within KTOs and in related and connected structures (e.g. contamination labs, incubators, accelerators). For new activities, new competencies are required. For example, research managers should integrate their competencies—at least the basic skills of IP management.

The macro process of start-up and spin-off creation is segmented into numerous sub-activities requiring different abilities and skills. These activities include: training researchers and organizing events to raise awareness about the possibility of starting up new companies based on their research results; organizing initiatives to foster the setting up and development of business ideas; putting in place new structured services and offices (e.g. contamination labs, fab labs, maker spaces) and supporting students and researchers in their idea-generation processes.

The aims and expected results of this process are twofold: creation of an entrepreneurial culture and de facto job orientation actions, and creation of new start-up enterprises.

Additional strategic competencies required in a KTO are communication, marketing and team management skills. Take as an example the establishment and management of an alumni network, which has often been neglected in the Italian context. We know from international experience, however, that this is a source of opportunities both for direct investment by alumni start-ups and for their presence and support in coaching and mentoring entrepreneurial initiatives.

The KS domain, within the broader TM, encompasses different activities and services and requires different skills and approaches, but emphasizes the need and added value of good communication and true sharing of information, data, knowledge and relationships among people.

In addition to this 'horizontal' expansion of competencies, a better definition of the KTO manager's professional profile is needed, with certified training courses that allow for the necessary evolution of a context that is changing with increasing speed. In this activity, the role of national KTO networks (briefly described in the next chapter) and international certification bodies (see ATTP[9]) is fundamental.

It is evident in the differences in performance among countries and in widely used indicators summarized in the most common international rankings[10] (and taken up by some international networks and national evaluation agencies). The gap is especially clear in the recognition of these professionals—recognition that also concerns contractual classification, economic treatment (wages), the possibility of having a well-defined career path and the possibility for mobility from the public to the private sector and vice versa.

These should be the priorities of every country that wants to address the challenges of KS strategically and seriously. It is necessary to build structured training courses that will lead to the establishment of consolidated and recognized professionalism in all public and private, national and international contexts, leading to the introduction of incentive and salary schemes that, if not advantageous, are at least non-discriminatory.

In this regard, we would like to bring attention to a recent training initiative in which both the authors of this book are involved: the Master in Intellectual Property Valorisation for Knowledge Exchange and Impact (KEI). This programme aims to: train participants to acquire theoretical and practical managerial knowledge and skills for the management of IP and the main TT activities; create opportunities for discussion and growth via networking; raise awareness of the national innovation ecosystem through visits organized with partner universities throughout the country; and analyse in the context of project work a topic of interest, guided by professionals in the sector.

To conclude, the main issues relating to KTO competencies include:

- Set up the right mix of skills related to the type of KTO organizational model
- Invest in training activities for supporting the quick growth of young and small KTOs
- Establish relationships with stakeholders and organize processes that exploit different and external competencies (specifically in advanced contexts or territories), also with the aim of sharing some services and activities.

References

Brescia, F., Colombo, G., & Landoni, P. (2016). Organizational structures of knowledge transfer offices: An analysis of the world's top-ranked universi-ties. *The Journal of Technology Transfer, 41*, 132–151. https://doi.org/10.1007/s10961-014-9384-5

[9] https://attp.info

[10] www.reuters.com/graphics/EUROPE-UNIVERSITY-INNOVATION/010091N02HR/index.html

Campbell, A., Cavalade, C., Haunold, C., Karanikic, P. & Piccaluga, A. (2020). Knowledge Transfer Metrics - Towards a European-wide set of harmonised indicators. In Karlsson Dinnetz, M. Editor(s), EUR 30218 EN, Publications Office of the European Union, Luxembourg, ISBN 978-92-76-18885-8, https://doi.org/10.2760/907762

Carlsson, B., Dumitriu, M., Glass, J. T., Nard, C. A., & Barrett, R. (2008). Intellectual property (IP) management: Organizational processes and structures, and the role of IP donations. *The Journal of Technology Transfer, 33*, 549–559. https://doi.org/10.1007/s10961-008-9082-2

Evans, J., Klofsten, M., Andersson, E., & Pandya, D. (1999). Creating a bridge between university and industry in small European countries: The role of the industrial liaison office. *R&D Management, 29*(1), 47–56. https://doi.org/10.1111/1467-9310.00116

Huyghe, A., Knockaert, M., Wright, M., & Piva, E. (2014). Technology transfer offices as boundary spanners in the pre-spin-off process: The case of a hybrid model. *Small Business Economics, 43*, 289–307. https://doi.org/10.1007/s11187-013-9537-1

Leydesdorff, L., & Etzkowitz, H. (1998). The triple helix as a model for innovation studies. *Science and Public Policy, 25*(3), 195–203. https://doi.org/10.1093/spp/25.3.195

Litan, R. E., Mitchell, L., & Reedy, E. J. (2007). Commercializing university innovations: Alternative approaches. *Innovation Policy and the Economy, 8*, 31–57. https://doi.org/10.1086/ipe.8.25056198

Netval. (2020). *Rapporto Netval 2021 - Netval*. Accessed from https://netval.it/en/doc/rapporto-netval-2020/

Radicic, D., & Pugh, G. (2017). R&D programmes, policy mix, and the 'European paradox': Evidence from European SMEs. *Science and Public Policy, 44*(4), 497–512. https://doi.org/10.1093/scipol/scw077

Siegel, D. S., Waldman, D. A., Atwater, L. E., & Link, A. N. (2004). Toward a model of the effective transfer of scientific knowledge from academicians to practitioners: Qualitative evidence from the commercialization of university technologies. *Journal of Engineering and Technology Management, 21*(1–2), 115–142. Accessed from https://doi-org.ezproxy.unibo.it/10.1016/j.jengtecman.2003.12.006

Individuals in Knowledge Share

5

In this chapter we explore individual-level characteristics in relation to knowledge share. Although individuals are at the heart of KS as engines of knowledge production, diffusion and socialization, they have been given less attention in the literature on technology and knowledge transfer and in the KS domain, which has instead devoted more room to organizational mechanisms and policy/environmental factors.

Nonaka and Takeuchi (1995) hold that knowledge sharing will not be successful within an organization without the active engagement of humans. People's knowledge is created and expanded through social interactions and creative activities. In the process of knowledge sharing, individuals generate and receive knowledge (as sender and recipient, respectively). They generate knowledge by exchanging their ideas and experience through socialization, suggesting that networks play an important role in sharing knowledge.

Despite the context in which individuals operate (internal or external to a university/public research organization), for them to be effectively involved in KS, it is important to have appropriate skills and competencies.

Also personnel motivation is key. Social exchange theory (Blau, 1964) assumes that individuals form their knowledge sharing behaviour based on future expectations, meaning that individuals will not share when they perceive activities to be mere costs, but they will share when positive returns are expected. The consequence is that individuals may not get involved in knowledge sharing unless they view the outcomes as being positive. This suggests that universities and PROs, while defining strategies in support of KS, should devote attention to their human capital, to engage personnel, to have employees motivated so to combine organizational prosperity with individual level growth.

Another key concept is trust. Individuals will not consider certain activities when they feel uncertain about future associated returns. However, most of the time in KS, individuals interact with people they do not know or about whom they do not have any prior evaluation. This applies to researchers in their interactions with

G. Conti, R. Grimaldi, *Knowledge Share: the (R)evolution of Technology Transfer*, SxI - Springer for Innovation / SxI - Springer per l'Innovazione 16,
https://doi.org/10.1007/978-3-031-51384-8_5

external companies and other external stakeholders. Though it regards also internal interactions, among researchers from different departments, among professionals from different areas, between researchers and KTO professionals, etc. In all these cases trust plays a central role in formulating the decision to engage to begin with and then to collaborate.

The focus above on trust and expectations of positive rewards are only two examples of the many organizational factors to be considered to smooth barriers to collaboration, openness and sharing. The point is that, for effective KS to be in place, it is desirable to understand individual-level characteristics and consider micro-organizational dynamics within the work context in which individuals operate, paying specific attention to individual behaviours, traits, skills, abilities, and motivations. We will explore some of these factors below.

5.1 Individuals Within Universities and PROs

Who are the individuals involved in KS within universities and PROs? It is useful to recall our definition of KS: *proactive and collaborative behaviours encompassing the distribution, connection and co-production of knowledge, through a circular, multi-sourced and multidirectional process that unfolds in both an intentional and an unintentional way.* This description of behaviours and actions is important for defining the individuals involved in the process of KS. Regarding universities and PROs, individuals expected to have an active role in KS (Fig. 5.1) include scientists/researchers, technicians, and administrative personnel (mainly KTO personnel). For universities, students are additional (non-employee) individuals who can be actively involved in KS. Finally, individuals sitting on the management board/governance (they can be internal to universities/PROs or may come from abroad and include

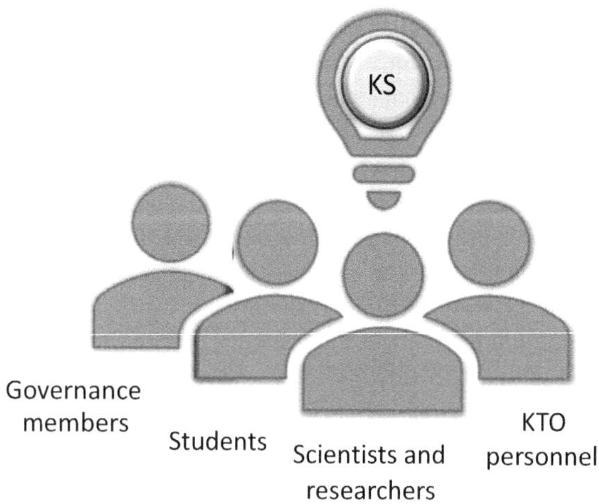

Fig. 5.1 Most important individuals in knowledge share

both academics and non-academics) are key for creating internal legitimacy, defining norms, and creating organizational conditions for KS to happen.

5.1.1 Scientists and Researchers

Scientists and researchers producing knowledge through research activities are the engine of knowledge production. All of them participate in KS within their institutional, research-driven mission. They normally produce and co-produce knowledge and distribute and socialize it through their research activities, papers, conferences, etc. within scientific/academic communities.

Among them is a subset of scientists who are also engaged in the valorisation of research results (TM activities), usually less than 20% of the total number. These individuals may be involved in producing, co-producing, distributing and socializing knowledge in collaboration with non-academic communities (e.g. private companies, public entities, financial institutions, other institutions/individuals), on top of generating research impact through their publications. We are interested in this latter category of scientists because they are relevant for knowledge sharing and impact. A relevant question for us to explore is: why do they get engaged? Under what circumstances?

Scientists who engage in TM activities while investing in basic research, are generally also very attentive in selecting research projects and activities through which they can address societal challenges and find solutions to problems to generate economic, societal, environmental, and cultural impact. They have developed over the years a set of skills and competencies that enable them to produce research results which are of interest to external communities and are worth being commercially valorised. They can create value for both the academic community—through their publications—and the non-academic audiences and society at large—through applications of their research results and scientific discoveries.

The literature has explored scientists' engagement in the valorisation of research results in relation to 'more traditional' technology transfer (TT) activities. Specifically, the role of human capital in TT has been acknowledged in the past (Wright et al., 2007), regarding new technology-based venture creation (Colombo & Grilli, 2010). Allen et al. (2007) conducted an empirical test of human capital theory by analysing data on the propensity of American academics to engage in entrepreneurial activity via patenting. Their findings show that older faculty and those with tenure are more likely to engage in entrepreneurial activities. According to this view, the degree of scientists' cumulated expertise and know-how can explain the likelihood of their engagement with KS.

Following this line of reasoning, the scientist life-cycle model (Audretsch & Stephan, 2000) suggests that, early in their careers, scientists invest heavily in human capital to build a scientific reputation (Levin & Stephan, 1991). In the later stages of their career, scientists trade or leverage on their reputation to generate economic returns. Therefore, early in their career, scientists invest in the creation of scientific knowledge and publications, to establish a reputation that signals the value of that knowledge to the scientific community. As scholars mature from a scientific point of view, some of them start thinking about ways to appropriate the economic value of the new knowledge. Thus, academic scientists may seek to commercialize their scientific research within a life-cycle context. The life-cycle model of the scientist implies that, *ceteris paribus*, a scientist's reputation should play a role in the decision to commercialize (Audretsch & Aldridge, 2009).

In relation to the life-cycle model (and somehow in contrast with it), it is worth mentioning that young scholars (particularly PhD students) may become engaged in the valorisation of their research results via the establishment of new spin-offs because they struggle in finding opportunities for academic career. The creation of a new independent venture is a mechanism for them to exploit their research results to meet market opportunities, leveraging on the knowledge that they have built over the years. This may appear to contradict the seniority and reputation effect that we talked about above, yet the life-cycle model refers to academics formally enrolled within universities and tenured. Doctorate students represent the step immediately before entering a formal, more structured, academic career path.

Audretsch and Aldridge (2009) suggest that locational factors can also influence the propensity for scientists to engage in commercialization activities. Jaffe (1989) and Audretsch and Feldman (1996) show that knowledge tends to spill over within geographically bounded regions and that scientists working in regions with a high level of investment in new knowledge can more easily access and generate new scientific ideas.

Organizational contextual factors are also relevant—e.g. characteristics of the work setting in which the scientists operate. In a study looking at the commercialization activities of scientists at Johns Hopkins and Duke Universities, Bercovitz and Feldman (2004) showed that the likelihood of scientists engaging in commercialization activities (measured through disclosures) is influenced by the commercialization behaviour and attitudes exhibited by the chair and peers in their departments. Bercovitz and Feldman (2008) also found that TT behaviour is calibrated by the experience of those in similar positions in terms of academic rank and departmental affiliation. If individuals can observe others of their academic rank disclosing, then they are more likely to do the same.

In a similar line of reasoning, Tartari et al. (2014) hold that academic scientists' industry engagement is influenced significantly by the behaviour of their peers—that is, the behaviour of colleagues of similar seniority. Using insights from social psychology, they hypothesize that these peer effects are produced by the mechanism of social comparison. In an analysis of data from multiple sources for 1370 UK academic scientists and engineers, they found that peer effects are stronger for early-career individuals and weaker for star scientists. An implication of their study is that peers can be a source of inspiration and benchmark for the engagement of early career scientists.

More generally speaking, depending on their scientific discipline (Mosey & Wright, 2007), scientists vary in how outward-looking they are and their inclination towards investing in open innovation practices.

We have so far presented different studies highlighting factors that can influence scientists' engagement. Besides competencies, behaviours and socialization issues, the starting point for scientists' willingness to engage in KS is the availability of incentives to engage. Motivational factors become relevant in this regard. Which are the incentives for scientists to be engaged in KS?

There is evidence (Lee, 1996; Glaser & Bero, 2005) that academics at highly rated research universities tend to be sceptical about having excessive commercial involvement for fear that it will undermine their academic productivity. The rationale for this is that industry engagement, for instance, may require specific skills and organizational capabilities for managing resources, time, people, constraints, etc., which are different and far removed from those required in academia (Bercovitz & Feldman, 2008). Also, an excessively outward-looking attitude, attention to problem-solving and involvement in networks and external relations with non-academic communities could distract scientists from pursuing basic and fundamental research.

On the other hand, there are studies that show a positive relationship between the quality of academic research and engagement in patenting and academic entrepreneurship (Geuna & Nesta, 2006; Siegel et al., 2007), suggesting that there is 'no paradox' between the inclination towards patenting and entrepreneurial acting, and making high-quality scientific contributions. According to Meyer (2000), patenting activities do not appear to have an adverse impact on the publication and citation performance of researchers.

Still on this aspect, Poege et al. (2019) showed the findings of a large-scale matching exercise between 4.8 million patent families and 43 million publication records. They found a strong positive relationship between the quality of the scientific contributions referenced in patents and the value of the respective inventions. Their findings clearly imply that what is considered excellent within the scientific sector also leads to outstanding outcomes in the technological and commercial realms. Apparently, there is no paradox between patenting and high-quality research.

Nevertheless, we should not forget that patenting is only one of several channels for academic engagement. According to Perkmann et al. (2013), the 'no paradox' results cannot be generalized to other channels for sharing knowledge, such as university–industry collaboration, contracts and collaborative research (D'Este & Patel, 2007; Cohen et al., 2002), which might require more time, attention and commitment to ongoing research, compared to patenting and new venture creation that can be considered by-products or externalities of past research. Perkmann et al. (2013), in a study looking at university–industry engagement, held that scientists' engagement may be more strongly driven by complementarities achieved by working with industrial partners and pursuing academic research, rather than by a single-minded focus on commercial success. Moreover, the authors found that the search for additional resources motivates scientists to engage in university–industry collaborations. Academics can use funding gained from industry contracts to supplement grants from public sources. The search for additional research resources might be more pronounced in some disciplines (e.g. engineering or biotech) than in others.

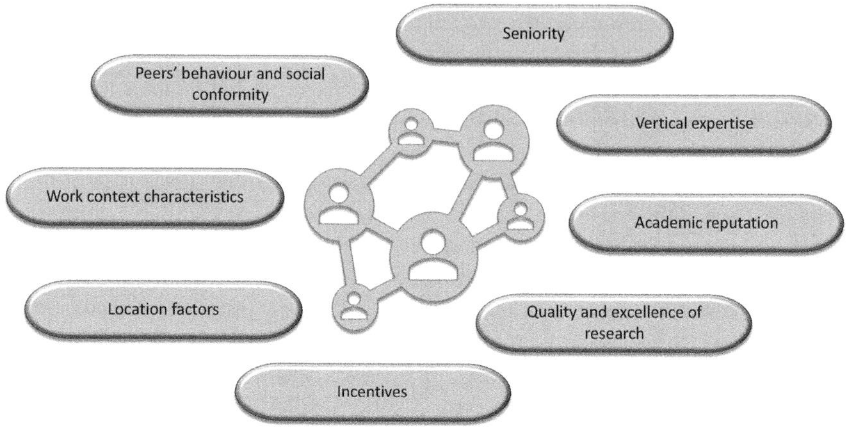

Fig. 5.2 Most important individual drivers of academic engagement

In line with the studies reviewed above, Fig. 5.2 summarises the main drivers of engagement for scientists.

Overall, we think that for universities and PROs wanting to favour their scientists' engagement in KS, it is necessary to introduce rules and incentive schemes that guarantee a balance between research needs/objectives and institutional expectations. Incentive schemes should be coherent with strategic plans' goals. If KS is a desirable direction in a university/PRO roadmap, then it is important to create coherent internal organizational conditions driving individuals' behaviours towards the achievement of KS goals. Here we focused mainly on engagement in relation to commercial valorisation of research results. Though, we know that academics' engagement is a broader concept, accounting also for public engagement and the generation of forms of impact, other than economic and financial. Hence, Universities and PROs wanting to be key players in the KS domain, should work to design and implement internal conditions driving academics and scientists' engagement at large with regard to both the commercial valorisation of research results and the production of public goods for a broader non-academic community.

5.1.2 KTO Personnel

KTO personnel, or more generally speaking, administrative personnel working in universities and PROs within the TM, play a key role in contributing to KS. On top of being directly involved in KS most of the time, since they work in close collaboration with scientists/researchers to support them in different activities (e.g. licensing, patenting, collaborating with industries, new venture scouting, proof of concept, organization of events), perhaps more importantly, through their daily work they implement actions and put in place procedures that create the organizational conditions for knowledge to be shared (e.g. managing contracts according to national regulations and university/PRO-level internal rules, putting in place internal support mechanisms, defining internal regulations).

The ultimate success of entrepreneurial strategies of universities and PROs depends to a great extent on KTO personnel. They act as boundary-spanners and need to be able to reach different audiences. On the one hand, they need to understand the potential of technologies and inventions from different disciplines; they should be continuously connected within the internal research community to be knowledgeable about research activities and results that could generate external impact. On the other, KTO personnel need to reach external communities, speak the language of the market, understand market dynamics and grasp end users' needs to continuously generate opportunities for commercializing science and research outputs. Balancing the internal and external perspectives might not be easy.

The extant literature has devoted significant attention to KTOs (Siegel et al., 2007), in terms of both outcomes and organization, but scant attention has been paid to the characteristics of KTO personnel, with some exceptions. Soares et al. (2019), while exploring the relationship between the background of Technology Transfer Office (TTO) staff and TT outcomes, showed that TTO professionals with different backgrounds affect the early and late stages of the TT process differently. Employees with a doctoral degree are positively associated with new invention disclosures but have no effect on new licensing agreements. On the other hand, professionals with a master in Business Administration (MBA) have a positive and significant impact on new licensing agreements but appear to have no (or only a little) influence on new invention disclosures. They also found that employees with industry experience negatively affect licensing outcomes.

One of the authors of this book has recently studied the motivational aspects of KTO personnel with two colleagues (Pohle et al., 2022). We know that in general motivational characteristics are relevant in work settings, where individuals must act under challenging conditions that could undermine the interest, magnitude, direction and maintenance of effort in their job. This is pretty much the case for KTOs, most of which are characterized by the presence of different institutional logics, low routinization, fast-changing contexts, and significant exposure to external dynamics, but at the same time are highly dependent on internal rules and regulations. Because of the exposure to internal (community of researchers) and external (public and private stakeholders) audiences, KTO personnel have to face competing institutional logics in the form of balancing different interests, goals, cultural backgrounds and behaviours (Pache & Santos, 2013).

Pohle et al. (2022) showed that having motivated KTO personnel can be a challenge for universities and PROs. They should pay attention to skills updating—e.g. having their employees always in flow (Nakamura & Csikszentmihalyi, 2014), guaranteeing a balance between their competences and the typology of tasks that they are assigned. This balance may vary over time because of different factors: employee growth, upskilling and evolution of competencies; changes in the governance of universities, new policies and new objectives and actions that are not necessarily in line with those of the past; changes in the management structure of the

KTO, etc. As these factors evolve over time, it is important to find new forms of match by guaranteeing the fulfilment of employees' general needs.

The study by Pohle et al. (2022), drawing on self-determination theory (Cerasoli et al., 2014; Ryan & Deci, 2000), identifies three basic psychological needs that must be satisfied to achieve intrinsic motivation:

- need for autonomy—individuals' need to act in line with their own will, which for KTO personnel means having the possibility to work on innovative projects and actions, feel in charge, be in the position to make decisions also in uncertain conditions.
- need for competence—individuals' need to feel that they are effective in their work and that their competencies are useful, which for KTO personnel means feeling they have the knowledge to act as boundary spanner, but also that their work-context provides them with the opportunity to grow and to learn and acquire new competences.
- need for relatedness—individuals' need to feel connected to and cared for by others as members of a group, which for KTO personnel means being connected with different communities, individuals, entities—including those within their universities/PROs and those outside. It also means having the possibility to work with an open-minded approach, in searching and activating external collaborations.

KTO managers have a central role to play in this regard, to the extent that they should continuously orchestrate human capital and pay attention to employee motivation to achieve better performance. It is desirable for KTO personnel to have the opportunity to put their technical competencies to work and to avoid being overwhelmed by daily routine and administration. On the skills side, KTO personnel should be equipped with soft skills and relational competencies, to manage change, leverage on different networks of relations, with the aim to stay updated and be ready to catch environmental trends and opportunities. KTOs personnel, though, can have a crucial role for the success of technology and knowledge transfer strategies, not only through the competence and skills that they bring, but also through their motivation, passion, and through other individual level traits and organizational behaviours dimensions. Person-organization fit (P-OF) is one such factors that has not been sufficiently explored. P-OF refers to the compatibility between people and organizations (Kristof, 1996) and occurs when an individual perceives correspondence between his or her own values and goals, and those of the organization (Hamstra et al., 2019). P-OF has been also associated to greater organizational performance. If P-OF is low or absent, the employees and the organization face values incongruence, ineffective communication, lack of trust and opportunistic behavior (Hamstra et al., 2019). In other words, P-OF represents an important aspect for success. In a recent paper by one of the authors of this book (Grimaldi & Villani, 2023), the authors show that the "nature" of the goals and the values that are at the basis of the P-OF within KTOs, are critical to observe the positive relationship between P-OF and performance. Specifically, the fit between employees and organization can build on motivational values and goals or on hygienic goals and values. P-O fit deriving from an alignment of hygienic factors (e.g. salary, status, job conditions) is not leading to KTO performance. For P-OF to lead to KTO success, an alignment of motivational values and goals (e.g. challenging job/tasks, personal growth and achievement, autonomy) needs to be at place.

Often, specifically in public and bureaucratic organizations, like universities and PROs can be, KTO personnel need to be resilient in the face of slow career progressions. After all, they are civil servants who feel they have a role in generating impact. Universities and PROs wanting to play an active role in the KS domain should invest in these professionals and support the growth of their competencies through specific training programmes.

In this regard, the two authors have played a key role in launching one of the first master's programmes in Italy targeting KTO personnel, as President of NETVAL and as Scientific Director of this programme. The first edition of the Master in Intellectual Property Valorisation for Knowledge Exchange and Impact started in March 2022. The idea behind the programme is to train individuals working within KTOs to develop a variety of skills in different fields of third mission. For the reasons explained above, KTO personnel need to develop holistic approaches towards knowledge sharing and be knowledgeable about different, though related, aspects.

More specifically, the master's programme aims to: train participants to acquire theoretical and practical managerial knowledge and skills for the management of intellectual property and the main TT activities; create opportunities for discussion and growth via networking; and raise awareness of the national innovation ecosystem through visits organized with partner universities throughout the country. This programme has been developed in collaboration with the Italian Patent and Trademark Office, NETVAL and the University of Bologna.

5.1.3 Students

Students can play a key role in the KS domain. While not being universities' formal employees like scientists and KTO personnel, they represent an important component of academic communities. The knowledge they produce in their internships, stages, theses, and through participating to other learning activities is rich and varied and, in many circumstances can be worth to be commercially valorised. During their curricula, within courses, students have several opportunities to work in teams; they get to know students from other disciplines, work closely with their mentors and professors, visit companies and become familiar with challenges and problems that industries and other external stakeholders are facing. They are exposed to a variety of sources of knowledge and information and networks of relations, which often lead them to develop and co-generate new knowledge that is valuable for the market and has potential for commercial application. Also, through this exposure, students get to know problems looking for solutions and have a better understanding of societal needs that are waiting to be addressed.

Students are becoming more and more aware of the importance of engagement and increasingly involved in new venture creation. They develop novel ideas that are not research based but can be considered outcomes of the competencies they have acquired during their curricula undertaken at their universities to promote innovation and entrepreneurship. They are becoming increasingly active in KS activities.

The challenge for universities is to have their students engaged in a continuous and structured way. This can be done by investing in TM actions, and teaching activities that stimulate students' creativity and leverage their innovative potential. Many universities are investing in training their students in so-called soft skills so as to complement the vertical background that is offered by traditional curricula with horizontal and transversal competencies. This is particularly important within specialized and vertical curricula. The aim is to promote heterogeneity and interdisciplinarity to maximize the chances that new knowledge will be co-created and shared.

In many countries around the world, students' engagement in entrepreneurship is common, notwithstanding the uncertainties and difficulties that characterize the entrepreneurial process and the high likelihood of failure. In many schools and universities there is a culture in support of student entrepreneurship. Failure is increasingly seen as a learning opportunity, part of the journey, and acceptance of failure nurtures a culture that supports innovation.

These cultural aspects are central to explaining the different rates of student entrepreneurship across countries. Italy, like other European countries, has been lagging behind the American experience, but it is quickly catching up.

The AlmaLaurea report[1] provides interesting insights on student entrepreneurship in Italy. The sample includes 61,115 undergraduate (bachelor) and graduate (master) students, who graduated between September and December 2014 from the 64 Italian universities members of the AlmaLaurea Consortium. Data show that 1664 (2.7%) are student entrepreneurs (i.e. students who have created a new venture during their university study or before starting university), 2232 (3.8%) are nascent entrepreneurs (i.e. students who are currently engaged in some entrepreneurial activities), and 57,219 (93.5%) are non-entrepreneurs (i.e. students who are not engaged in any entrepreneurial activity. Overall, the most relevant evidence suggests that: even if more males currently engage in entrepreneurship, the rate of female entrepreneurship among students is double that of female entrepreneurship in Italy; student entrepreneurship does not happen in STEMM disciplines only; entrepreneurship from social sciences is tantamount the one spurring from hard science; even if Italian universities are not fully receptive in terms of foreign-born students, their rate doubles among entrepreneurs and nascent entrepreneurs.

What can be done to make students more engaged? Policymakers are responsible for creating supportive organizational conditions. Decision-makers at universities can foster the development of strategies and design actions in support of student entrepreneurship. Organizational-level effort (universities in this specific case),

[1] https://www.almalaurea.it/sites/almalaurea.it/files/docs/universita/altro/imprenditorialita2016/student_entrepreneurship_in_italy.pdf

coupled with external dynamic ecosystems, can foster student engagement in entrepreneurship.

Increasing student entrepreneurship is desirable not only because it is expected to increase the number of new start-ups, but also, and perhaps more importantly, because it generates an entrepreneurial mindset, a positive orientation towards change and individuals' confidence in governing uncertainty and risk. This is going to be even more desirable in the KS domain, where students' willingness to co-create and collaborate with the academic community, as well as the external community (ahead of graduation) of private companies, financing institutions, public entities and other players in the ecosystem, will be key for the production and socialization of new knowledge.

5.1.4 Governance Members

Another category of individuals playing a key role in KS dynamics is decision-makers within the research organization and universities. In the majority of cases, the governance is made up of faculty members (professors and/or research community members).

In every research organization, governance members are in charge of designing the future evolution of the organizations they lead, their missions and their long-term objectives. The governance is also responsible for the organizational design meant to support the strategic choices.

They have a very delicate role in making KS happen. The strategies they design are likely to influence the organizational culture of their organizations. When the governance decides to invest in third mission—for example, within a university—new support actions are designed. Investments and resources to foster TT and KS at large act as incentives for the entire academic community. Moreover, there is a sense of legitimization, which makes individuals' academic engagement compliant with the values of the organization they work for.

Bercovitz and Feldman (2008), while addressing the role of leadership in TT, argue that leaders influence behaviour in organizations both by building culture and by acting as role models. The behaviour of leaders drives organizational culture by signalling what actions are expected, valued and are likely to be rewarded. Moreover, the authors shed light on the fact that individual behaviour is shaped by the observation and imitation of others in a social context. Through vicarious learning, we all learn what activities are deemed legitimate and worthy of emulation by observing the actions of our leaders (Bandura, 1977, 1986). Therefore, governance members are key not only to defining strategic goals and creating organizational conditions, but also as a source of inspiration and for the legitimization of behaviours.

On top of the governance, in academic departments there are other individuals who may have an influential role: for instance, department chairs are leaders too. If the chair is active in TT, as demonstrated by his or her prior disclosures, then he or she sends a signal that TT is a valuable activity. In this case, other members of the department may be more likely to be engaged.

All this suggests that governance members and all those in 'visible' and leading positions can inspire their communities to a great extent. When they are in favour of an outward-looking attitude and engagement, they are explicitly defining TM objectives in their institutions' strategic plans; this motivates their organizations and staff. When they are less in favour of this, they might not make TM objectives explicit in their strategic plans. It would be important in this last case not to mitigate bottom-up initiatives in the direction of academic engagement and to support them anyway.

5.2 Individuals Outside Universities and PROs

As well as scientists, KTO personnel, students and governance members, there are individuals outside universities and PROs who are involved in KS. These include all the employees (e.g. researchers, technicians, administrative staff) of external public and private institutions, firms and other third parties, collaborating on research projects and interested in the valorization and impact of research results and public knowledge.

Also, there are additional external actors, working for business incubators, science parks, bridging institutions and financing institutions (e.g. business angels and venture capitalists) who are interested in scouting out promising entrepreneurial ideas and technologies worthy of commercial exploitation, as well as other external stakeholders (e.g. individuals working for banks, foundations, associations). Venture capitalists are incentivized to collaborate with universities to scout out early-stage technologies, and scientists can benefit from their expertise to fine-tune their technologies or find applications for markets that they could not even imagine on their own.

Local municipalities and regional government staff also play a key role. Often they bridge citizen expectations and needs with activities provided by university scientists and other local stakeholders.

In a similar vein, private companies should appoint individuals to dialogue with universities and research centres in a steady and structured way. This is already happening in some private context where selected employees are identified as responsible for university–industry interactions and to identify collaboration opportunities with PROs and universities. Many of these interact directly with KTOs.

In their interactions with these players (direct or mediated through KTOs) scientists may identify possibilities for commercial exploitation of their research results. At the same time, they can get hints and ideas for future research or examples to feed their teaching. Companies can benefit from personal relationships with scientists and PhD students, creating possibilities for student internships, theses, and recruitment at large.

The challenge for universities and PROs is to build internal capacity in terms of the personnel and resources (mainly within KTOs) in charge of managing relationships with this plethora of different actors, all of whom have different expectations and institutional missions. It is important to create appropriate networks and to manage them over time, creating sound, reliable and trustful relationships to maximize the likelihood of successful KS.

5.3 The Stakeholder Approach

Radko et al. (2022) have conceptualized the stakeholder approach by identifying four types of entrepreneurial university stakeholders involved in knowledge spillover. We think this framework is interesting because it identifies different roles in a knowledge ecosystem that are important for making KS happen within universities and PROs.

- Knowledge enablers: Organizations and individuals who facilitate knowledge manipulation (e.g. influential people from industry and government) (Klingbeil et al., 2019)
- Knowledge providers: Organizations and individuals who produce and spill over knowledge within the entrepreneurial university (e.g. university students and faculty) (Boardman & Gray, 2010)
- Knowledge codifiers: Organizations and individuals who actively seek new channels and forms of knowledge transfer, and facilitate knowledge spillover outside the university (e.g. TTOs and KTOs)
- Knowledge facilitators: Organizations and individuals who facilitate entrepreneurial incentives (Fayolle & Liñán, 2014) and encourage knowledge spillover within the university and into the ecosystem (e.g. research and science parks, business incubators, accelerators) (Amoroso & Hervás Soriano, 2019; Wright et al., 2019; Wright & Westhead, 2019); these stakeholders may also raise finance (e.g. venture capitalists)

We think Radko et al.'s (2022) conceptualization is very useful for understanding how different individual stakeholders contribute to knowledge sharing dynamics (Cunningham et al., 2021). Specifically, Radko et al.'s (2022) model shows that effective knowledge flows require support at different stages in the process of new knowledge development, and collaboration among stakeholders including those who create knowledge and those who codify and facilitate knowledge spillover outside university boundaries. All these types of support are provided by different stakeholders and are needed by individuals within academia (e.g. professors, students, staff) to act on opportunities and manage the business effectively (Davies et al., 2021).

The stakeholder approach suggests that the interaction of individuals from different organizations is important for innovation to occur. Different actors play different and complementary roles, have different competencies and abilities, and bring different information and resources to the entrepreneurial and innovation journey, also from a value-chain perspective. As in the open innovation approach, the ultimate success of innovation, entrepreneurial and, more generally, knowledge generation processes requires overcoming 'not-invented-here' syndrome and being aware of the importance of having specialized knowledge in different fields (e.g. technologies, marketing, communications), and even more importantly, having the ability to orchestrate inputs from different perspectives and coordinate them into a whole that is greater than the sum of single contributions.

The challenge for a university's top management lies in working out how to best manage and balance stakeholders' interests in order to maximize the entrepreneurial outputs and knowledge spillover.

In conclusion, we believe that individual-level factors (e.g. competencies, skills, motivations, abilities, networks of relations) can be important drivers of KS. On top of understanding everyone's role and contribution, it is important to have an idea of how to orchestrate everyone within a coherent system to maximize the incentives for all participants and to create the conditions for KS to happen.

References

Allen, S. D., Link, A. N., & Rosenbaum, D. T. (2007). Entrepreneurship and human capital: Evidence of patenting activity from the academic sector. *Entrepreneurship Theory and Practice, 31*(6), 937–951.

Amoroso, S., & Hervás Soriano, F. (2019). An international perspective on science and technology parks. In *Science and technology parks and regional economic development: An international perspective* (pp. 1–8). Springer. https://doi.org/10.1007/978-3-030-30963-3_1

Audretsch, D. B., & Aldridge, T. T. (2009). Knowledge spillovers, entrepreneurship and regional development. In *Handbook of regional growth and development theories*. Edward Elgar. https://doi.org/10.4337/9781848445987.00019

Audretsch, D. B., & Feldman, M. P. (1996). R&D spillovers and the geography of innovation and production. *The American Economic Review, 86*(3), 630–640.

Audretsch, D. B., & Stephan, P. E. (Eds.). (2000). *The economics of science and innovation*. Edward Elgar.

Bandura, A. (1977). Self-efficacy: toward a unifying theory of behavioral change. *Psychological Review, 84*(2), 191.

Bandura, A. (1986). The explanatory and predictive scope of self-efficacy theory. *Journal of Social and Clinical Psychology, 4*(3), 359–373.

Bercovitz, J., & Feldman, M. (2004). *Academic entrepreneurs: Social learning and participation in university technology transfer*. Hubert H. Humphrey Institute of Public Affairs, University of Minnesota.

Bercovitz, J., & Feldman, M. (2008). Academic entrepreneurs: Organizational change at the individual level. *Organization Science, 19*(1), 69–89. https://doi.org/10.1287/orsc.1070.0295

Blau, P. (1964). *Exchange and power in social life*. Wiley.

Boardman, C., & Gray, D. (2010). The new science and engineering management: Cooperative research centers as government policies, industry strategies, and organizations. *The Journal of Technology Transfer, 35*, 445–459. https://doi.org/10.1007/s10961-010-9162-y

Cerasoli, C. P., Nicklin, J. M., & Ford, M. T. (2014). Intrinsic motivation and extrinsic incentives jointly predict performance: A 40-year meta-analysis. *Psychological Bulletin, 140*(4), 980. https://doi.org/10.1037/a0035661

Cohen, W. M., Nelson, R. R., & Walsh, J. P. (2002). Links and impacts: The influence of public research on industrial R&D. *Management Science, 48*(1), 1–23. https://doi.org/10.1287/mnsc.48.1.1.14273

Colombo, M. G., & Grilli, L. (2010). On growth drivers of high-tech start-ups: Exploring the role of founders' human capital and venture capital. *Journal of Business Venturing, 25*(6), 610–626. https://doi.org/10.1016/j.jbusvent.2009.01.005

Cunningham, J. A., Lehmann, E. E., Menter, M., & Seitz, N. (2021). Regional innovation, entrepreneurship and the reform of the Professor's privilege in Germany. In *Technology transfer and entrepreneurial innovations: policies across continents* (pp. 175–205). Springer. https://doi.org/10.1007/978-3-030-70022-5_9

D'Este, P., & Patel, P. (2007). University–industry linkages in the UK: What are the factors underlying the variety of interactions with industry? *Research Policy, 36*(9), 1295–1313. https://doi.org/10.1016/j.respol.2007.05.002

Davies, G. H., Flanagan, J., Bolton, D., Roderick, S., & Joyce, N. (2021). University knowledge spillover from an open innovation technology transfer context. *Knowledge Management Research and Practice, 19*(1), 84–93. https://doi.org/10.1080/14778238.2020.1746204

Fayolle, A., & Liñán, F. (2014). The future of research on entrepreneurial intentions. *Journal of Business Research, 67*(5), 663–666. https://doi.org/10.1016/j.jbusres.2013.11.024

Geuna, A., & Nesta, L. J. (2006). University patenting and its effects on academic research: The emerging European evidence. *Research Policy, 35*(6), 790–807. https://doi.org/10.1016/j.respol.2006.04.005

Glaser, B. E., & Bero, L. A. (2005). Attitudes of academic and clinical researchers toward financial ties in research: A systematic review. *Science and Engineering Ethics, 11*(4), 553–573. https://doi.org/10.1007/s11948-005-0026-z

Grimaldi, R., & Villani, E. (2023). The role of person-organization fit within knowledge transfer offices: A comparative case-study approach. In *Paper presented at 39th EGOS colloquium, Cagliari, Italy*.

Hamstra, M. R., Van Vianen, A. E., & Koen, J. (2019). Does employee perceived person-organization fit promote performance? The moderating role of supervisor perceived person-organization fit. *European Journal of Work and Organizational Psychology, 28*(5), 594–601. https://doi.org/10.1080/1359432X.2018.1485734

Jaffe, A. B. (1989). Real effects of academic research. *The American Economic Review, 79*(5), 957–970.

Klingbeil, C., Semrau, T., Ebers, M., & Wilhelm, H. (2019). Logics, leaders, lab coats: A multi-level study on how institutional logics are linked to entrepreneurial intentions in academia. *Journal of Management Studies, 56*(5), 929–965. https://doi.org/10.1111/joms.12416

Kristof, A. L. (1996). Person-organization FIT: An integrative review of its conceptualization, measurement and implications. *Personnel Psychology, 49*(1), 1–49. https://doi.org/10.1111/j.1744-6570.1996.tb01790.x

Lee, Y. S. (1996). 'Technology transfer' and the research university: A search for the boundaries of university-industry collaboration. *Research Policy, 25*(6), 843–863. https://doi.org/10.1016/0048-7333(95)00857-8

Levin, S. G., & Stephan, P. E. (1991). Research productivity over the life cycle: Evidence for academic scientists. *The American Economic Review, 81*, 114–132.

Meyer, M. (2000). What is special about patent citations? Differences between scientific and patent citations. *Scientometrics, 49*(1), 93–123. https://doi.org/10.1023/a:1005613325648

Mosey, S., & Wright, M. (2007). From human capital to social capital: A longitudinal study of technology–based academic entrepreneurs. *Entrepreneurship Theory and Practice, 31*(6), 909–935.

Nakamura, J., & Csikszentmihalyi, M. (2014). *Flow and the foundations of positive psychology* (pp. 239–263). Springer.

Nonaka, I., & Takeuchi, H. (1995). *The knowledge-creating company: How Japanese companies create the dynamics of innovation*. Oxford University Press.

Pache, A. C., & Santos, F. (2013). Inside the hybrid organization: Selective coupling as a response to competing institutional logics. *Academy of Management Journal, 56*(4), 972–1001. https://doi.org/10.5465/amj.2011.0405

Perkmann, M., Tartari, V., McKelvey, M., Autio, E., Broström, A., D'este, P., Fini, R., Geuna, A., Grimaldi, R., Hughes, A., Krabel, S., Kitson, M., Llerena, P., Lissoni, F., Salter, A., & Sobrero, M. (2013). Academic engagement and commercialisation: A review of the literature on university–industry relations. *Research Policy, 42*(2), 423–442. https://doi.org/10.1016/j.respol.2012.09.007

Poege, F., Harhoff, D., Gaessler, F., & Baruffaldi, S. (2019). Science quality and the value of inventions. *Science Advances, 5*(12), eaay7323. https://doi.org/10.1126/sciadv.aay7323

Pohle, A., Villani, E., & Grimaldi, R. (2022). Personnel motivation in knowledge transfer offices: The role of university-level and organizational-level antecedents. *Technological Forecasting and Social Change, 181*, 121765. https://doi.org/10.1016/j.techfore.2022.121765

Radko, N., Belitski, M., & Kalyuzhnova, Y. (2022). Conceptualising the entrepreneurial university: The stakeholder approach. *The Journal of Technology Transfer, 48*(1), 1–90. https://doi.org/10.1007/s10961-022-09926-0

Ryan, R. M., & Deci, E. L. (2000). Intrinsic and extrinsic motivations: classic definitions and new directions. *Contemporary Educational Psychology, 25*(1), 54–67. https://doi.org/10.1006/ceps.1999.1020

Siegel, D. S., Veugelers, R., & Wright, M. (2007). Technology transfer offices and commercialization of university intellectual property: Performance and policy implications. *Oxford Review of Economic Policy, 23*(4), 640–660. https://doi.org/10.1093/oxrep/grm036

Soares, T. J. C. C., Vitale, A. L., & Nagano, M. S. (2019). TTO's human capital and technology transfer: Examining staff's experience and educational background. *Academy of Management Proceedings, 2019*, 13316. https://doi.org/10.5465/AMBPP.2019.13316abstract

Tartari, V., Perkmann, M., & Salter, A. (2014). In good company: The influence of peers on industry engagement by academic scientists. *Research Policy, 43*(7), 1189–1203. https://doi.org/10.1016/j.respol.2014.02.003

Wright, M., & Westhead, P. (2019). Science technology parks and close relations: Heterogeneity, context and data. In *Science and technology parks and Regional economic development: An international perspective* (pp. 39–60). Springer. https://doi.org/10.1007/978-3-030-30963-3_4

Wright, M., Hmieleski, K. M., Siegel, D. S., & Ensley, M. D. (2007). The role of human capital in technological entrepreneurship. *Entrepreneurship Theory and Practice, 31*(6), 791–806.

Wright, M., Link, A. N., & Amoroso, S. (2019). Lessons learned and a future research and policy agenda on science parks. In *Science and technology parks and regional economic development: An international perspective* (pp. 211–219). Springer. https://doi.org/10.1007/978-3-030-30963-3_12

The Entrepreneurial University

6

In this chapter we address the topic of entrepreneurial universities. The concept of entrepreneurial universities is central to knowledge share (KS). Universities, and more generally public research organizations (PROs), are producers of knowledge. Many of them are active in the diffusion of such knowledge and frontier research results. The attention that universities have been paying to reaching out to different audiences and generating impact through KS has increased over the years.

In order to accomplish this 'new' and 'more entrepreneurial' mission (as compared to the more traditional missions of education and research), they have been facing important internal organizational changes, to be more central and visible in society and generating impact.

6.1 Entrepreneurial Universities and Knowledge Spillover

The extant literature defines entrepreneurial universities as universities that contribute to local economic, social and cultural development (Clark, 1998). In other words, universities with a Third Mission (TM) other than research and education (Etzkowitz, 1998); universities that, facilitating academic entrepreneurship, 'generate regional economic and social development through the added value created by the identification and exploitation of entrepreneurial opportunities' (Shane, 2004).

The entrepreneurial universities are entities that offer opportunities, practices, cultures and, overall, a context that encourages entrepreneurship and the commercialization of research. Entrepreneurial universities practice academic entrepreneurship, such as the development of commercialization beyond the traditional focus on licensing and innovation, including the creation of new ventures that involve the spinning-off of technology and knowledge generated by universities (Wright et al., 2007). At the same time, they can implement internal procedures for knowledge valorization, going beyond commercial exploitation and encompassing public

G. Conti, R. Grimaldi, *Knowledge Share: the (R)evolution of Technology Transfer*, SxI - Springer for Innovation / SxI - Springer per l'Innovazione 16, https://doi.org/10.1007/978-3-031-51384-8_6

engagement activities, generating social, environmental and cultural impact and targeting society at large.

The concept of knowledge spillover is central for defining entrepreneurial universities. Knowledge spillover is a flow of knowledge from one party, where the knowledge is generated, to another party, where the knowledge is used (Acs et al., 2013; Audretsch & Lehmann, 2006). University spin-offs and start-ups are considered to be mechanisms for knowledge spillover, as they are based on university-produced knowledge (Acs et al., 2009) and are channels through which this knowledge reaches the market to generate impact. Within universities' TM strategies, knowledge spillovers may occur through commercial exploitation channels (including, on top of spin-offs and start-ups, university–industry collaborations, contract research, licensing, etc.) to generate economic impact, as well as through non-commercial exploitation channels, including public engagement initiatives and the generation of public goods with cultural, social and environmental impact.

When the spillovers are the outcome of deliberate processes of commercialization of research results, we talk about academic entrepreneurship.

Universities practising academic entrepreneurship can act as hubs, connecting different stakeholders within the local environment to facilitate knowledge spillover (Davies et al., 2021). Within ecosystems surrounding universities, actors are connected by the constant flow of knowledge via different channels that enable knowledge spillover (Siegel et al., 2003). Universities have an important role to play in connecting these external actors. This suggests that for knowledge spillovers to happen, the role of the external context is not secondary and knowledge ecosystems, as we will discuss later, are key for entrepreneurial universities to exist.

In defining entrepreneurial universities Guerrero and Urbano (2012), identify two main 'conditioning' dimensions: (a) environmental factors; (b) internal factors.

Environmental factors refer to 'contextual' organizational characteristics and include: the organization and governance structure of universities (its internal management structures, decision-making mechanisms, and leadership functions), a range of support measures developed within the universities to support new firm creation (including KTOs), entrepreneurship education programs, exchange programs and collaboration strategies between university and industry, reward systems, etc.

Internal factors include resources and competencies like: leaders with strong management capabilities, as well as leadership traits in the governance, academics as critical human resources for the development of educational quality and generation of innovation in research, financial resources, social capital, networks, alliances, etc. The internal factors highlight the importance of accessing resources and competencies and indirectly point to the importance of locations in which universities are settled.

Entrepreneurial universities are more likely to emerge in ecosystems favouring access to critical expertise, networks and knowledge (Saxenian, 1991). This is to say that, location is a significant factor which explains the innovative activities of firms, as the cost of transferring the knowledge is a function of geographic distance and gives rise to localized externalities. This is in line with the entrepreneurial university framework[1] of the European Commission-OECD (2012) that considers that external relationships for knowledge exchange and internationalization among the most relevant external strategic aspects for universities. Knowledge exchange and collaboration support organizational innovation, teaching and research, and local development, creating value for higher education and society in general.

These 'conditioning' dimensions favour the emergence of entrepreneurial universities, as entities that implement several strategies and new institutional configuration to work together with the government and industries to facilitate the generation and exploitation of knowledge and technology (Leydesdorff & Meyer, 2003). Entrepreneurial universities are focused on their contribution to social development and economic growth (Schulte, 2004) and on generating impact.

6.2 The Debate Around Entrepreneurial Universities

Over the past three decades, university entrepreneurship has been a topic of substantial policy debate. To what extent should universities evolve towards being entrepreneurial organizations? Is this trend negatively affecting the autonomy and freedom of fundamental research?

The rationale in support of entrepreneurial universities is that, in an increasingly globalized world where economic activity is becoming more knowledge intensive, universities serve as significant catalysts for economic and technological growth and innovation. Also, the introduction of civil society and the media in the quadruple helix (Carayannis & Campbell, 2009) highlights the university's role as a link between the innovation ecosystem and civil society.

The advocates of entrepreneurial universities hold that universities can and should take a proactive role in advancing the technological and economic growth of countries through the valorization of research results. As we illustrated in Chap. 2, to this end the Bayh–Dole Act is generally regarded as having been successful in promoting the commercialization of university research brought about through federal funds. Even though there is no general agreement that the Bayh–Dole Act has been the primary driver behind university patenting, it has nonetheless provided a significant incentive for universities to patent and license their research and establish technology transfer offices (TTOs/KTOs) that facilitate the transfer of research to industry.

Nevertheless, it is these new institutional roles—patenting, licensing and technology transfer—that raise concerns about the notion of the entrepreneurial university. The conflict lies in balancing university support for entrepreneurial activities with their primary roles of education, research and public service. Through close cooperation between industry and academia augmenting university funding, revenue and profit, there is a risk that the integrity of university researchers, their research and the university itself may be compromised.

[1] https://www.utadeo.edu.co/files/collections/documents/field_attached_file/ec-oecd_entrepreneurial_universities_framework.pdf

At the heart of the debate around entrepreneurial universities is the idea that commercializing university research potentially might come at the detriment of universities' primary aims of education and community outreach.

Questions emerge as to whether research faculty's involvement in entrepreneurial activities diverts priorities away from scientific exploration and towards work on applied research with more practical applications and technological innovations. Moreover, there are concerns that research will be driven into areas where there are market incentives for innovations in products and processes.

On top of this, there are concerns about increased secrecy and publication delay on the part of university researchers (and advocated for by private companies) because of the potential commerciality and profitability of their research and innovations. This would discourage and impede the advancement of knowledge—a key prerogative of the traditional university system—which would therefore reduce the pursuit of scientific progress and in turn slow industrial innovation.

In the face of these warnings, those in favour of entrepreneurial universities hold that there is no evidence in support of these concerns or of a shift towards applied research away from basic research. Indeed, data gathered by the National Science Foundation found that the split between basic and applied research expenditure has not changed despite the growing entrepreneurial role of universities (Compagnucci & Spigarelli, 2020).

The advocates of entrepreneurial universities hold that universities, instead of coming into conflict with their traditional mission, are evolving into a new mission: to become knowledge factories that catalyse development, capability, and innovation within a larger innovation system. This mission synthesizes and requires the bringing together of both their traditional and entrepreneurial roles, which perhaps may complement and reinforce each other.

The debate around entrepreneurial universities, while bringing together different and contradicting views, highlights the importance for universities to maximize their impact through technology, innovation, research and education. Our own definition of entrepreneurial universities is very much related to the notion of impact. Entrepreneurial universities generate impact (economic, technological, social, environmental, cultural, etc.) through leading, addressing, managing and organizing change. Through such entrepreneurial behaviours, they generate externalities/impact going beyond third mission and also affecting research and education.

But what does it take for universities to act entrepreneurially? Below we will explore the role of internal entrepreneurial abilities, external innovation ecosystems and university entrepreneurial strategies. These all influence each other. Strategy should build on internal resources and entrepreneurial abilities, as well as on the specificities of the supportive external environment (i.e. ecosystem). The ecosystem is in turn influenced by entrepreneurial strategies, as their outcomes often land in the external ecosystem to generate impact. Internal entrepreneurial abilities are built over the years and are important for defining an entrepreneurial strategy.

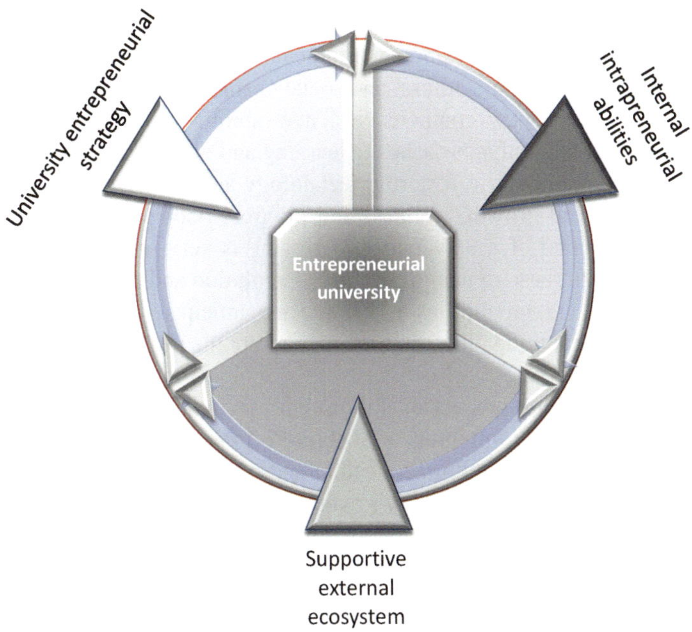

Fig. 6.1 Factors characterizing entrepreneurial universities

6.3 What Does It Take to Be an Entrepreneurial University?

Entrepreneurial universities perform institutional activities aimed at generating impact. Under what circumstances does this happen? And what does it take for universities to be entrepreneurial? We believe there are at least three factors (some others might be required, but these three are the foundations for entrepreneurial universities to come to place): internal intrapreneurial abilities, a supportive external ecosystem and university entrepreneurial strategy. These three factors (Fig. 6.1) are strictly intertwined so that thy influence each other. Below we will explore these factors in three separate sections.

6.3.1 Internal Intrapreneurial Abilities

In order to be entrepreneurial, universities should develop internal intrapreneurial abilities within their settings (Klofsten et al., 2021). The concept of an intrapreneurial ability is not new in the literature, though scant attention has been devoted to it within universities or PROs.

University intrapreneurial abilities are the *abilities to orchestrate internal resources and competencies and leverage on external ones, to lead, manage and implement change within universities, in response to (and coherently with) the evolution of the environment/ecosystem.*

Universities, like other public educational institutions, are continuously challenged by the external context and environmental dynamics, including technological and economic evolution, cultural and social changes. The changing demands of the labour force (i.e. new competencies, new abilities, better interactions with industry, smart and digital approaches to learning and working) require universities to evolve to engage better in fostering technology and knowledge transfer and to contribute to societal growth, wellness and progress (Compagnucci & Spigarelli, 2020). The likelihood of a university progressing is very much dependent on its ability to cope with these dynamic patterns of evolution and requires internal individual and organizational abilities to manage and anticipate change, to orchestrate the factors underpinning the notion of entrepreneurial universities (Flores et al., 2024).

Universities with intrapreneurial abilities have the potential to lead, manage and implement change. Their intrapreneurial ability is important to generate innovation outcomes within research, within education and/or within third mission/academic entrepreneurship and, more generally speaking, within KS. They are a key ingredient for generating innovative outputs in all the three possible missions of any university. At the same time their development is influenced by what goes on within the three missions.

University intrapreneurial abilities (Flores et al., 2024) can be developed in response to either a top-down strategic impulse (institutional activities supporting continuous change and putting entrepreneurial and innovative culture at the heart of strategic actions, which are part of official strategic plans) or bottom-up initiatives (initiatives stemming from individual scholars/professors within their own courses and teaching activities or within their research projects or their engagement activities with companies, local entities, etc.). Intrapreneurial abilities build on existing university internal resources and competencies (human capital, scientific and technological endowments, financial resources, internal and external networks, alliances, etc.).

For these abilities to emerge in response to a stimulus, regardless of its origin (top-down or bottom-up), it is important to have a socialization process in place, aimed at connecting, legitimizing, and engaging academic communities (e.g. professors, students, professionals). Through these innovation-oriented behaviours, intrapreneurial abilities emerge that are long-lasting and dynamic (Klofsten et al., 2021). To the extent that innovative behaviours are continuously practiced, legitimized, socialized across areas and disciplines, they become embedded, part of the DNA of the organization. For a concrete example of how intrapreneurial abilities emerge within a university see the paper by Flores et al. (2024) presenting the case of the University of Bologna.

Another important element for these abilities to emerge is continuity of action with regard to strategies and organization design. The process takes time, as intrapreneurial abilities come to life through consolidated behaviours, requesting continuity of values, goals, and organizational mechanisms and practices.

University intrapreneurial abilities are meant to identify and fulfil the real needs of society, going beyond the traditional educational offering and research activities.

The result is a dynamic path in which the entrepreneurial efforts of universities strengthen their relationship with the ecosystem, generating impact on the local society and its innovation capability. In turn, the external environment will support the universities' competitiveness (Centobelli et al., 2019) and influence the development of intrapreneurial abilities.

We hold there is a relation between intrapreneurial abilities and entrepreneurial universities. Those universities having developed internal entrepreneurial abilities can have better performance in their entrepreneurial strategies and as entrepreneurial universities more generally speaking. Future studies could explore this relation.

6.3.2 Supportive External Ecosystem

The concept of ecosystem has been extensively adopted in the literature of innovation management and entrepreneurship, highlighting the importance of collaborative actions and of bringing together diverse resources for innovation to occur. Successful innovation is highly influenced by organizations' ability to find and exploit external knowledge (Cohen & Levinthal, 1990). Chesbrough (2006) highlighted that the more internally focused a firm remains, the greater its likelihood of losing out on innovation opportunities.

Innovation ecosystems arise from complex relationships of cooperation, communication and feedback among organizations (e.g. governments, universities, industry) in line with the triple helix idea (Carayannis & Campbell, 2009). They also arise at the interface of different dimensions (individual, organizational and environmental), bringing in different factors to be orchestrated (see Chap. 1 for a more detailed explanation of these three levels).

The literature has also highlighted the important role of universities in innovation ecosystems, and in turn the role of ecosystems for the existence of entrepreneurial universities. The impact generated by knowledge, technologies and resources transferred from universities to local territories on industrial upgrading and innovation activities has been widely acknowledged (Giunta et al., 2016). Universities play a key role in forging human capital, shaping the new labour force that will feed into industries and nurturing the existing workforce through reskilling and upskilling teaching programmes, designed ad-hoc for industries.

Good et al. (2019) developed a typology consisting of three types of technology transfer ecosystem: introverted, externalized and allied.

In an *introverted ecosystem* most of the organizational components are large and internal to the university. Components are internal organizational units, typically highly centralized and designed to deliver services to the internal community (with an inward focus), only interacting with external components on a formal basis.

In an *externalized ecosystem* all the components vary in size and are independent, external organizations with multiple owners. This ecosystem is structured in a highly independent fashion and is externally oriented.

An *allied ecosystem* is characterized by typically small organizational components that are both internal and external to the university. The components in such an ecosystem are highly specialized and coordinated.

Regardless of the existence of different ecosystem models, universities should be aware that supportive ecosystems are nurtured by human capital educated by universities and by the knowledge and research results that universities produce. At the same time, they continuously trigger and feed universities providing stimuli and challenges for them to grow. Therefore Universities, in order to actively participate to their ecosystems, should develop an open-minded attitude, so to be permeated by the surrounding environment, and develop what we called 'intrapreneurial abilities' to orchestrate internal resources, people, activities from different disciplines and areas (i.e. education, research, third mission) in a coordinated manner and in synergy with external stakeholders.

In a recent paper (Audretsch et al., 2024) on University and Innovation Entrepreneurial Ecosystems (UIEE), it is suggested that these ecosystems consist of a mix of educational programmes, infrastructure (e.g. incubators, research parks, TTOs, business development and employment offices), regulatory factors (relating to business establishment and property rights), culture (e.g. role models, attitudes towards entrepreneurship) and relationships with government, investors, industry and other socio-economic agents (Wright et al., 2017). These four pillars of UIEE are illustrated in Fig. 6.2. The notion of the UIEE (Special Issue by Feldman, Siegel et al., 2023 for Academy of Management Perspectives) is interesting because it focuses on making connections from an internal perspective and in relation to factors that universities can control or influence in a direct way (Feldman et al., 2019). Different academic communities make up UIEEs, including students, alumni, academics and administrative and technical staff, in the exploration and exploitation of

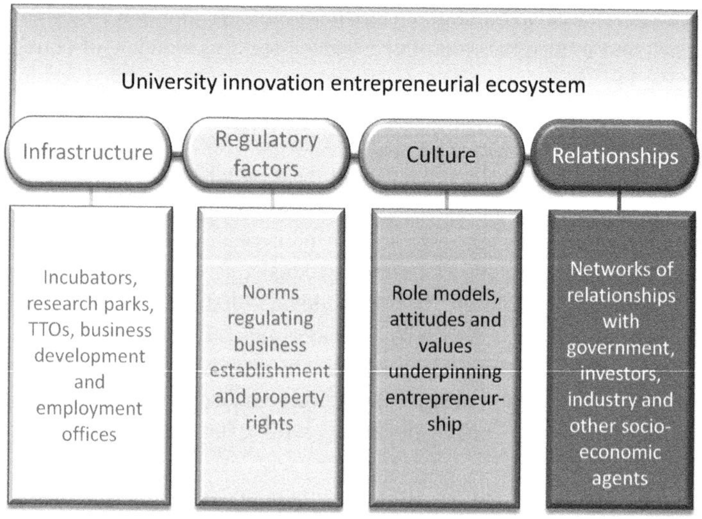

Fig. 6.2 The university innovation and entrepreneurial ecosystem

innovative and entrepreneurial initiatives (Guerrero & Urbano, 2012). These communities act entrepreneurially, interact with the outside environment (community/region) in an entrepreneurial manner (Audretsch, 2014) and with the intention of generating impact.

In the following section, we will focus on the internal activities to be performed by entrepreneurial universities, within a coherent entrepreneurial strategy.

6.3.3 University Entrepreneurial Strategy

So far, we have presented the idea that for entrepreneurial universities to exist, it is important to have internal intrapreneurial abilities and to be part of a fertile supportive external ecosystem (that will nurture them and vice versa). A third important ingredient is university entrepreneurial strategy (UES).

What does it mean for a university to have an entrepreneurial strategy? Entrepreneurial strategies should contribute to generating external impact mainly in the form of newly established companies (research spin-offs and students' start-ups) and should also aim at nurturing an internal innovation and entrepreneurial mindset, which ultimately contributes to the rise of intrapreneurial abilities. As we have already said, UES are influenced by the existence of internal intrapreneurial abilities and by external supportive ecosystem and, in turn, contribute to shaping both.

We do not explore here in detail the role of resources supporting the definition of strategy (and its subsequently implementation), though we give for granted their role and importance. Resources (economic resources, human capital, technologies, infrastructures, etc.) are key, as they set the boundaries for what can be done and what cannot be realized. As such, the formulation of any strategy should move from a detailed analysis of the status quo and of the resources available or likely to be acquired.

UES should work on (at least) three main pillars (see Fig. 6.3): definition of goals; design of actions; communication. The foundation of any strategy starts with the definition of goals to be achieved based on the internal resources already available, new investments and partnerships. A prerequisite for this to happen is a clear vision, which in the specific case of UES should reflect the willingness and intention to embrace an entrepreneurial attitude and foster an entrepreneurial culture in the long run. Mission statements are also important to provide guidance in the short term for specific goals to be reached and for activities to be designed coherently

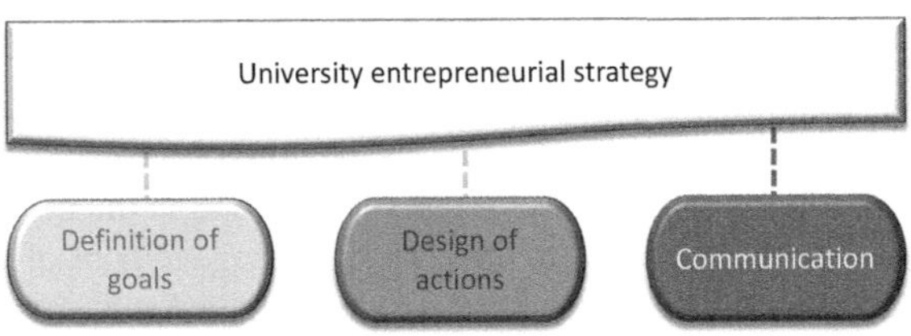

Fig. 6.3 Three ingredients of university entrepreneurial strategy—UES

with short-term UES goals. (In Chap. 3 we provided concrete examples of vision, mission statements for the UES at the University of Bologna.)

Following a clear declaration of vision and mission, and the definition of coherent goals, UES should design the main actions to invest in to achieve goals (in both the short and long term). Universities should create the organizational conditions for these actions to be implemented and orchestrated in a coherent and meaningful way. Therefore, UES should define actions, considering the strategic goals on one hand and the internal resources and organizational endowment available (and its future evolution) on the other. The design of actions will be further detailed in the following chapter.

The third important aspect of UES is communication. Any strategy needs to be communicated in the right way, both internally within the university and externally to the rest of the world. It is important to socialize internally the strategy to support the development of entrepreneurial culture within universities, to let people (e.g. students, professors, staff) know what is going on and what opportunities their universities provide in support of entrepreneurship. Many universities do not pay attention to internal communication. However, there are situations in which scholars, faculty members and students ignore the existence of KTOs and the opportunities for them to leverage on their knowledge and generate impact through the commercial exploitation of their ideas. To have them engaged it is important to let them know, disseminate the strategic intents and communicate the actions in support.

Communication to the rest of the world is important, then, to position universities in their surrounding innovation ecosystems and to leverage on external resources and opportunities to maximize the likelihood of success in commercializing academic knowledge and generating impact. We will come back to this aspect below, but it is important to bear in mind that effective communication strategies are key for UES to be successful. The orchestration of various channels (e.g. networking events, websites, physical leaflets and brochures, social media) is desirable to reach different communities and socialize entrepreneurial outcomes in an effective way.

As Fig. 6.3 shows, UES should be concerned with three aspects: define the goals, design coherent actions, and work out a communication plan coherent with the goals and the actions. In the following section we will detail take a closer look to designing actions.

6.4 Designing Effective Actions in University Entrepreneurial Strategies

The heart of any UES is the actions designed in line with the goals, to be communicated internally and externally. We believe there are two main building blocks in around which UES actions (i.e. support mechanisms) can be designed.

The first encompasses actions and initiatives aimed at generating and diffusing an internal entrepreneurial culture. The second is the actions, initiatives and tools that will be implemented to encourage the engagement of university communities (e.g. faculty, students, administrative and technical staff) in academic entrepreneurship.

The idea of the two-block strategy in support of entrepreneurship comes from the prior experience of the two authors at the University of Bologna, as Deputy Rector for entrepreneurship and Head of the Knowledge Transfer Office (KTO). (In Chap. 3 we described the University of Bologna's strategy, articulated through five pillars and specific support actions for spin-offs and start-ups.)

The two-blocks strategy that we present here comes from that experience and build on it with the aim of providing a more general framework that can fit a large number and different types of universities and other research organizations.

Figure 6.4 illustrates the two-blocks strategy in support of entrepreneurship.

6.4.1 The First Block: Nurturing Internal Entrepreneurial Culture

As expected, this is the most challenging part. What does it mean for a university to have an entrepreneurial culture and how can its emergence be encouraged? How can universities create internal intrapreneurial abilities?

Organizational culture is about values, practices, expectations, beliefs, and behaviours. Universities willing to promote entrepreneurial culture should design strategies (and related goals and actions) driven by values that favour change, evolution, openness and an outward-looking attitude, in line with their missions and their specificities and in respect to the past and tradition.

It is difficult to make a pre-defined list of values, as many of them depend on the specificities of the university and its history. Nevertheless, it is fair to say that universities embracing an entrepreneurial culture have some traits in common: an outward-looking attitude; a positive attitude towards change, evolution, and innovation (rather than fear); and an orientation towards inclusion, diversity and openness. In 'true' entrepreneurial universities these values are *shared* and *diffused* across the different communities, are *drivers of individuals' behaviour* and, to the extent that they are rooted in organizational routines, contribute to the emergence of *intrapreneurial abilities*.

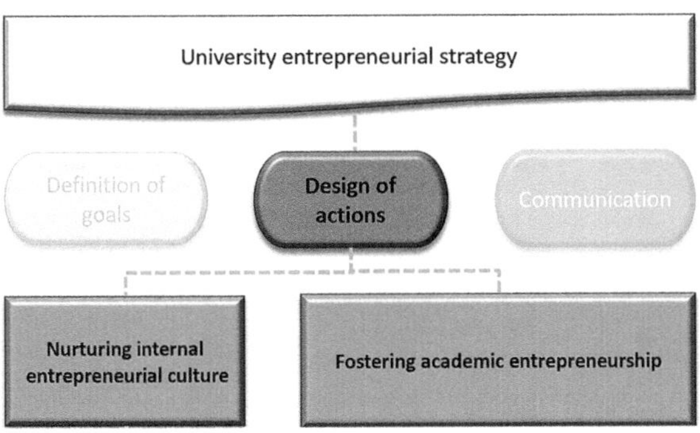

Fig. 6.4 Actions of university entrepreneurial strategy: two-building blocks

Entrepreneurial universities can be both newly established organizations and old ones with long histories and traditions. The former do not have pre-existing boundaries and often have more flexibility and are more dynamic and quicker to address the challenges brought about by the future. The latter often face the challenge of combining tradition with innovation, negotiating between advocates of the past and evangelists of novelties. The challenge for them is to find the right balance. Conversely to what common sense would suggest, it is often the case that the stronger their identity, history and tradition, the less they fear the future and the risks and opportunities it may offer, and the more likely they are to act in an entrepreneurial way.

The entrepreneurial culture should permeate all the areas (as illustrated in Fig. 6.5) in consideration of the fact that universities generate impact through their three missions: teaching, research and third mission (Mtawa et al., 2016). Indeed, universities' social mission is not separate from teaching and research but rather is integrated with them (Etzkowitz, 2013).

In the *research area*, universities can create internal measures to support interdisciplinary or applied research and research projects in collaboration with other universities or private companies. These initiatives can be independent (based on the university's budget) or activated within European or national projects. In fact, significant attention is paid by individual countries and at the European level to the commercial valorization of research results and to promoting academic entrepreneurship.

In the *education area*, much can be done through entrepreneurial education (EE—see Sect. 6.6 for more details on this topic). It is important to recall here that EE can have different targets and goals. Specifically, it can support the creation of an entrepreneurial culture to the extent that it encourages the engagement of all the

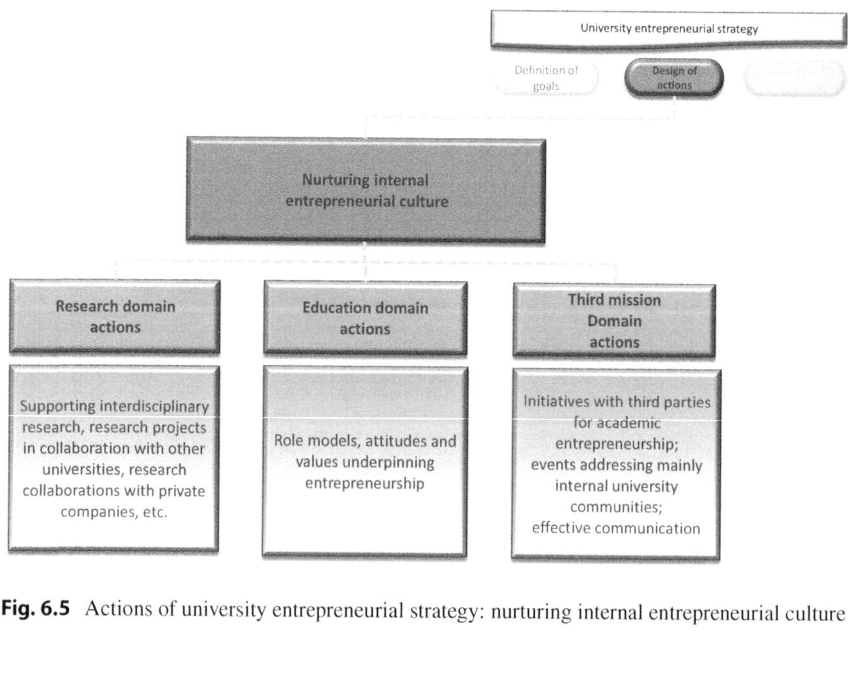

Fig. 6.5 Actions of university entrepreneurial strategy: nurturing internal entrepreneurial culture

different academic communities (i.e. students, faculty, administrative and technical staff). Turning to different goals, we tend to think of academic spin-offs and start-ups as the principal outcomes of EE. The creation of independent ventures is highly desirable, though it represents a limited outcome. There is evidence that only a limited number of students exposed to EE end up creating start-ups. The most important goal of EE is the possibility of shaping human capital and educating people to have outward-looking attitudes and an entrepreneurial mindset. What does this mean? Through their EE programmes, universities can contribute to creating T-shaped people, with a vertical specialization and a horizontal set of soft skills, among which is an entrepreneurial mindset. These skills are becoming increasingly important in the face of the exponential evolution of technology and society at large, requiring individuals to cope with and lead change. This applies to students (who will become the workforce of the near future), professors and scholars (who are increasingly stimulated by open innovation, collaboration with other universities and research organizations and industrial partnership) and staff (who can be involved in academic entrepreneurship and may play a key role in addressing, guiding and supporting both professors and students in the commercial exploitation of their knowledge, specifically those working in KTOs). Finally, given that entrepreneurship can happen across all disciplines, it is important to have dedicated training sessions to let students know about the opportunities their universities provide.

In the TM area (and at the interface with research and education), actions such as events and initiatives with third parties (e.g. companies, as well as Non Governmental Organizations—NGOs—and other public entities) aim to bring together diverse communities (academic and non-academic) to work together or raise awareness and promote dialogue and discussion on topics of interest for society at large (having implications for entrepreneurship and offering opportunities for academic entrepreneurship).

In between education and third mission (in line with both training and disseminating objectives), it is desirable to run events (mainly catered towards internal university communities, but also external ones) aimed at socializing the mechanisms that the university puts in place to support entrepreneurship. It is surprising to see that professors, scholars, students, and staff are often unaware of what goes on within their mother organizations because nobody tells them. Communication through seminars, events and in collaboration with external partners is key to spreading information and motivating individuals to participate and to feel that entrepreneurship is part of their university's culture. Also, in line with this, it is important to invest in effective communication: dedicated websites, internal brochures and leaflets, newsletters and intensive use of social media.

6.4.2 The Second Block: Fostering Academic Entrepreneurship

The commercialization of academic knowledge can take place through various channels, one of which is academic entrepreneurship. We stick to the definition provided by Shane (2004), according to which academic entrepreneurship involves the founding of a firm with the objective to commercially exploit a patented invention, or in some cases a body of unpatented expertise (Shane, 2004). Other definitions include the licensing of a patented or otherwise protected invention against the contracted receipt of royalties (Jensen & Thursby, 2001). Commercialization means that an academic invention is exploited with the objective of generating financial rewards. Also, more general academic knowledge, not in the form of inventions or patents, can be the object of commercialization.

The actions that universities can put in place to support academic entrepreneurship, as detailed in Chap. 3, vary based on the characteristics of the organization: geographical location, size, specialization, age, inclusion of a medical school, etc. There is no upfront formula that can fit all of them. As we mentioned above, a successful UES should be specific in leveraging on the key characteristics and resources of universities and enhance their uniqueness.

Provided that it is important to consider the peculiarities of individual universities, there are some key general actions that universities should invest in if they want to support academic entrepreneurship and leverage the entrepreneurial potential of their employees and students. Actions in support of entrepreneurial processes should be designed in consideration of the interrelations among them. Most actions, as in a value chain, are sequential and are meant to generate additional value at every step of the entrepreneurial process, starting from the identification of the idea, all the way to setting up a new venture and accelerating its growth.

Actions within a UES can be designed from inception as targeting two different communities: students, who are mainly involved in educational activities and likely to generate student entrepreneurship, and those who can be assimilated as employees, who are mainly involved in research activities (e.g. faculty members, scholars, PhD students) and are more likely to come up with research-based entrepreneurship. Both student and research-based entrepreneurship can have intellectual property (IP) contents or can be based on a body of unpatented expertise or knowledge. Having separate actions for (at least) these two separate targets helps with delivering value in a more accurate way and with implementing more effective measures, addressing the different needs that different audiences may have. Of course, this is not to suggest that the student and researcher communities should be kept separate and treated as silos. Separate actions should be accompanied by 'get-together' moments, events, and actions, with the aim of supporting cross-contamination and reinforcing the entrepreneurial potential.

On top of these 'separate' actions designed for two specific targets, it would be desirable to have in place additional support mechanisms designed around a third hybrid target, bringing together researchers (from universities and other PROs), students (including PhDs) and companies. This is, in part, what already happens in many universities investing in open innovation programmes, such as hackathons, which encourage the development of new solutions starting from a concrete problem. We think that more specific actions can be designed around these open innovation activities with the specific goal of establishing new research-based companies based on collaboration between research organizations, private companies, and students. Open innovation with a push approach to technology could be designed

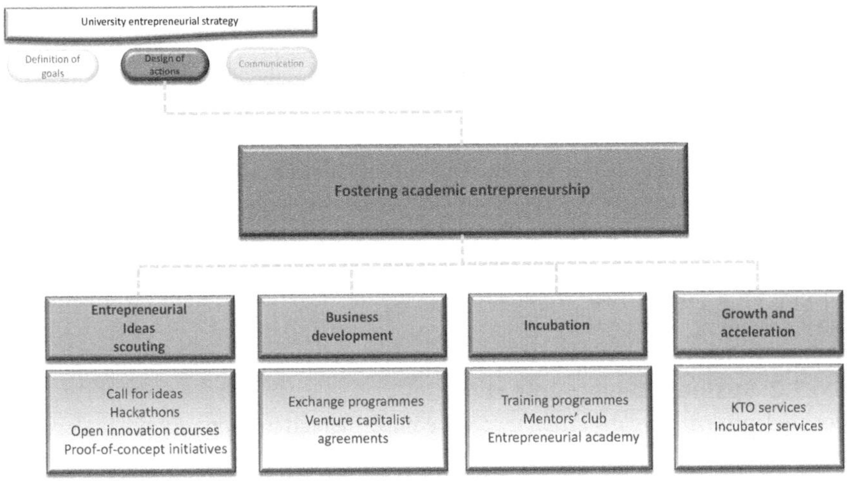

Fig. 6.6 Actions of university entrepreneurial strategy: fostering academic entrepreneurship

around research organizations' unexploited patents to favour their commercialization. This approach would be beneficial not only to universities but also to PROs, which lack the student component.

Below we suggest four categories of actions within the second building block of fostering academic entrepreneurship: entrepreneurial ideas scouting, business development, incubation, and growth and acceleration. For each category, we provide some examples. A summary is offered in Fig. 6.6.

6.4.2.1 Entrepreneurial Ideas Scouting

For students, a *call for ideas* works well, specifically when it is designed to offer support with the refinement of the ideas, understanding potential markets and their needs, bringing out the 'distinctive value', running a competitive analysis, searching for complementary knowledge and resources, establishing a team of founders and presenting the ideas. A call for ideas should be run each year so to create a steady and continuous approach to academic entrepreneurship and to allow time for potential candidates to think carefully about their projects and apply at the right time to catch the 'opportunity window'.

On top of a call for ideas, other actions include *hackathons* and *challenge-based initiatives*, and *open innovation courses* (also in collaboration with companies) where students from different disciplines come together to work in interdisciplinary teams. All these initiatives can offer students grants to work more on their ideas.

Specific *physical locations*—e.g. fab labs, maker spaces, coworking spaces—can be put in place to encourage teamwork and projects, as well as cross-contamination with students from different disciplines and between students, professors and staff, aimed at creating deal flow of ideas.

For the research-based community, a specific *call for research-based ideas* can work to identify IP and non-IP research-based projects with the potential for commercial exploitation. These calls for action can be accompanied by small training sessions so to allow candidates to apply and, for instance, present a rudimentary business model or competitor analysis. These calls should also offer grants or other awards (e.g. money to be spent on resources/tools to further develop the idea or understand its potential, or to activate research assistant grants).

Another important action finalized at scouting ideas is *proof of concept*, which is meant to enhance the development of early-stage technologies, to raise their technology readiness level and to further investigate their commercial potential. Through Proof of concept grants are offered to scholars to develop their IP-based technologies so as to unveil their commercial potential in terms of spin-off creation or out-licensing.

6.4.2.2 Business Development

For students, *training programmes* can be implemented to support them in developing their business ideas. These programmes can be run in collaboration with incubators, maker spaces or fab labs and should target teams of aspiring founders. The training should be designed to include plenary sessions followed by one-to-ones so that expert mentors can provide feedback in a more dedicated way to specific entrepreneurial projects. These programmes should be devoted to students who already have a business idea and are looking for support in developing it. In many universities these training sessions take the form of a 'university academy', in which educators can be internal professors (mainly experts in business models and management and entrepreneurship) and staff (mainly KTO staff), as well as experts from outside, bringing in vertical knowledge and experience in specific fields of interest for business idea exploitation.

The creation of *mentors' clubs* goes hand in hand with these training programmes. Mentors can be professors or scholars with some expertise in the subject (e.g. managers, entrepreneurs, people from the market, business developers, IP experts, business angels), who can assist with the development of ideas into viable business plans and also consider formal participation in the new ventures.

For the research-based community, similar activities to those for students should be designed ad hoc. *Training sessions* can be associated with proof-of-concept beneficiaries such that, in addition to grants, scientists also receive support to further develop the market potential of their technologies. Business development training sessions can also be associated with spin-off calls, taking into consideration the fact that spin-off ideas might be at different stages of development. Within this academy, one-to-one training can be organized with experts addressing vertical issues. Those who are more advanced can move straight into establishing a company, while those lagging behind can benefit from specific training to refine their business plans and then proceed towards spin-off creation.

6.4.2.3 Incubation

For both students and the research-based community, support can be offered by *KTO divisions* (ideally those in charge of supporting new venture creation) in establishing start-ups and spin-offs. University-owned (or partially owned) or external *incubators* should be put in place to guarantee initial assistance in terms of basic services (e.g. legal, administrative, secretarial) and offer office spaces at affordable prices but also access to external funds/investments.

Also for incubation services we do not hypothesize a distinction between students and the research community because the nature of the services is such that there are no distinctions between the two categories of companies: student-based start-ups and research-based spin-offs. On the contrary: cross-contamination in the same physical space between different companies operating in different sectors can be highly beneficial.

6.4.2.4 Growth and Acceleration

For both students and the research-based community, post-new venture creation, universities can offer additional services to start-up companies to promote their growth. First, they can give them access to research networks and create ties that will be beneficial to those companies still requiring investment in research to further advance their solutions. *Specific agreements* can be set up with universities and other centres around the globe, allowing founders' mobility and exchange programmes so that companies from different countries can be exposed to different ecosystems. Also, universities can set up *strategic agreements* with venture capitalists to facilitate exposure to finance and invest in their own internal funds.

On the acceleration side, it has become very popular to create partnerships with *accelerators*. Accelerators are fixed-term, cohort-based programmes that include mentorship and educational components and culminate in a public pitch event or demo day. Accelerators can be either privately or publicly funded and cover a wide range of industries. The application process for seed accelerators is open to anyone but is highly competitive and selective. There are specific accelerators, such as corporate accelerators, which are often subsidiaries of or programmes in larger corporations that act like seed accelerators.

6.5 The 4S UES Framework

In our view an effective UES should have at least four key properties. The four properties of UES are illustrated in Fig. 6.7.

Specific: taking inspiration from successful UESs implemented in other parts of the world, a UES should maintain its specificity, adhering to the story, 'soul' and characteristics of the university in which it is designed and implemented. While it is important to look around for best practices and learn from benchmark universities, it is a mistake to emulate a formula that works elsewhere in other geographies and organizational settings. A successful UES should be based on local resources and specificities and should reflect the values and the culture of the organization in which it is rooted. The roots, specificities, peculiarities and uniqueness of the organization are strengths to be valorised.

Systemic: a UES should bring together separate parts (e.g. actions, tools, people, organizational divisions, areas, stakeholders) in an attempt to create a system in

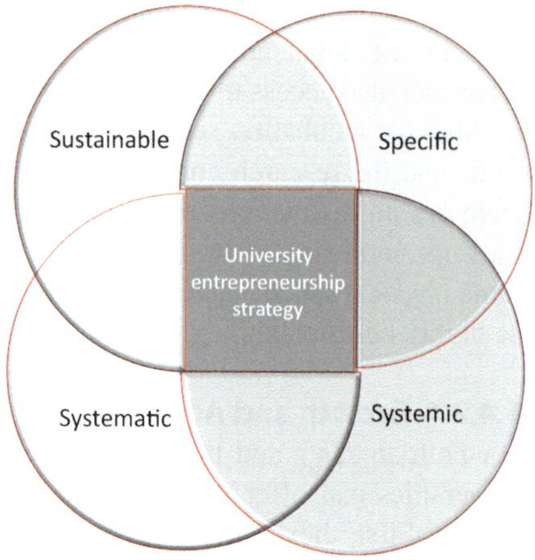

Fig. 6.7 The 4S university entrepreneurial strategy framework

which the nodes are connected and interact, so as to create a whole that is bigger than the sum of its parts. This systemic attitude applies both internally and externally. With regard to the former, a UES is transversal to different missions that universities might have (i.e. teaching, research, third mission). A UES should link these diverse missions, areas and organizational divisions with their actions, projects, and tools under the overarching umbrella of innovation and entrepreneurship. Some of these factors can generate synergies if they work in parallel; others generate wealth if they work along a value chain. No matter how, it is important to create connections for internal dimensions, with the underlying common contents of innovation and entrepreneurship to be connected and orchestrated.

The same reasoning applies to a university's surrounding external context. In this chapter we recall the concept of the ecosystem several times. Having a systemic UES starts with universities being aware that they are nodes in a larger external ecosystem to which they can contribute. Then, it is important for universities to understand how they can contribute to the ecosystem and coherently design and implement actions in collaboration with external stakeholders.

Systematic: a strategy is a plan that identifies long-term goals and the resources and investments to be used to achieve them. Successful UES strategies require the socialization of goals within the organization and the generation of a context in which, every day, everyone understands how they are contributing to the whole, so that they feel they are part of the whole and contribute to it in a steady and continuous way. In other words, the contribution that each part (e.g. actions, tools, people, organizations, units, stakeholders) brings to the system, on top of being orchestrated with a systemic approach, should also provide continuity so as to guarantee reliable actions and replicability and generate internal routines imbued with the values and behaviours underpinning the entrepreneurial culture. Some ad-hoc designed events and actions might be desirable. Continuity creates patterns in which individuals and organizational actions meet and find meaning, to the point that they become shared and structural parts of the organization. Systematic approaches create internal legitimacy, which is essential for a university to be acknowledged externally in the role(s) it wants to have. Only universities that manage to convey to the outside world this systematic entrepreneurial attitude succeed in effectively positioning themselves in the external ecosystem.

Sustainable: any strategy needs to be sustainable. Sustainability means investing in activities and actions that, after the start-up stage, can generate resources (tangible or intangible) that can support the future evolution of the actions. The idea of sustainability is central to every industrial plan for private and public organizations. Within a UES, only some of the returns on investment in entrepreneurship are financial/economic (and are expected to be reinvested in internal activities and actions). Other results are more difficult to measure; they are not financial/economic and take the form of general knowledge spillover, a more innovative mindset for facing change, a widening of the network of relations, a changing of the culture in favour of better external collaborations and greater attention paid to the generation of impact.

6.6 Internal Ecosystems

For universities wanting to be entrepreneurial it is important to put forward a coherent set of objectives and related activities in line with the two-block UES that we described above. The basic idea of UES is to describe organizational mechanisms that should be implemented to support the emergence of entrepreneurial universities. These mechanisms not only need to stay under a unique frame (UES), but they also need to be connected and work in synergies.

While it is important to have different actors and organizational units specialized in specific phases of the entrepreneurial process, it is also desirable to create bridges to link together these different activities governed by universities. Each of the two building blocks of UES describes organizational mechanisms that do not work in isolation and call for integrations and synergies. It is desirable to adopt a process perspective to connect and orchestrate all the actors operating along the different stages of the academic entrepreneurial journey. A lack of synchronization could lead to failure in generating the recommended spill over effects at the heart of any effective knowledge transfer process.

To stress the potential of these connections, we introduce the notion of *internal ecosystems* that can be defined as internal organizational *meta-contexts* creating links across mechanisms (actions, events, programs) governed by the university in support of entrepreneurship, which means bridging: a) personnel working in different organizational units, different areas (research, education and third mission); b) different university governed entities, like incubators, foundations, agencies (controlled or participated by universities) or different departments, that care about entrepreneurship, invest in it and are in charge of mechanisms (or parts of them).

Internal university ecosystems in support of entrepreneurship are important because they:

- Create connections across all the mechanisms in support of entrepreneurship or likely to impact and influence entrepreneurship
- Reinforce awareness of the relevance of academic entrepreneurship within the academic community
- Make universities' efforts in academic entrepreneurship more visible and valuable for the internal community, by presenting it as a coordinated efforts.

We believe that for effective internal ecosystems to exist there are two important prerequisites:

- A portfolio of heterogeneous mechanisms working in support of entrepreneurial universities, targeting different academic communities and students, at different stages of the entrepreneurial process
- Attitude/orientation towards collaboration in different departments, organizational units, as well as area (research, education and third mission)
- The availability of internal 'glues' that somehow connect the actions and contribute to generating diffused organizational learning and awareness of supporting entrepreneurial outcomes.

The notion of internal ecosystems is related to the intrapreneurial abilities that we discussed in relation to successful entrepreneurial universities in this chapter. When intrapreneurial abilities are available, the creation of such internal ecosystem in support of entrepreneurship can be straightforward. As we said intrapreneurial abilities have to do with orchestration of resources and competencies to lead, manage and implement change in different areas and missions of universities and, as such, they are an important driver for the emergence of internal ecosystems.

6.7 Entrepreneurial Education

Entrepreneurial education (EE) has become a very popular topic, capturing the interest of universities, instructors, students, scholars, private companies, policymakers, and independent individuals looking for jobs, having business ideas or just interested in new possibilities for the future.

Originally, EE referred to teaching, learning and pedagogical techniques applied by higher education institutions to degree programmes related to the field of entrepreneurship, with the intention of creating new businesses (Bolzani & Luppi, 2021). Recent advancements, however, view EE as a more complex, transversal construct, generating interest across different disciplines and, more importantly, not necessarily aimed at new venture creation.

EE aims to develop new competencies and skills as well as an entrepreneurial mindset—the ability to adapt to changing contexts in order to promote flexibility, creativity and continuous innovation (Haynie & Shepherd, 2007; Naumann, 2017; Ireland et al., 2003).

EE is important for entrepreneurial universities to emerge, for encouraging the emergence of both an entrepreneurial culture and accompanying strategic actions in support of academic entrepreneurship at large. It is also key for positioning universities in the external ecosystem. More specifically, EE can influence the three basic ingredients of entrepreneurial universities (Fig. 6.1) and can be instrumental to:

- Creating better ecosystems (with training program based on innovation and entrepreneurship targeting non-academic community, companies and external stakeholders at large)
- Favouring the emergence of intrapreneurial abilities and internal ecosystems (facilitating raise awareness on entrepreneurship and internal connections, with training events designed to bring together different disciplines and targeting faculty, students and personnel from different departments and organizational divisions)
- Supporting the development of a strategy in support of entrepreneurship, UES, accompanying the design and implementation of its actions, specifically those targeting faculty and students and aimed at generating the valorisation of research results through spin-offs and the creation of start-ups).

The portfolio of EE initiatives can include different initiatives targeting various audiences and having different goals.

6.7.1 Generating Entrepreneurial Awareness Within the Academic Community

These actions are meant to support the development of an entrepreneurial culture by making it possible for academic communities of students, researchers, and staff (specifically, but not limited to KTO personnel) to be part of an entrepreneurial project. At the same time these initiatives can aim at socializing successful and unsuccessful stories from other students/faculties/scientists from around the globe with interesting stories to share. The target is the entire academic community.

The modality is via seminars, inspirational speeches, events, and think-tanks. This is, in general, an informal modality. Everybody can join when they want, if they feel like to attend.

6.7.2 Developing an Entrepreneurial Mindset and Raising Entrepreneurial Self-efficacy of Students

These actions encompass formal courses in entrepreneurship targeting students with the aim of developing their entrepreneurial mindset, raising their personal entrepreneurial self-efficacy and improving their ability to work in teams on the development of innovative solutions to a problem (challenge-based courses). Courses in entrepreneurship and innovation management follow in this category; they should be formal courses that provide credits. Given their transversal character, they have become very popular in almost all disciplines and curricula, where once they could be found mainly in management, finance, and economics types of studies.

6.7.3 Supporting the Development of Business Plans Within the Academic Community Towards the Establishment of New Ventures

These actions encompass business development training aimed at turning promising ideas into viable business models. They target members of the academic community (e.g. students, professors, staff) who have ideas and want to assess their commercial viability. These are more 'hands-on', often one-to-one training sessions, where would-be entrepreneurs and their teams are supported by experts and business developers through the development of their ideas to craft them, determine their potential and work out a formal business plan. This training is, in general, not part of institutional curricula; it is rather offered as an add-on, often in collaboration with incubators, KTOs and/or other university-related entities in charge of supporting entrepreneurship. Examples are training sessions for students and research communities (*advanced academies*), which we mentioned above in the business development actions to accompany the development of business ideas within a UES.

6.7.4 Supporting the Development of Business Plans by *External* Would-Be Entrepreneurs

These actions include training sessions often developed in collaboration with external third parties (e.g. private companies, other public or private organizations working within the external ecosystem to support entrepreneurship) and fall under the umbrella of universities' continuous education (programmes designed for working people to upgrade their skills). Programmes in support of entrepreneurship (e.g. entrepreneurial culture promotion, business plan development) can be designed for external customers within formal partnerships.

6.8 Student Entrepreneurship

Over the last 30 years there has been a worldwide proliferation of courses in entrepreneurship in many universities, accompanied by an increasing number of university-based start-ups, many of them stemming from students (student entrepreneurship). As we saw above, student entrepreneurship can be part of a more general university strategy in support of entrepreneurship.

Universities are interested in generating new student-based firms for different reasons, the most important including enhancing local/regional economic development, encouraging employment, creating new job opportunities and, last but not least, making themselves more attractive to current or prospective faculty members and future students (Wright et al., 2019; Mustar, 2021).

In many countries, entrepreneurship is an attractive employment option for university graduates. This is shown by the increasing rate of new venture creation by students and the rising global demand for entrepreneurship education programmes and support structures at universities (OECD, 2015). There is growing interest in designing and evaluating student entrepreneurship programmes and initiatives from both a managerial and a public policy standpoint.

While most academic studies of university entrepreneurship have emphasized the commercialization of technology through start-ups based on formal university-owned IP, there is evidence that students from all disciplines, including the social sciences, business administration, arts and humanities, are engaging in entrepreneurial activity that does not necessarily depend on IP, formal or informal, generated by the university (Fini et al., 2016).

In this section on student entrepreneurship, we rely on the magnificent work of Wright et al. (2019) to summarize the state of the art on this topic. The authors selected some universities from a dozen countries and based on detailed case studies, they conclude that there is substantial heterogeneity in universities' strategies for promoting student entrepreneurship.

They show that in some cases strategies in support of student entrepreneurship have resulted from bottom-up initiatives, while others have been based on top-down policies. Few universities have devoted substantial resources to supporting student entrepreneurship, both from inside and outside the institution, while others manage them on a modest budget. Actions in support of student entrepreneurship can be centrally managed or can be promoted and implemented directly by departments and in some cases by single professors with passion and competence on entrepreneurship. In other situations, actions in support of student entrepreneurship are ideated and implemented directly by students.

Overall, Wright et al. (2019) identify four different models of student entrepreneurship: student run, missionary professor run, supporting entrepreneurship across the university and internally integrated.

6.8.1 Student Run

The student-run model relies on students as the main engine of action in support of entrepreneurship. This may happen when there is weak or absent university strategy or support. Students gather into student entrepreneurship societies, student clubs or student associations to drive entrepreneurial activities. These societies, clubs or associations have a crucial role in developing activities to support entrepreneurial projects and entrepreneurial mind-set. They support student entrepreneurship by organizing networking events to create links between students from different departments and sometimes different universities.

This model relies heavily on volunteers (among the students) to organize events, contact speakers, etc. The support of faculty, while not central in this model, is desirable, as they may provide a bridge to useful contacts. Also, the support and endorsement received by some 'influential' academics may be crucial for gaining access to resources.

6.8.2 Missionary Professor Run

When there is no university-level strategy to support student entrepreneurship, some faculty members (with the tacit or explicit approval of the department) can take an active role in promoting student entrepreneurship. These faculty members often come from business and engineering schools, as well as some science departments. The latter may be more focused on faculty and postdoctoral entrepreneurship. There is evidence that faculty with entrepreneurial experience have played a significant role in supporting other faculty who are new to the spin-off process (Mosey & Wright, 2007). Similarly, such faculty may possess important experience-based skills that can make them more effective as coaches and mentors for student entrepreneurs. Adjunct or visiting professors, entrepreneurs in residence and professors of practice may also be well placed to perform this role. They can be sources of inspiration to their students during their courses and can help them in their entrepreneurial projects during their internships or thesis.

6.8.3 Supporting Entrepreneurship Across the University

This model allows for the existence of a plethora of different initiatives in support of student entrepreneurship. Different departments, schools and other institutions (controlled or participated, like incubators, foundations, etc.) within universities may have different goals regarding entrepreneurship and may seek to construct their own approaches to entrepreneurship in a top-down way. There is no central strategy but a coexistence of different institutional measures. In this case, there is no central strategy supporting student entrepreneurship, but there are several initiatives spread and diffused which build on separate budget and resources and also reflect diversity of intents, competencies and approaches of a variety of actors. This is desirable to have in case of supporting student entrepreneurship in specific vertical domains (specialized actors can generate more and vertical value added), though, at some stage, the contamination and heterogeneity is necessary to provide different views and competencies requested by entrepreneurial projects.

6.8.4 Internally Integrated

The integrated model is a powerful centre for entrepreneurship (across all schools and all disciplines). The objective of this model is to provide an internally integrated set of support mechanisms aimed at students within and across the university. The focus is both to educate students in entrepreneurship and to offer them all the necessary resources to realize their projects through to the start-up phase. The model is characterized by having a high level of resources: a strong and structured team of professionals, different spaces (e.g. coworking spaces, fab labs, incubators, accelerators) and significant funds from rich alumni, the university and corporates.

The success of a top-down, internally integrated activity model relies heavily on the strategic commitment of the university to provide finance, space, and human resources. It also relies on the governance. There is a need to align the goals and incentives of different departments with those of the university as a whole. University KTOs also need to be part of the integrated activities.

The four models and their main characteristics are summarized in Table 6.1, which has been adapted from Wright et al. (2019). The four models can co-exist or, in many cases, reflect different stages of supporting student entrepreneurship in situations starting in a more informal way (less institutional) with the first two models and then evolving towards more formalized and institutional models (the last two).

With regard to the different models for supporting student entrepreneurship (Wright et al., 2019), we believe that top-down approaches are best suited for contexts in which, in the absence of a strong attitude towards entrepreneurship on the student side and/or the surrounding external context, some coordinated and institutional nudging is desirable to generate signals and create an initial institutional framework to provide legitimacy to students' entrepreneurial behaviours. The case of the University of Bologna illustrated in Chap. 3 is an example of this.

In contexts where there is already a widespread entrepreneurial culture and the surrounding context is fertile enough to pull from and call for entrepreneurial initiatives from students, entrepreneurial behaviours from students might emerge in a natural way, with no need for specific top-down strategies. The adoption of one model (out of the four) depends very much on the characteristics of both the university and the external local context. We believe that institutional top-down support (even to a small extent) is desirable for creating a framework within which students can feel identification and legitimation. Then it can be relaxed when an internal culture in support of student entrepreneurship has been developed and in presence of supportive ecosystems that provide all forms of support to aspiring entrepreneurs.

Table 6.1 Characteristics of the four models for managing student entrepreneurship at universities

IP Protection process

People/Structure	Objective	Focus	Initiatives	Resources	Activities
Student entrepreneurship societies, student clubs	Support student entrepreneurial projects	Narrow: Student start-ups, creation of companies by students	Bottom-up	Limited, based on voluntary service (some exceptions)	Business plan competitions, conferences
Business schools, science departments, individual faculty members	Support mechanisms beyond the traditional classroom offerings	Narrow: Thematic spin-offs	Bottom-up (looked upon benevolently by the university management)	Limited: One or two missionary professors, a small space, low financial support	Broad range: entrepreneurial education, competitions, events, conferences
A light structure in a large or new university without a long entrepreneurial tradition	Support and development for student entrepreneurship	Narrow: students and recent graduates	Top-down from the university management	Very small team with modest space and low financial support	Mentorship, training programmes, access to coworking spaces
A powerful centre for entrepreneurship (across all schools and disciplines)	Provision of an integrated set of support mechanisms	Education of students in entrepreneurship and support with their start-ups	Top-down	High: Strong team, different spaces, funds from the university, rich alumni and corporate sponsors	Outreach programmes, events, infrastructure and state-of-the-art facilities, academics

References

Acs, Z. J., Audretsch, D. B., & Lehmann, E. E. (2013). The knowledge spillover theory of entrepreneurship. *Small Business Economics, 41*(4), 757–774. https://doi.org/10.1007/s11187-013-9505-9

Acs, Z. J., Braunerhjelm, P., Audretsch, D. B., & Carlsson, B. (2009). The knowledge spillover theory of entrepreneurship. *Small Business Economics, 32*(1), 15–30. https://doi.org/10.1007/s11187-008-9157-3

Audretsch, D. B. (2014). From the entrepreneurial university to the university for the entrepreneurial society. *The Journal of Technology Transfer, 39*(3), 313–321. https://doi.org/10.1007/s10961-012-9288-1

Audretsch, D. B., & Lehmann, E. (2006). Entrepreneurial access and absorption of knowledge spillovers: Strategic board and managerial composition for competitive advantage. *Journal of Small Business Management, 44*(2), 155–166. https://doi.org/10.1111/j.1540-627X.2006.00161.x

Audretsch, D., Khurana, I., Dutta, D. & al. (2024). Creating effective university innovation and entrepreneurial ecosystems: a commitment system perspective. Journal of Technology Transfer https://doi.org/10.1007/s10961-024-10090-w

Bolzani, D., & Luppi, E. (2021). Assessing entrepreneurial competences: Insights from a business model challenge. *Education+Training, 63*(2), 214–238. https://doi.org/10.1108/ET-04-2020-0072

Carayannis, E. G., & Campbell, D. F. (2009). 'Mode 3' and 'Quadruple Helix': Toward a 21st century fractal innovation ecosystem. *International Journal of Technology Management, 46*(3–4), 201–234. https://doi.org/10.1504/IJTM.2009.023374

Centobelli, P., Cerchione, R., & Esposito, E. (2019). Exploration and exploitation in the development of more entrepreneurial universities: A twisting learning path model of ambidexterity. *Technological Forecasting and Social Change, 141*, 172–194. https://doi.org/10.1016/j.techfore.2018.10.014

Chesbrough, H. W. (2006). The era of open innovation. *Managing Innovation and Change, 127*(3), 34–41.

Clark, B. R. (1998). *Creating entrepreneurial universities: Organisational pathways to transformation*. IAU Press and Pergamon.

Cohen, W. M., & Levinthal, D. A. (1990). Absorptive capacity: A new perspective on learning and innovation. *Administrative Science Quarterly, 35*, 128–152. https://doi.org/10.2307/2393553

Compagnucci, L., & Spigarelli, F. (2020). The Third Mission of the university: A systematic literature review on potentials and constraints. *Technological Forecasting and Social Change, 161*, 120284. https://doi.org/10.1016/j.techfore.2020.120284N

Davies, G. H., Flanagan, J., Bolton, D., Roderick, S., & Joyce, N. (2021). University knowledge spillover from an open innovation technology transfer context. *Knowledge Management Research and Practice, 19*(1), 84–93. https://doi.org/10.1080/14778238.2020.1746204

Etzkowitz, H. (1998). The norms of entrepreneurial science: Cognitive effects of the new university–industry linkages. *Research Policy, 27*(8), 823–833. https://doi.org/10.1016/S0048-7333(98)00093-6

Etzkowitz, H. (2013). Anatomy of the entrepreneurial university. *Social Science Information, 52*(3), 486–511. https://doi.org/10.1177/0539018413485832

Feldman, M., Siegel, D. S., & Wright, M. (2019). New developments in innovation and entrepreneurial ecosystems. *Industrial and Corporate Change, 28*(4), 817–826. https://doi.org/10.1093/icc/dtz031

Fini, R., Meoli, A., Sobrero, M., Ghiselli, S., & Ferrante, F. (2016). *Student entrepreneurship: Demographics, competences and obstacles*. Technical Report – Almalaurea Consortium.

Flores, M. C., Grimaldi, R., Poli, S., & Villani, E. (2024). Entrepreneurial universities and intrapreneurship: A process model on the emergence of an intrapreneurial university. *Technovation*, Forthcoming. https://doi.org/10.1016/j.technovation.2023.102906.

Giunta, A., Pericoli, F. M., & Pierucci, E. (2016). University–industry collaboration in the biopharmaceuticals: The Italian case. *The Journal of Technology Transfer, 41*(4), 818–840. https://doi.org/10.1007/s10961-015-9402-2

Good, M., Knockaert, M., Soppe, B., & Wright, M. (2019). The technology transfer ecosystem in academia. An organizational design perspective. *Technovation, 82*, 35–50. https://doi.org/10.1016/j.technovation.2018.06.009

Guerrero, M., & Urbano, D. (2012). The development of an entrepreneurial university. *The Journal of Technology Transfer, 37*, 43–74. https://doi.org/10.1007/s10961-010-9171-x

Haynie, M., & Shepherd, D. A. (2007). *Exploring the entrepreneurial mindset: Feedback and adaptive decision-making*. Frontiers of Entrepreneurship Research.

Ireland, R. D., Hitt, M. A., & Sirmon, D. G. (2003). A model of strategic entrepreneurship: The construct and its dimensions. *Journal of Management, 29*(6), 963–989. https://doi.org/10.1016/S0149-2063(03)00086-2

Jensen, R., & Thursby, M. (2001). Proofs and prototypes for sale: The licensing of university inventions. *American Economic Review, 91*(1), 240–259. https://doi.org/10.1257/aer.91.1.240

Klofsten, M., Urbano, D., & Heaton, S. (2021). Managing intrapreneurial capabilities: An overview. *Technovation, 99*, 102177. https://doi.org/10.1016/j.technovation.2020.102177

Leydesdorff, L., & Meyer, M. (2003). The Triple Helix of university-industry-government relations. *Scientometrics, 58*, 191–203. https://doi.org/10.1023/A:1026276308287

Mosey, S., & Wright, M. (2007). From human capital to social capital: A longitudinal study of technology–based academic entrepreneurs. *Entrepreneurship Theory and Practice, 31*(6), 909–935. https://doi.org/10.1111/j.1540-6520.2007.0020

Mtawa, N. N., Fongwa, S. N., & Wangenge-Ouma, G. (2016). The scholarship of university-community engagement: Interrogating Boyer's model. *International Journal of Educational Development, 49*, 126–133. https://doi.org/10.1016/j.ijedudev.2016.01.007

Mustar, P. (2021). *L'entrepreneuriat en action: Ou comment de jeunes ingénieurs créent des entreprises innovantes*. Presses des Mines via OpenEdition.

Naumann, C. (2017). Entrepreneurial mindset: A synthetic literature review. *Entrepreneurial Business and Economics Review, 5*(3), 149–172. https://doi.org/10.15678/EBER.2017.050308

OECD. (2015). *OECD skills outlook 2015: Youth, skills and employability*. OECD Publishing.

Saxenian, A. (1991). The origins and dynamics of production networks in Silicon Valley. *Research Policy, 20*(5), 423–437. https://doi.org/10.1016/0048-7333(91)90067-Z

Schulte, P. (2004). The entrepreneurial university: A strategy for institutional development. *Higher Education in Europe, 29*(2), 187–191. https://doi.org/10.1080/0379772042000234811

Shane, S. A. (2004). *Academic entrepreneurship: University spinoffs and wealth creation*. Edward Elgar Publishing.

Siegel, D. S., Waldman, D. A., Atwater, L. E., & Link, A. N. (2003). Commercial knowledge transfers from universities to firms: Improving the effectiveness of university–industry collaboration. *The Journal of High Technology Management Research, 14*(1), 111–133. https://doi.org/10.1016/S1047-8310(03)00007-5

Wright, M., Hmieleski, K. M., Siegel, D. S., & Ensley, M. D. (2007). The role of human capital in technological entrepreneurship. *Entrepreneurship Theory and Practice, 31*(6), 791–806. https://doi.org/10.1111/j.1540-6520.2007.00202.x

Wright, M., Mustar, P., & Siegel, D. (2019). *Student start-ups: The new landscape of academic entrepreneurship* (Vol. 1). World Scientific Books. https://www.worldscientific.com/worldscibooks/10.1142/11494

Wright, M., Siegel, D. S., & Mustar, P. (2017). An emerging ecosystem for student start-ups. *The Journal of Technology Transfer, 42*(4), 909–922. https://doi.org/10.1007/s10961-017-9558-z

Conclusions

The main idea behind this book was to collect and share our thoughts on knowledge share (KS), its origins and its future trajectories. Also, we aimed to raise awareness on this topic to help individuals and organizations address, manage, engage with and generate impact through KS.

We brought in two different perspectives: one more theoretical and grounded in 20 years of research activities, which was applied over the course of 6 years within the University of Bologna, in terms of policymaking in support of innovation, valorisation of research results and academic entrepreneurship; and the other more applied, based on 20 years in the field and aimed at creating organizational conditions for (first) TT and (then) KS to happen. This double perspective is at the heart of the book, reflecting discussions and conversations between the authors, which eventually merged into this book project.

We believe this to be a distinctive feature of the book, representing a point of strength. We have brought together the theoretical perspective, which is necessary for developing awareness, providing context and gaining a better understanding of KS, and the practitioners' perspective, which is relevant for making things happen.

As we declared in the opening pages, an important driver for us to write this book was that we noticed the lack of a comprehensive approach to the analysis of KS. There are reports and studies that focus on single aspects of KS—specific characteristics of the environmental system (e.g. laws, funding, country characteristics), the organizations involved (their strategies, actions, incentives and tools) or the people involved (their individual characteristics, traits, personalities and motivations)—but we couldn't find a broad, comprehensive picture bringing together all these factors into a unitary framework. In creating this, we also wanted to generate awareness about how KS can positively influence our lives and economic, cultural, social and human progress.

The idea to focus on KS emerged also from a detailed analysis of the state of the art in published papers, studies, reports and books. Among the many documents that we have been reading over the years, both of us found very valuable the book 'University Technology Transfer' by Tom Hockaday (2020). His notion of 'expanding word of university technology transfer' has been for us a source of inspiration

G. Conti, R. Grimaldi, *Knowledge Share: the (R)evolution of Technology Transfer*, SxI - Springer for Innovation / SxI - Springer per l'Innovazione 16,
https://doi.org/10.1007/978-3-031-51384-8

for our evolutionary model of technology transfer towards knowledge share. The idea of continuous growth and expansion of contents, which are the object of sharing, calls for a reflection on the terminology that we use and for an evolution of the language to better grasp the complexity of the phenomenon. We are very grateful to Tom also for accepting to write the foreword to this book.

We believe we offer here a new concept of KS. In the book we often talk about a new KS domain, referring to a novel way of generating knowledge and of learning, socializing, and implementing it. This new KS domain is based on the actions listed above, through which knowledge is shaped. KS unfolds through a circular approach, bringing together different players contributing in different ways and from different perspectives to generating value and impact through their actions in knowledge sharing.

We are also aware that the concept of KS has continued to change as we wrote this book. We are aware that there are many aspects that we do not address here and that would be very important to include, such as: comparative analysis of international best practices and KS stories; a detailed overview of the indicators and metrics of KS, moving from the specificities of different countries and discipline-based peculiarities towards more standardized measures, enabling comparative analyses. Future studies and research exploring these directions are very much desirable.

In this line, the major challenges we see for the future are:

- Better collaborations between public research organizations (PROs) and universities at the research level. Over the last 30 years we have seen increasing attention be paid to collaborations with private companies in an attempt to push research results further. We see opportunities for more collaboration among research actors and between the research system and the innovation demand. This is a case of pre-clinic and clinic research, which would benefit from a unique process and integrated system technology and KS activities.
- Better collaboration within big European research projects and European networks, which could lead to clusters of research results being created and of intellectual property being made more visible and easily accessible to private companies to support development and economic and technological progress.
- PROs becoming more open to external, non-research communities. Unlike universities, which can rely on the community of students to bring them closer to research, PROs only have research employees. In order, to foster cross-contamination and maximize the likelihood of commercial exploitation of research results, we should work out more open innovation initiatives to expose 'other' non-research communities to stimuli, knowledge, and technologies for ideating new solutions/applications. This will be easier for universities, which can rely on student communities, but we should work on enabling other PROs to have such exposure.
- More events working on the hybridization of diverse domains, laboratories and calls to action, bringing together researchers and their technologies, students and companies (willing to invest in proof of concept) through vertical calls, with the

specific goal of working out new applications to be commercialized by establishing new companies.
- Investing more energy and resources in scouting. It is true that universities and PROs have huge potential, much of which is still hidden. We often suggest that the knowledge and technologies that are 'visible' and accessible for commercial exploitation are only the tip of the iceberg, the rest of which remains submerged. What can we do to unveil this potential? Given that each research organization has its own iceberg, it is important for each of them to establish internal organizational mechanisms devoted to unveiling the iceberg. This means investing in organizational-level mechanisms to create a better and more highly qualified deal flow of ideas.
- Invest in ad-hoc training programs targeting KTO professionals with the aim to increase their awareness on the multifaceted nature of KS and make them more effective in their daily activities.
- Have Universities and PROs hire more KTO professionals so to reach a minimum scale to run internal operations more efficiently and also to guarantee better interactions with external stakeholders.

Of course, all these challenges will require more researchers and more resources for research activities. It is important for researchers to develop better awareness of the commercial potential of their research activities. This is not to say that they have to be 'obsessed' with pursuing economic returns. Their first 'obsession' should be with generating impact and helping to progress the world we live in.

Unveiling the potential commercial exploitation of research results will also require more and better qualified personnel within KTOs, who play a fundamental role in scouting out promising ideas in the very early stages. However, we will need to train them so that they can develop the competencies to observe, scout, talk to researchers and imagine future market applications. For this to happen, it is important to invest in the professionalization of human capital working within KTOs.

To address these goals, in 2021 we launched a training programme targeting KTO personnel. The master's programme is a NETVAL (Italian Network for Research Valorisation), National Patent and Trademark Office (UIBM) - Ministry of Economic Development and University of Bologna initiative.

We hope this book can help to nurture the debate about the importance of KS and contribute to a conversation that will continue in the future.

GPSR Compliance

The European Union's (EU) General Product Safety Regulation (GPSR) is a set of rules that requires consumer products to be safe and our obligations to ensure this.

If you have any concerns about our products, you can contact us on ProductSafety@springernature.com

In case Publisher is established outside the EU, the EU authorized representative is:

Springer Nature Customer Service Center GmbH
Europaplatz 3
69115 Heidelberg, Germany

Batch number: 10732632

Printed by Printforce, the Netherlands